George Orwell

Animal Farm

Nineteen Eighty-Four

EDITED BY DANIEL LEE

Consultant editor: Nicolas Tredell

Published by
PALGRAVE MACMILLAN
Houndmills, Basingstoke, Hampshire RG21 6XS and
175 Fifth Avenue, New York, N. Y. 10010
Companies and representatives throughout the world

PALGRAVE MACMILLAN is the global academic imprint of the Palgrave Macmillan division of St. Martin's Press, LLC and of Palgrave Macmillan Ltd. Macmillan® is a registered trademark in the United States, United Kingdom and other countries. Palgrave is a registered trademark in the European Union and other countries.

First published 2001 by Icon Books Ltd

ISBN 1–84046–254–X

This book is printed on paper suitable for recycling and made from fully managed and sustained forest sources.

A catalogue record for this book is available from the British Library.

10   9   8   7   6   5   4   3   2   1
12   11   10   09   08   07   06   05   04   03

Printed in China

Contents

Provides an overview of Orwell's reputation amongst popular and critical audiences; begins the debate over the diverse interpretations of *Animal Farm* and *Nineteen Eighty-Four* and over the relationship between Orwell and his work; discusses the prevalence of Orwellian concepts in contemporary culture.

Summarises the early critical response to *Animal Farm* and *Nineteen Eighty-Four* through reviews published in Britain, America and the Soviet Union; establishes the controversy over Orwell's political affiliations; charts the beginnings of a literary critical debate on the novels; examines Orwell's posthumous reception through obituaries by V.S. Pritchett and Arthur Koestler.

Contextualises the novels within generic traditions by examining extracts from Robert Elliott and Krishan Kumar; establishes how Orwell simultaneously writes within and against conventional literary form; Lynette Hunter discusses the nature of allegory with relation to *Animal Farm*; Vita Fortunati considers the subversive trangression of utopian traditions in *Nineteen Eighty-Four*.

Explores the macrostructure of Orwell criticism by examining three key areas of debate; reveals the extent to which Orwell's novels have been appropriated to support divergent ideological causes; John Rodden on Raymond Williams and the ambivalence of the British Left; John Mander and Keith Alldritt on debates over the relationship between the biographical details of Orwell's life and his last fictions; analyses the significance of the transformation from Eric Blair to George Orwell and the notion of authorial 'honesty'; considers the criticisms of Orwell's characterisation of women by feminist writers; Daphne Patai on the patriarchal structures inherent in *Animal Farm*; John Newsinger and John Rodden on the defence of Orwell's 'masculinity'.

Modes of Criticism 2
Subjecting the Form – Forming the Subject

Focuses more closely on clusters of thematised criticism around *Animal Farm* and *Nineteen Eighty-Four*; considers the 'simplicity' of the fable and presents Keith Alldritt and Laraine Fergenson on how that straightforwardness undermines the political commentary; Patrick Reilly and Lynette Hunter on the sophisticated manipulation of genre in *Animal Farm*; considers the portrayal of totalitarianism in *Nineteen Eighty-Four* through discussions of power dynamics, selfhood and language corruption; Erika Gottlieb and Alan Kennedy on the centrality of Room 101 to the exercise of power; Robert Lee and Alok Rai on the corruptibility of language under totalitarian regimes.

1984 – The Orwellian Moment

Approaches the revival of interest in Orwell around the year 1984; John Rodden on the commercialisation of Orwell in popular culture; tackles the welter of criticism comparing the worlds of *Nineteen Eighty-Four* and 1984; Raymond Williams and George Woodcock on the similarities between the political systems of book and year; Mark Crispin Miller on the correspondences between telescreens and television culture; Anthony Burgess discusses the sexual revolution as indicative of an Orwellian separation of love and sex; Tom Winnifrith and William Whitehead analyse the connections between 'Newspeak' and contemporary forms of expression; Donald McCormick on the intrusion of Big Brother into the private lives of the general public.

Watching Big Brother Watching: Orwell on the Screen

Explores the histories of *Animal Farm* and *Nineteen Eighty-Four* on the big and small screen; John Sutherland on the controversy around the first BBC TV production of *Nineteen Eighty-Four*; David Sylvester's insightful criticisms of the 1955 film animation of *Animal Farm*; discusses the impact of Orwell's fiction on recent films; shows the prevalence of Orwell imagery in contemporary culture through the presentation of two test cases of recent TV programmes: *Room 101* and *Big Brother*.

A NOTE ON REFERENCES AND QUOTATIONS

All references to *Animal Farm* and *Nineteen Eighty-Four* are given in brackets in the text of this Guide. All other references are given in endnotes.

All quotations from Orwell's novels have been amended to accord with the most recent editions of the novels (Penguin Books, 1989). These are the authoritative editions and are the most easily available in the UK.

In the extracts in this Guide, insertions by the editor are in square brackets and standard type. Definitions of words, where provided in editorial insertions, have been taken from the *Collins Dictionary of the English Language* and *The New Shorter Oxford English Dictionary*, unless otherwise stated in the endnotes. Insertions in square brackets and bold type in the extracts are by the respective authors themselves.

In any quotation, a row of three dots indicates an editorial ellipsis within a sentence or paragraph, and a row of six dots (that is, two ellipses) indicates an editorial omission of a paragraph break, or of one or more paragraphs.

INTRODUCTION

IN 1947 George Orwell described his reasons for writing:

■ All writers are vain, selfish and lazy, and at the very bottom of their motives there lies a mystery. Writing a book is a horrible, exhausting struggle, like a long bout of some painful illness. One would never undertake such a thing if one were not driven on by some demon whom one can neither resist nor understand. For all one knows that demon is simply the same instinct that makes a baby squall for attention. And yet it is also true that one can write nothing readable unless one constantly struggles to efface one's own personality. Good prose is like a window pane. I cannot say with certainty which of my motives are the strongest, but I know which of them deserve to be followed. And looking back through my work, I see that it is invariably where I lacked a *political* purpose that I wrote lifeless books and was betrayed into purple passages, sentences without meaning, decorative adjectives and humbug generally.[1] □

To begin this Guide to Orwell's two most famous fictions with an explanation of the motivations behind those texts seems entirely appropriate. The essay 'Why I Write' was composed two years after the publication of *Animal Farm* (1945) and two years before the publication of *Nineteen Eighty-Four* (1949). It shows Orwell in reflective mood as he contemplates a career in literary production that has encompassed journalism, documentary-writing, editing, reviewing, reportage as well as fiction. With little more than three years still to live and with serious health problems arising from tuberculosis, Orwell was nonetheless poised to become one of the most celebrated and controversial writers of the century. With the ideas and plans for *Nineteen Eighty-Four* filling his mind, he writes movingly about the painful process of writing and how that process is driven by a deep-seated, demonic force which cannot be resisted. Writing becomes an unwilled, necessary action over which the author has little control, an action which is dictated from without, but which possesses the author as mouthpiece. For Orwell, writing should reflect not the author's personality, but the truths which lie in the external world. His admonition to us as readers is to treat prose as a window pane: to look through rather than at it.

From a distance of over fifty years, the irony of the above invocation seems almost unbearably poignant. Looking at the history of Orwell's reputation, one sees only the palpable chasm between Orwell's idea of the writer as self-effaced and the actuality of his own intrinsic involvement in the production of two of the most significant signposts of twentieth-century literature. Orwell has never achieved the status of the self-effacing artist who can stand 'above his handiwork, invisible, refined out of existence, indifferent, paring his fingernails'.[2] And in Orwell's description of the process of creation as he experienced it, there is perhaps an indication of why his literary personality has been so perplexing and fascinating to scholars. The contention that the drive to create comes from within is immediately contradicted by his suggestion that if his writing is worth anything, then it is because it has been motivated from without – by politics. Orwell constructs an image of the intrinsic connection of writing to the process of being, and yet undermines that by suggesting that good writing always looks outwards. It is this kind of self-contradictory statement that has fuelled much of the debate around Orwell's political and social values and led to a critical discourse centring on the marked paradoxes of his own personality. That personality is inextricably intertwined with the reception of Orwell's texts and with the cultural lives that they have assumed long after their moments of production. The continued prevalence of phrases such as 'Big Brother', 'Thought Police', 'Doublespeak' and widespread popular awareness of concepts such as 'Room 101' and 'All animals are equal but some are more equal than others' attest both to the ongoing relevance of *Nineteen Eighty-Four* and *Animal Farm* and to the status of cultural icon bestowed upon their creator. Orwell is, and has always been, common property in the sense that his novels' significance has far outgrown the political contexts within which they were written, and they have become cross-cultural symbols of the contest between the individual and the state. What this Guide aims to show is the process by which that common 'ownership' of Orwell has come about.

That such a condition exists is partly evidenced by the very production of a Guide to *Animal Farm* and *Nineteen Eighty-Four*. These are two texts which, despite being over fifty years old, regularly feature in lists of readers' most influential and enjoyable books. Many of those reading this Guide will be doing so either in preparation for school/college/university assignments, or because their interest has been piqued by having encountered the books in their earlier educational lives. Most of us have been introduced to *Animal Farm* at school; the clear moral message and the attractive use of animal fable lend themselves perfectly to the teaching of the political history of the Russian Revolution. Many more will have read

Nineteen Eighty-Four as a natural progression from the allegory of *Animal Farm* and, if it has lost some of its power since the passing of the year 1984, it remains a potent reminder of the possibilities for the corruption of power under totalitarian regimes. The continued appearance of these texts on the educational syllabi in many countries points not just to their immediate accessibility, but also to their status as icons of political satire. In many ways they encapsulate the mood of the post-war political stand-off which quickly degenerated into ideological oppositionalism between the United States and the Soviet Union. They are texts which articulate a Cold War paranoia even though they were written before the Cold War had been properly engaged. That they are still considered relevant in the twenty-first century is an indication of their enduring values as teaching texts, and of their ability to reflect the changing conditions of political anxiety even in the post-Soviet world. It is in their ability to mutate to confront new political realities that *Animal Farm* and *Nineteen Eighty-Four* are most valuable. These are texts which, despite their historical specificity, contemplate the broader nature of power itself and, in particular, explore the potential for corruption by power that Orwell saw to be at the heart of humankind.

Yet one of the main things that this Guide will do is to show how little control and direction Orwell had on the trajectories of his texts. His death shortly after the publication of *Nineteen Eighty-Four* inspired a vigorous reappraisal of his significance to the literary world, and began a process of interpreting the novels which has taken them a substantial distance from the readings which Orwell himself advocated. In itself this discrepancy is not a problem for criticism, particularly as much recent theoretical thinking has decentred authorial intention in favour of the intrinsic systems of signification and meaning in the text. However, with Orwell, the decentring of the author has become a critical issue in itself. Almost from the day it was published, *Nineteen Eighty-Four* has been appropriated to support wildly divergent ideological concerns. Its ostensible criticism of a Soviet-style society in England led critics of the political Right to pronounce Orwell a supporter of the forces of capitalism and conservatism. It was a claim that the ailing Orwell strove to dispute, stating instead that the novel related to *all* totalitarian states and not simply the Soviet Union. The warning of the novel, he argued, was against the possibility of totalitarian states emerging in the West. Despite these caveats, the novel began to assume its own political life independent of its author's intentions, and was used as an instrument of propaganda against the Eastern bloc. At the same time, critics of the Left were struggling to equate Orwell's claims to be a socialist with his bleak and austere presentation of life under a dictatorship so closely resembling that of Stalin. It was a dispute that re-ignited debates that had raged over Orwell's politics on the publication of *Animal Farm* in 1945. Then, the attack on the outcomes of the Russian Revolution was widely seen as a clear indication of Orwell's conservative credentials, a claim he hotly denied. The Left reviled the fable, the Right embraced it and, somewhere in between, Orwell's protestations were ignored.

The subsequent critical histories of *Animal Farm* and *Nineteen Eighty-Four* have largely mirrored the early confusion. As this Guide shows, criticism has tended to be dominated by political readings of Orwell which are inevitably polarised. A consequence of this bitter feud over the legacy of Orwell is that there is a certain stagnation in studies relating to him. It is true that different concerns emerge at specific times, such as the feminist attention of the 1970s and 1980s, but, in many cases, the same issues of political ownership emerge as the dominant mode of criticism across the decades. This Guide pays full attention to that debate, and also explores the other key areas of appraisal. These often revolve around the figure of Orwell, even though the texts are the intended focal points of discussion. As suggested, one of those areas is the nature of Orwell's socialism, which he vehemently proclaimed but which some critics have attempted to discredit. Political commitment is an issue which runs throughout Orwell's writing career and is perhaps best articulated in the confessional sections of *The Road to Wigan Pier* (1937). When he turned his gaze upon the Russian Revolution, however, his critical conclusions led some to question the depth of his socialist affiliation.

Another important concern which will be addressed is the relationship between the man and his work. Much criticism, which we might call psychobiographical, has focused on the correspondences between themes and motifs of the last novels and recurrent features of Orwell's life. Pre-eminent amongst these is the transformation that Eric Blair underwent to become George Orwell. A great deal of attention has been paid to the crisis of identity inherent in the last fictions, and the extrapolation of Orwell's own identity-change has become a fruitful path for critics. The last key trope which guides the following discussion is the interrogation of Orwell's status as a literary giant. Given the significance of *Animal Farm* and *Nineteen Eighty-Four* within Western culture, it would be reasonable to anticipate Orwell's ascendancy to a position of canonicity within twentieth-century literature. That his reputation as a writer is still in doubt in some circles attests both to the exclusiveness of the academy and to the negative judgements made on his professional writing. Orwell was first and foremost a journalist, a branch of literary production which has struggled to attain credibility within institutions of literary scholarship. Questions about Orwell's writing abilities have been raised which have led to further questions about the generic categorisation of his work. As a skilled writer who continually experimented with different forms, Orwell crosses over generic boundaries, destabilising those boundaries in the process. This has led to a degree of confusion as to how we should best read his work: for instance, is *Nineteen Eighty-Four* a novel, a utopia, a political tract or a satire? Although these categories are not mutually exclusive, their interpenetration has unsettled some critics.[3]

Almost inevitably when discussing two texts by an author, there is a degree of conflation and comparison, and whilst this eventuality is not wholly desirable, such interlinking can and does have positive outcomes. *Animal Farm* and *Nineteen Eighty-Four* complement each other extremely well and their comparison reveals a development of Orwell's thought between 1945 and 1949 which is beneficial to the discussion. Having said that, it is unsurprising that one particular text will dominate the extracts, and in this case it is *Nineteen Eighty-Four*. This eventuality has been striven against, but any imbalance also indicates an imbalance in the relative quantities of criticism of the texts. *Animal Farm* has generated a significant body of criticism, but it is far outweighed in number and diversity of approaches by *Nineteen Eighty-Four*. That this Guide reflects that historical domination is deemed not only a necessary choice by the editor, but also a positive indication of the impact on popular and critical culture of *Nineteen Eighty-Four*.

The first chapter of the Guide discusses the early critical responses to the publications of *Animal Farm* and *Nineteen Eighty-Four*. These range from the laudatory to the condemnatory, and immediately characterise the subsequent struggle for Orwell's memory. Efforts have been made to present a politically balanced range of reviews in order to show the divergence of opinion inspired by the texts. Critics from Britain, America and the Soviet Union clash over the intended targets for Orwell's satire, and, in many cases, use the review as an opportunity to promote the egalitarianism of their own lived ideology. The reviewing process therefore becomes an exercise in propagandist sabre-rattling and indicates the highly charged political atmosphere in which Orwell was intervening. The first chapter also begins the examination of Orwell's posthumous reputation and establishes the hagiographic reception that characterised much early criticism.

In Chapter Two, the focus is broadened to explore the generic traditions to which *Animal Farm* and *Nineteen Eighty-Four* conform, but which they also, simultaneously, subvert. Critics have, as suggested above, consistently struggled to find specific categories of literature in which to place *Animal Farm* and *Nineteen Eighty-Four*. This does reveal the inflexibility of a literary criticism which seeks to define texts by certain established criteria, but it also points towards the protean qualities of Orwell's last novels. By considering the most common genres within which Orwell's work is categorised – allegory, fable, utopia – it is possible to see how *Animal Farm* and *Nineteen Eighty-Four* exploit readerly expectations in order to question the impermeability of those generic boundaries. That Orwell writes across genres threatens the stability of those genre conventions and demands some renegotiation of the parameters of traditional forms. Focusing principally on the history of allegory in relation to *Animal Farm* and of utopia with reference to *Nineteen Eighty-Four*, this chapter explores Orwell's experiments with genre and addresses critical material that postulates his radical challenge to conventional literary modes.

Chapters Three and Four should be read as complementary, in that they attempt to synthesise the body of critical writing on *Animal Farm* and *Nineteen Eighty-Four* into a series of broad modes of criticism. The intention here is to provide an overview of the most significant strands of argument about the novels and to indicate how those strands are, more often than not, interdependent. Chapter Three seeks to analyse the macrostructure of Orwell criticism and, to that end, breaks down into three main categories the approaches that seem to have dominated debate around Orwell, and, in particular, around his last novels. Those categories are political criticism, psychobiographical criticism and feminist criticism. Whilst not encompassing all critical postures towards Orwell, these categories encapsulate many of the recurring issues which have emerged around discussions of the man and his work. Chapter Four develops on this approach by analysing separately, and in more depth, the specific strands of criticism which have tackled *Animal Farm* and *Nineteen Eighty-Four*. In the case of *Animal Farm*, these debates often revolve around formalistic concerns, but they also provoke debate about whether the novel is worthy of the acclaim with which it has been received. The extracted passages on *Nineteen Eighty-Four* examine the crucial themes of totalitarianism and the politics of power, and explore the way in which the novel articulates those ideas through the deracination of selfhood and the corruption of language.

The focus of Chapter Five is 1984, or as it is described, 'the Orwellian moment'. The eponymous year of Orwell's last novel was fated to produce a frenzy of interest in Orwell and his vision of the future. While the most precarious years of the Cold War had perhaps passed, tension between the Soviet Union and the United States was still extremely high, and the critique of totalitarianism contained in *Nineteen Eighty-Four* ensured vigorous reiteration in the West of the iniquities of Communism, and of the inequalities of capitalism in the Eastern bloc. This chapter considers both the renewal of mass interest in Orwell and some of the more thoughtful critiques of *Nineteen Eighty-Four*, in the light of the realities of 1984. In the build-up to the year of the book, much attention was expended upon how similar the world of 1984 was to that projected by Orwell. In many instances, this gave rise to astute analyses of the superpowers and of their engagement in ideological and often territorial conflict through smaller surrogate states. The approach of the year also gave rise to less sober comparisons between the book and the year. Clearly represented here, these critiques attempted to show how the worst examples of 'Newspeak', 'doublethink' and 'Big Brother-ism' were no longer fantasies but lived realities.

The final chapter of this Guide engages with the presence of Orwell in popular culture throughout the late twentieth century and into the twenty-first century. Examining the screen versions of *Animal Farm* and *Nineteen Eighty-Four*, Chapter Six suggests that Orwell's continued relevance to society has largely been supported by the appearance of his novels on the small and big screen. Charting a history of controversy around those adaptations, it is argued that the novels have become independent cultural icons, separate and increasingly distanced from Orwell. This autonomy is then examined through the prevalence of direct or indirect references to *Animal Farm* and *Nineteen Eighty-Four* in television and film in recent decades. Finally, by taking two Orwellian case-studies from popular culture, the BBC's comedy chat-show, *Room 101*, and Channel Four's *Big Brother*, it is argued that not only have the novels outgrown Orwell, they have also outgrown their original contexts and meanings.

The reader of this Guide will, to whatever extent, already be educated about George Orwell, even if only casual interest has motivated him or her to browse this book over others. Yet even those who have never heard of Orwell, or who can make no connection between the man and the work, will probably have been exposed to the legacy of Orwell. The powerful iconography of *Animal Farm* and *Nineteen Eighty-Four* has been repeatedly employed to describe the conditions of contemporary society. The image of Big Brother is associated with a culture of surveillance that incorporates Closed Circuit Television (CCTV) and even the Internet. 'Orwell' and 'Orwellian' have become standard terms for the intrusion of state offices on individual freedom, and recent televisual events such as *Big Brother* foreground our deep-seated fear of – but also fascination with – the loss of private selfhood. Whether or not Big Brother is watching you, you are almost certainly watching him.

CHAPTER ONE

Early Reviews and Responses

GEORGE ORWELL died of complications arising from tuberculosis on 21 January 1950. A long-term sufferer from ill-health, he succumbed at the highest point of his popular and critical acclaim. Fellow writers, philosophers and liberal intellectuals hastened to proclaim him a genius, a prophet, even a saint. None waxed more lyrical than writer V. S. Pritchett:

■ George Orwell was the wintry conscience of a generation which in the 'thirties had heard the call to the rasher assumptions of political faith. He was a kind of saint and, in that character, more likely in politics to chasten his own side than the enemy. His instinctive choice of spiritual and physical discomfort, his habit of going his own way, looked like the crankishness which has often cropped up in the British character; if this were so, it was vagrant rather than puritan. He prided himself on seeing through the rackets, and on conveying the impression of living without the solace or even the need of a single illusion.

There can hardly have been a more belligerent and yet more pessimistic Socialist; indeed his Socialism became anarchism. In corrupt and ever worsening years, he always woke up one miserable hour earlier than anyone else and, suspecting something fishy in the site, broke camp and advanced alone to some tougher position in a bleaker place; and it had often happened that he had been the first to detect an unpleasant truth or to refuse a tempting hypocrisy. Conscience took the Anglo-Indian out of the Burma police, conscience sent the old Etonian among the down and outs in London and Paris, and the degraded victims of the Means Test or slum incompetence in Wigan; it drove him into the Spanish civil war and, inevitably, into one of its unpopular sects, and there Don Quixote saw the poker face of Communism. His was the guilty conscience of the educated and privileged man, one of that regular supply of brilliant recalcitrants which Eton has given us since the days of Fielding; and this conscience could be allayed only by taking upon itself the pain, the misery, the dinginess and the pathetic but hard vulgarities of a stale and hopeless period. ... ...

He has gone; but in one sense, he always made this impression of the passing traveller who meets one on the station, points out that one is waiting for the wrong train and vanishes. His popularity, after *Animal Farm*, must have disturbed such a lone hand. In *1984*, alas, one can see that deadly pain, which had long been his subject, had seized him completely and obliged him to project a nightmare, as Wells had done in his last days, upon the future.[1] □

The adulation that characterises this retrospective summation is in sharp contrast to the standing which Orwell enjoyed only five years previously. Prior to the publication of *Animal Farm*, Orwell's reputation as an essayist and political commentator was growing steadily, but his renown as a novelist was waning. In 1940, the distinguished critic Q.D. Leavis wrote positively of Orwell's writing skills, but recommended that he concentrate his energies on non-fiction and abandon the novel form.[2] Exigencies of time and financial necessity ensured that Orwell's wartime writing was largely journalistic: letters to the left-liberal journal *Partisan Review*; book reviews and a regular column in *Tribune* entitled 'As I Please'. Along with *The Lion and the Unicorn* (1941), this work earned him increasing respect from sections of the literary establishment. Yet his fiction was widely supposed inferior to his journalism and was coolly received by an unwelcoming public. His last novel, *Coming Up For Air*, had been published in 1939 before the outbreak of war and, although favourably reviewed, sold out its moderate print-run of 3,000 copies within two years. In comparison, *Animal Farm*, published on 17 August 1945, had sold its initial print-run of 4,500 copies by November of the same year, when a second impression of 10,000 copies was produced to meet a colossal demand.[3] The novel transformed Orwell's reputation, brought him to the attention of an American audience and elevated his status within intellectual circles on both sides of the Atlantic.

Animal Farm – Early Reviews

It was a work that Orwell had struggled to publish. Although completed in February 1944, the manuscript went unpublished for seventeen months as Orwell was confronted by problems of both a practical and political nature. The conditions of war meant that paper was in desperately short supply – a factor that delayed publication until after the conclusion of the conflict. In addition, the overtly political nature of the fable caused publishers anxiety as to its potential reception from a politically volatile public. Orwell's condemnation of the Stalinist betrayal of the Russian

Revolution would be likely to receive a frosty reception from a readership for whom Stalin's Soviet Union still had an integral part to play in the destruction of Nazi Germany. The radical polarisation of ideological commitment throughout the 1930s – coming to a point for Orwell as for many others in the Spanish Civil War – had opposed Hitler and Mussolini's brand of right-wing fascist politics with Stalin's hard-line Communist governance. Within English intellectual circles, Communist sympathies had been widespread throughout the decade and Stalinism seemed to find its natural enemy in Hitler's aggressive stance towards Eastern Europe. The British reader, aware of the more geographically immediate threat of Germany, tended towards the benign images of Uncle Joe Stalin and the Russian bear. This faith was severely shaken by the Germano–Russian pact of 1939, but with Hitler's fateful decision to invade Russia, and its terrible consequences, British public opinion turned once again to favour the power of the Soviet Union. With the war at a crucial stage and the support of Stalin fundamental to the destabilisation of Hitler, Orwell's anti-Stalinist diatribe found little favour within a pusillanimous publishing industry. Many of the large publishing houses in Britain and at least a dozen in America rejected *Animal Farm*. In his letter of rejection, the highly respected publisher Jonathan Cape hinted at high-level pressure to suppress the manuscript in such a changeable political context:

■ I mentioned the reaction that I had had from an important official in the Ministry of Information with regard to ANIMAL FARM. I must confess that this expression of opinion has given me seriously to think. My reading of the manuscript gave me considerable personal enjoyment and satisfaction, but I can see now that it might be regarded as something which it was highly ill-advised to publish at the present time. If the fable were addressed generally to dictators and dictatorships at large then publication would be all right, but the fable does follow, as I see now, so completely the progress and development of the Russian Soviets and their two dictators, that it can apply only to Russia, to the exclusion of other dictatorships. Another thing: it would be less offensive if the predominant caste in the fable were not pigs. I think the choice of pigs as the ruling caste will no doubt give offence to many people, and particularly to anyone who is a bit touchy, as undoubtedly the Russians are . . . [4] □

Orwell, insulted by rejection and half-amused by the objection to the portrayal of the Revolutionary leadership as pigs, moved to publish *Animal Farm* at his own expense. Secker and Warburg spared him this onerous and costly task and eventually published the fable only days after the war in the Far East culminated in the dropping of the atomic bomb on Hiroshima.

Early reviews of the novel are characterised by their enthusiastic approbation for Orwell's satire of the Russian Revolution, but are simultaneously tinged by a roseate residue of ideological romanticism. Cyril Connolly's review for *Horizon* is an interesting riposte to Orwell's criticism, which to a distanced reader may seem to contain elements of a willed self-deception:

■ Mr Orwell is a revolutionary who is in love with 1910. This ambivalence constitutes his strength and his weakness. Never before has a progressive political thinker been so handicapped by nostalgia for the Edwardian shabby-genteel or the under-dog. It is this political sentimentality which from the literary point of view is his most valid emotion. *Animal Farm* proves it, for it truly is a fairy story told by a great lover of liberty and a great lover of animals. The farm is real, the animals are moving. At the same time it is a devastating attack on Stalin and his 'betrayal' of the Russian revolution, as seen by another revolutionary. The allegory between the animals and the fate of the revolution (they drive out the human beings and plan a Utopia entrusted to the leadership of the pigs – Napoleon-Stalin, Snowball-Trotsky – with the dogs as police, the sheep as yes-men, the two cart-horses, Boxer and Clover, as the noble hard-working proletariat), and the Russian experiment is beautifully worked out, perhaps the most felicitous moment being when the animal 'saboteurs' are executed for some of the very crimes of the Russian trials, such as the sheep who confessed to having 'urinated in the drinking pool' or the goose which kept back six ears of corn and ate them in the night. The fairy tale ends with the complete victory of Napoleon and the pigs, who rule *Animal Farm* with a worse tyranny and a far greater efficiency than its late human owner, the dissolute Mr Jones.

Politically one might make to Mr Orwell the same objections as to Mr Koestler for his essay on Russia in *The Yogi and the Commissar* – both allow their personal bitterness about the betrayed revolution to prejudice their attitude to the facts. But it is arguable that every revolution is 'betrayed' because the violence necessary to achieve it is bound to generate an admiration for violence which leads to the abuse of power. A revolution is the forcible removal of an obsolete and inefficient ruling-class by a vigorous and efficient one which replaces it for as long as its vitality will allow. The commandments of the Animal Revolution, such as 'no animal shall kill any other animal' or 'all animals are equal' can perhaps never be achieved by a revolutionary seizure of power but only by the spiritual operation of reason or moral philosophy in the animal heart. If we look at Russia without the particular bitterness of the disappointed revolutionary we see that it is an immensely powerful managerial despotism – far more powerful than its Czarist predecessor – where, on the whole, despite a police system which we should find intolerable, the masses are happy, and where great strides in material progress have been made (i.e. independence of women, equality of the sexes, autonomy of racial and cultural minorities, utilization of science to improve the standard of living, religious toleration, etc.). If Stalin and his regime were not loved as well as feared the *Animal Farm* which comprises the greatest land-mass of the world would not have united to roll back the most efficient invading army which the world has ever known – and if in truth Stalin is loved then he and his regime cannot be quite what they appear to Mr Orwell (indeed Napoleon's final brutality to Boxer – if Boxer symbolises the proletariat – is not paralleled by any incident in Stalin's career, unless the Scorched Earth policy is indicated). But it is unfair to harp on these considerations. *Animal Farm* is one of the most enjoyable books since the war, it is deliciously written, with something of the feeling, the penetration and the verbal economy of Orwell's master, Swift. It deserves a wide sale and a lengthy discussion. Apart from the pleasure it has given me to read, I welcome it for three reasons, because it breaks down some of the artificial reserve with which Russia is written about, or not written about (a reserve which we do not extend to America – nor they to us), because it restores the allegorical pamphlet to its rightful place as a literary force, and lastly because it proves that Mr Orwell has not been entirely seduced away by the opinion-airing attractions of weekly journalism from his true vocation, which is to write books.[5] □

Connolly's bitter-sweet review characterises Orwell as a wavering revolutionary whose subversive politics are countermanded by a deep-rooted and nostalgic conservatism. The criticism (which is also deemed an artistic strength) that Orwell is 'a revolutionary who is in love with 1910' positions him as an idealist to the point of being naïve, whose perceptions of revolution are distanced from the realities of power by an ingenuous belief in the principles of collectivist democracy. While acknowledging the potency of Orwell's satire, Connolly argues that Orwell is divorced from the *realpolitik* of governance and, in suggesting that all revolutions are betrayed, intimates that Stalin's end of social, scientific and militaristic improvement justifies the brutal, oppressive means necessary to achieve it. With twenty-first century hindsight, it is not difficult to dismiss Connolly's review as itself naïve – his arguments based upon superficial propagandist images of a progressive Soviet Union – but the review does show the positive light in which Stalin's Soviet Union was viewed in certain circles of the British public and press during the 1940s. This attitude would have changed dramatically by the time Orwell published *Nineteen Eighty-Four* in 1949. One criticism that reappears throughout reviews of both *Animal Farm* and *Nineteen Eighty-Four* is contained in Connolly's contention that the Commandments of the Animal Revolution cannot be perpetually enforced by revolution, but must be willingly adopted as part of a moral framework and a rational philosophy. This he uses as evidence of the complicit agreement of the Soviet peoples to Stalin's measures. As Orwell, however, was to show through the creation of 'Newspeak', 'doublethink', 'thoughtcrime' and 'Hate Week', acquiescence in extreme social policy does not always indicate conscious approval of these policies by autonomous subjects. The indoctrination and ideological conditioning of the people through repetitive overt and subliminal suggestion became an increasingly important focus for Orwell, but was one which many early reviewers and critics failed to address.

Connolly's implied disappointment with Orwell's revolutionary backsliding is mirrored by Kingsley Martin, who, in a *New Statesman and Nation* review, describes Orwell as a 'disillusioned idealist'. For Martin, the retreat from political idealism has not stopped at a loss of faith in the USSR, but has developed into a sceptical attitude towards all human motivations:

■ In a world choked everywhere with suffering, cruelty and exploitation, the disillusioned idealist may be embarrassed by the rich choice of objects for denunciation. He runs the risk of twisting himself into knots, as he discovers enemies, first to the Right, then to the Left and, most invigorating, at home amongst his friends. He may try to solve his dilemma by deciding on some particular Power-figure as the embodiment of Evil, concentrating upon it all his wealth of frustration and righteous indignation. If he remains only a critic and fails to turn his talent to the search for a practical remedy for a specific evil, he is likely, in time, to decide that all the world is evil and that human nature is itself incorrigible. The alternatives then – we see many contemporary instances – are cynicism or religion and mysticism.

Mr Orwell's Devils have been numerous and, since he is a man of integrity, he chooses real evils to attack. His latest satire, beautifully written, amusing and, if you don't take it too seriously, a fair corrective of much silly worship of the Soviet Union, suggests to me that he is reaching the exhaustion of idealism and approaching the bathos of cynicism. ....

There is plenty in the U.S.S.R. to satirise, and Mr Orwell does it well. How deftly the fairy story of the animals who, in anticipation of freedom and plenty, revolt against the tyrannical farmer, turns into a rollicking caricature of the Russian Revolution! His shafts strike home. We all know of the sheep, who drown discussion by the bleating slogans; we have all noticed, with a wry smile, the gradual change of

Soviet doctrine under the pretence that it is no change and then that the original doctrine was an anti-Marxist error. ... ...

The logic of Mr Orwell's satire is surely the ultimate cynicism of Ben, the donkey. That, if I read Mr Orwell's mind correctly, is where his idealism and disillusion has really landed him. But he has not quite courage to see that he has lost faith, not in Russia but in mankind. So the surface moral of his story is that all would have gone well with the revolution if the wicked Stalin had not driven the brave and good Trotsky out of Eden. Here Mr Orwell ruins what should have been a very perfect piece of satire on human life. For by putting the Stalin–Trotsky struggle in the centre he invites every kind of historical and factual objection. We are brought from the general to the particular; to the question why Stalin decided to attempt the terrific feat of creating an independent Socialist country rather than risk plunging Russia unprepared into a war of intervention by stirring up revolution in neighbouring countries. Mr Orwell may say it would have been better if this policy had prevailed, but a moment's thought will evoke in him the brilliant satire he would have written about the betrayal of the revolution, if Trotsky, who was as ruthless a revolutionary as Stalin, had won the day and lost the revolution by another route. This same error compels the reader to ask whether in fact it is true that the Commissar today is indistinguishable in ideals and privilege from the Tzarist bureaucrat and the answer is that though many traditional Russian characteristics survive in Russia, the new ruling class is really very different indeed from anything that Russia has known before. In short, if we read the satire as a gibe at the failings of the U.S.S.R. and realise that it is historically false and neglectful of the complex truth about Russia, we shall enjoy it and be grateful for our laugh.[6] □

Unlike Connolly, Martin does not hide Stalinist excess behind governmental expediency, but rather accuses Orwell of a selective rendition of this Revolutionary history. By presenting Stalin as the fount of political corruption, Martin believes Orwell to be eliding the role of Trotsky in the betrayal of idealism, thereby excising the past in exactly the same manner that he criticises in others. Martin's review is a sensitive and perceptive response to *Animal Farm*, illustrating the high degree of political awareness that typifies many of the British reviews. The fluctuating reputation of the USSR ensured that most reviewers, whether or not they agreed with Orwell's stance, were sensitive to the condemnation of tyrannical despotism and to the underlying theme of revolution betrayed. The perception of the USSR in the United States was wholly different: ideological preconceptions about the threat of Communism to individual freedom resulted in Orwell's novel receiving an altogether less considered response.

Published in America in August 1946, *Animal Farm* was selected as the Book-of-the-Month Club choice for September, a serendipitous occurrence which could be seen as a defining moment in Orwell's career. The huge audience which opened up before him, along with the enthusiastic promotion by the Club's president, Harry Scherman, ensured that the novel became an instant popular and critical success. Scherman went so far as to issue a special statement urging members to buy *Animal Farm* over any other book. His entreaties draw on the fable as an epochal moment in modern literature: 'Every now and then through history, some fearless individual has spoken for the people of a troubled time . . . Just so does this little gem of an allegory express, perfectly, the inarticulate philosophy of tens of millions of free men . . . Wherever . . . men are free to read what they want, this book and its influence will spread.'[7] The response to this emotional plea was enormous, and Orwell was transformed from an obscure British writer/journalist, of whom little was known in America, to an internationally recognised author and political commentator. However, whereas in Britain reviewers and critics tended to read the novel as the story of a justified revolution betrayed by the appeals to power and autocracy, American readers leaned towards an interpretation of the allegory as revealing the inherent weaknesses of socialist idealism. The hyperbole used by Scherman to promote the book undoubtedly encouraged readers to contextualise *Animal Farm* within simplistic discourses of ideological binarism in which capitalism equates to freedom whilst Communism/socialism equates to repression. The complex and intertwining histories of Marxism, socialism and Communism are elided and little distinction is made between the political philosophy of socialism and the practical politics of Communist rule. Orwell's intended separation of the moral justice of the revolution from the subsequent nefarious misappropriation of power was largely ignored in favour of the ostensible criticism of revolutionary methods. The widespread endorsement of his vision thus rebounded upon Orwell's own political attitudes and while public approbation brought him financial success and an international renown, it also brought him a frustrating degree of misunderstanding which was to grow with the publication of *Nineteen Eighty-Four*. The paradox of Orwell's critique of Soviet policy from within a socialist position has unsettled and baffled many readers, and it was a paradox of which he was conscious. In a letter to an American reader, he attempted to distance himself from the contention that *Animal Farm* was an attack on socialism *qua* socialism:

■ Re. your query about 'Animal Farm'. Of course I intended it primarily as a satire on the Russian revolution. But I did mean it to have a wider application in so much that I meant that *that kind* of revolution (violent conspiratorial revolution, led by unconsciously power-hungry people) can only lead to a change of masters. I meant the moral to be that revolutions only effect a radical improvement when the masses are alert and know how to chuck out their leaders as soon as the latter have done their job. The turning-point of the story was supposed to be when the pigs kept the milk and apples for themselves. . . . If the other animals had had the sense to put their foot down then, it would have been all right. If people think I am defending the status quo, that is, I think, because they have grown pessimistic and assume that there is no alternative except dictatorship or laissez-faire capitalism. . . . What I was trying to say was, 'You can't have a revolution unless you make it for yourself; there is no such thing as benevolent dictatorship.'[8] □

As hard as Orwell strove to assert that revolution itself was not *a priori* pernicious, the misapprehension persisted and Orwell began to be classed in certain quarters as a conservative and reactionary ideologue. The Canadian professor and literary critic, Northrop Frye, attacked the novel in *Canadian Forum* for its superficial condemnation of the symptoms of Communism and for failing to address the underlying doctrinal contradictions of Marxism:

■ The story is very well-written, especially the Snowball episode, which suggests that the Communist 'Trotskyite' is a conception on much the same mental plane as the Nazi 'Jew,' and the vicious irony of the end of Boxer the work horse is perhaps really great satire. On the other hand, the satire on the episode corresponding to the German invasion seems to me both silly and heartless, and the final metamorphosis of pigs into humans at the end is a fantastic disruption of the sober logic of the tale. The reason for the change in method was to conclude the story by showing the end of Communism under Stalin as a replica of its beginning under the Czar. Such an alignment is, of course, complete nonsense, and as Mr Orwell must know it to be nonsense, his motive for adopting it was presumably that he did not know how otherwise to get his allegory rounded off with a neat epigrammatic finish.

Animal Farm adopts one of the classical formulas of satire, the corruption of principle by expediency, of which Swift's *Tale of a Tub* is the greatest example. It is an account of the bogging down of Utopian aspirations in the quicksand of human nature. . . . But for the same reason it completely misses the point as a satire on the Russian development of Marxism, and as expressing the disillusionment which many men of goodwill feel about Russia. The reason for that disillusionment would be much better expressed as the corruption of expediency by principle. For the whole point about Marxism was surely that it was the first revolutionary movement in history which attempted to start with a concrete historical situation instead of vast *a priori* generalizations of the 'all men are equal' type, and which aimed at scientific rather than Utopian objectives. Marx and Engels worked out a revolutionary technique based on an analysis of history known as dialectic materialism, which appeared in the nineteenth century at a time when metaphysical materialism was a fashionable creed, but which Marx and Engels always insisted was a quite different thing from metaphysical materialism. . . . . . .

Official Marxism today announces on page one that dialectic materialism is to be carefully distinguished from metaphysical materialism, and then insists from page two to the end that Marxism is nevertheless a complete materialist metaphysic of experience, with materialist answers to such questions as the existence of God, the origin of knowledge and the meaning of culture. Thus instead of including itself in the body of modern thought and giving a revolutionary dynamic to that body, Marxism has become a self-contained dogmatic system, and one so exclusive in its approach to the remainder of modern thought as to appear increasingly antiquated and sectarian. Yet this metaphysical materialism has no other basis than that of its original dialectic, its program of revolutionary action. The result is an absolutizing of expediency which makes expediency a principle in itself. From this springs the reckless intellectual dishonesty which it is so hard not to find in modern Communism, and which is naturally capable of rationalizing any form of action, however ruthless.

A really searching satire on Russian Communism, then, would be more deeply concerned with the underlying reasons for its transformation from a proletarian dictatorship into a kind of parody of the Catholic Church. Mr Orwell does not bother with motivation: he makes his Napoleon inscrutably ambitious, and lets it go at that, and as far as he is concerned some old reactionary bromide like 'you can't change human nature' is as good a moral as any other for his fable. But he, like Koestler, is an example of a large number of writers in the Western democracies who during the last fifteen years have done their level best to adopt the Russian interpretation of Marxism as their own world-outlook and have failed.[9] □

Frye's review is a fascinating right-wing dismissal of Marxism as a purely self-referential ideology brought artificially into existence in response to a particular set of historical circumstances. Marxism and its progeny Communism are considered inauthentic philosophical postures by Frye because they have not arisen out of a 'body of modern thought' but have been instantaneously conceived, codified and applied to a concrete historical context. Frye's complaint against Orwell is that he opts for easy, identifiable targets, such as Stalin, without engaging with the systemic incongruities of Marxist thinking. Orwell, he suggests, sees the corruption of contemporary Communism as the result of individualistic intervention in a collective ideal. The assertion of the self over the community, and the concomitant urge for power which it induces, undermine the founding principles of socialist democracy and initiate a return of oligarchical rule. The roots of Communism's self-negation, according to Frye, are embedded in the contradictory impulses which inspired the Marxist revolution in the mid-nineteenth century, not in the resulting struggles for power. This is certainly one of the most intellectually sensitive reviews and, while it chides Orwell for a perceived lack of ambition in his satire, it does point the way towards *Nineteen Eighty-Four* in which Orwell widens his focus to consider, not specific instances of dictatorial corruption, but the nature of totalitarianism itself.

Nineteen Eighty-Four – Early Reviews

Evidence suggests that Orwell had been planning the novel which was to become *Nineteen Eighty-Four* since 1943, before he had begun writing *Animal Farm*.[10] As a result of the success of his allegory, however, he was flooded with journalistic work and with offers for social engagement which stand testament to his new status as a public figure. Work on the new novel, which he initially referred to as 'The Last Man in Europe', was suspended and delayed further by the death in March 1945 of his wife, Eileen. Orwell's own health was failing as he began the process of writing in the summer of 1946. Over the next two years, most of the novel was written at Orwell's home on the remote Scottish island of Jura, to which he increasingly retreated from the incessant demands of his journalistic existence. The cumulative effects of his tubercular condition, perhaps worsened by the harsh climate of the island, rendered the creative process slow and painful and, after completing the first draft, he spent seven months in hospital, dangerously ill. Once discharged, Orwell set about revising and typing the manuscript, work which reduced his level of energy still further. When the novel was eventually published in June 1949, Orwell was back in a sanatorium being informed that only complete rest could improve his 50 per cent chance of survival.[11] His spirits were doubtless raised by the warm reception that greeted the novel. In both Britain and America (where it was published simultaneously), critics applauded the book's interrogation of totalitarianism, and many recognised that Orwell's targets were not Communism or socialism in any narrow sense, but the structures of political power which underlie all ideologies. The following two extracts – the first by Diana Trilling in the left-wing journal, *Nation*, the second by Daniel Bell in *New Leader* – exhibit a perceptive awareness of the broadened themes of power and corruption in *Nineteen Eighty-Four*. Diana Trilling writes:

■ Even where, as in his last novel, *Animal Farm*, Mr Orwell seemed to be concerned only with unmasking the Soviet Union for its dreamy admirers, he was urged on by something larger than sectarianism. What he was telling us is that along the path the Russian revolution has followed to the destruction of all the decent human values there have stood the best ideals of modern social enlightenment. It is this idealism he has wished to jolt into self-awareness. In the name of a higher loyalty, treacheries beyond imagination have been committed; in the name of Socialist equality, privilege has ruled unbridled; in the name of democracy and freedom, the individual has lived without public voice or private peace – if this is true of the Soviet Union, why should it not eventually be equally true of the English experiment? In other words, we are being warned against the extremes to which the contemporary totalitarian spirit can carry us, not only so that we will be warned against Russia but also so that we will understand the ulti-mate dangers involved wherever power moves under the guise of order and rationality.

With this refusal to concentrate his attack upon Soviet totalitarian-ism alone Mr Orwell reasserts the ability, so rare among intellectuals of the left, to place his own brand of idealism above the uses of politi-cal partisanship. It is very difficult to pin a political label on the author of *Nineteen Eighty-Four*: if one has heard that Mr Orwell is now an anarchist, one can of course read his new novel as the work of an anarchist – but one can just as easily read it as the work of an un-fashionable, highly imaginative democrat or of an old-fashioned libertarian.[12] □

Here is Daniel Bell:

■ When Thomas More in 1516 described an imaginary island, he called it *Utopia*, which in Greek means, literally, 'nowhere.' The fright-ening aspect of George Orwell's imaginary world is that it is somewhere – in and around us. ... ...

What makes it a shuddering, sickening, gripping spectacle is the remorseless piling on of detail upon detail, like a fingernail drawn ceaselessly across a blackboard, of a human society stripped of the last shreds of community where even the sexual act is a cold, distasteful, jerky moment of copulation, performed because artificial methods are not yet sufficiently perfect to reproduce the species, and where fear and anxiety are the daily staple of life – not as in the concentration camps a dull and inured fear, but under the corrosive stimuli of hate, a high-tension twitching exhaustion from which dreams and even sleep offer no escape. ... The shrinking gap between imagination and reality is what heightens one's sense of fear in reading Orwell. Apparently there is nothing too extreme (either technically or psychologically) for the mind to contrive out of fantasy, that is not already present today . . . One last horror still remains, which is no less frightening for being metaphysical rather than real; for Orwell, actually, is not writing a tract on politics but a treatise on human nature. The secret of the inner party is that for the first time in human history, it has mastered the usage of pure power.

Once the secret of pure power is learned, Orwell suggests, the human being becomes completely malleable. And in that sub-mission, the small flickering flame of self-consciousness, the ability of detachment which distinguishes men from other animals becomes extinguished . . . . . .

Is this our world-to-be? Is this Socialism? Many will protest that Orwell has written an effective picture of totalitarianism, but not *demo-cratic* Socialism. But other than our protestations of sincerity and intentions of decency, what concrete dikes are we erecting against the rising flood-tide of horror? . . . One has to live *in* the world, and accept it in all its frightening implications. One has to live consciously and self-consciously, in the involvement and in the alienation, in the loyalty and in the questioning, in the love and in the critical appraisal. Without that persistent double image we are lost. At best we can live in paradox.[13] □

These reviews, both by American critics, acknowledge the horrific power of Orwell's vision, and both recognise that the Soviet Union is a looming influence on the world of Airstrip One. Diana Trilling's review is the more astute for its refusal to interpret *Nineteen Eighty-Four* as an attack solely on socialism. She acknowledges the powerful iconographic taint of the Soviet Union, but rightly divines Orwell's intention to be the disman-tling of the mythologies surrounding totalitarian state-systems. She also reads the novel primarily as a warning rather than a dystopian prophecy. ('Dystopian' is defined by the *OED* as 'of or pertaining to an imaginary place or condition in which everything is as bad as possible'. For a fuller description of dystopian fiction, see p. 35.) For Trilling, Orwell is positing the entirely possible cascade of the British democratic process into a fer-ment of political and social unrest out of which could emerge the same intolerant masters who had until recently dominated Germany and Italy, as well as those that continued to dominate in Spain and the Soviet Union. Few reviewers showed Trilling's perspicacity, and Daniel Bell's review contains some of the hallmarks of the hysterical reaction to the threat of socialism. Bell's reading of *Nineteen Eighty-Four* focuses largely upon the apolitical implications of Orwell's representation of the will to power. He tends to see the novel as relating not to the specific historical circumstances of mid-twentieth-century Europe, but to the atemporal condition of human greed. Nevertheless, he writes with a growing sense of panicked paranoia as he casts around him for examples of rampant state control from which to adduce the presence of the totalitarian in the contemporary world. Unlike Trilling, who acknowledges the potentiality of Orwell's vision with a detached objectivity, Bell attempts to erect 'safeguards' and 'checks' against the abuse of pure power. His review tends towards a prophetic reading of the kind which Orwell tried to discourage, and yet less intelligent reviewers gleefully seized on the apocalyptic vision of the novel as a paradigm of the world under Soviet control. While Bell does not attribute anti-socialist affiliations to Orwell, it is clear that he sees the Soviet Union as the most potent example of the misuse of power. In the mouths of less astute reviewers, this discomfort would become explicitly right-wing, anti-Soviet propaganda.

Orwell was disturbed to learn that his novel was being read in some quarters as a diatribe against the Soviet Union. Yet it would have been more surprising had readers not interpreted the novel as a prediction of Soviet ascendancy, particularly given the context of the deepening rifts between East and West. Orwell's own publishers partly anticipated the flexible meanings which would be attributed to the text. In his report on the manuscript, Frederic Warburg presents a reading of the political alignment of the text with which Orwell would surely have disagreed:

■ This is amongst the most terrifying books I have ever read. The savagery of Swift has passed to a successor who looks upon life and finds it becoming ever more intolerable . . . Orwell has no hope, or at least he allows his reader no tiny flickering candlelight of hope. Here is a study in pessimism unrelieved, except perhaps by the thought that, if a man can conceive *1984*, he can also will to avoid it. It is a fact that, so far as I can see, there is only one weak link in Orwell's construction; *he nowhere indicates the way in which man, English man, becomes bereft of his humanity* . . . . . .

For what is *1984* but a picture of man unmanned, of humanity without a heart, of a people without tolerance or civilization, of a government whose *sole* object is the maintenance of its absolute totalitarian power by every contrivance of cruelty. Here is the Soviet Union to the nth degree, a Stalin who never dies, a secret police with every device of modern technology . . . . . .

The political system which prevails is Ingsoc = English Socialism. This I take to be a deliberate and sadistic attack on socialism and socialist parties generally. It seems to indicate a final breach between Orwell and Socialism, not the socialism of equality and human brotherhood which clearly Orwell no longer expects from socialist parties, but the socialism of marxism and the managerial revolution. *1984* is . . . worth a cool million votes to the conservative party; it is imaginable that it might have a preface by Winston Churchill after whom its hero is named. *1984 should be published as soon as possible, in June 1949 . . . . . .*

1984 by the way might well be described as a horror novel, and would make a horror film which, if licensed, might secure all countries threatened by communism for 1000 years to come . . . It is a great book, but I pray I may be spared from reading another like it for years to come.[14] □

That Warburg misconstrued Orwell's intentions is evidenced by his assertion that *Nineteen Eighty-Four* was 'worth a cool million votes to the conservative party'.[15] By suggesting that the novel represents Orwell's very public dissociation of himself from Marxist politics, Warburg dramatises the self-evident critique of an increasingly unequal ideology of egalitarianism, but fails to appreciate the implicit extension of that critique to all systems of power. Ultimately, this partial reading epitomised a popular response which embraced the satire of socialism, but ignored the warning against autocracy in all guises. Readers of the left were swift to condemn Orwell as an apostate and a victim of a decadent capitalism. One such attack in the Soviet journal *Pravda* portrays Orwell as a misanthropic puppet, corrupted with snobbery and imperialistic arrogance:

■ Mr Orwell is in every way similar to Mr Huxley, especially in his contempt for people, in his aim of slandering man. And while the one cries out, 'The voice of the proletariat is the voice of the devil,' the other, slobbering with poisonous spittle, does not lag far behind him. For in describing a most monstrous future in store for man, he imputes every evil to the people. He is obliged to admit that in 1984, when the events in the novel take place, capitalism will cease to exist, but only for opening the way to endless wars and the degradation of mankind, which will be brought down to the level of robots called 'proles.' . . . . . .

Thus, gruesome prognostications, which are being made in our times by a whole army of venal writers on the orders and instigation of Wall Street, are real attacks against the people of the world . . . But the people are not frightened by any such fears of the instigators of a new war. The people's conscience is clearer today than ever before.

The foul maneuvers [*sic*] of mankind's enemies become more clearly understandable every day to millions of common people. The living forces of peace are uniting ever more firmly into an organized front in defense of peace, freedom and life. They are the only hope man has for the salvation of culture. Led by the Soviet Union, these forces are mighty and indomitable. They will assure mankind happiness and prosperity despite the monstrous intrigues of the imperialists, the instigators of war.[16] □

Interpretational demarcations were clearly drawn with little flexibility between positions. *Nineteen Eighty-Four* was increasingly claimed for any number of contradictory ideological stances, with scant attention paid to its thematic complexities. As a product of a specific cultural history, *Nineteen Eighty-Four* encapsulated the political *zeitgeist* of hostility and mistrust at the same time as it reflected the underlying similarities of capitalistic and communistic power structures. The deepening divisions between East and West were articulated through a cultural product which sought to expose the machinery of power in a non-politically specific manner. Rarely has an artistic object been so divergently manipulated to prove the legitimacy and justness of disparate ideological systems; the text entering the political forum to such an extent that terms such as 'Big Brother' and 'doublethink' have a wide and self-perpetuating discursive currency across many cultures. Orwell reacted with consternation to this textual autonomy and the casual appropriations of his novel for prejudiced political causes. So distressed was he by the tenor of some reviews that he felt compelled to issue a statement through his publishers:

■ It has been suggested by some of the reviewers of NINETEEN EIGHTY-FOUR that it is the author's view that this, or something like this, is what will happen inside the next forty years in the Western world. This is not correct. I think that, allowing for the book being after all a parody, something like NINETEEN EIGHTY-FOUR *could* happen. This is the direction in which the world is going at the present time, and the trend lies deep in the political, social and economic foundations of the contemporary world situation.

Specifically the danger lies in the structure imposed on Socialist and on Liberal capitalist communities by the necessity to prepare for total war with the USSR and the new weapons, of which of course the atomic bomb is the most powerful and the most publicized. But danger lies also in the acceptance of a totalitarian outlook by intellectuals of all colours.

The moral to be drawn from this dangerous nightmare situation is a simple one: *Don't let it happen. It depends on you.*[17] □

That Orwell deemed such clarification to be necessary indicates the seriousness with which he viewed the monstrously protean qualities of his creation, and also the immediacy with which the novel was seized upon, codified, and either canonised or reviled. Such early wrangling was a mere foretaste of the posthumous struggle for memory that would succeed Orwell.

Early Critical Responses

Orwell's death at the age of 46 occurred during his period of greatest artistic renown but, while obituary writers lauded his achievements, his elevation to a canon of academic and intellectual importance was, for many years, uncertain. The academy has frequently looked askance at the writerly disciplines of journalism and reportage and, while Orwell's last novels had propelled him into the literary spotlight, much of his reputation, in Britain particularly, was still founded upon his journalistic output. In his obituary, Arthur Koestler, a fellow writer and friend, was in no doubt about the acclaimed status which posterity would accord to Orwell:

■ *Animal Farm* and *1984* are Orwell's last works. No parable was written since *Gulliver's Travels* equal in profundity and mordant satire to *Animal Farm*, no fantasy since Kafka's *In the Penal Settlement* equal in logical horror to *1984*. I believe that future historians of literature will regard Orwell as a kind of missing link between Kafka and Swift. For, to quote [Cyril] Connolly again, it may well be true that 'it is closing time in the gardens of the West, and from now on an artist will be judged only by the resonance of his solitude or the quality of his despair'.[18] □

Popular success followed Orwell throughout the early 1950s: his earlier novels were re-released to much acclaim, and the publication of a collection of essays, *England Your England*, maintained his image in the public's consciousness long after his death. Meanwhile, adaptations of his last novel for radio (BBC, 1950), television (BBC TV, 1954) and screen (Columbia Pictures, 1956) brought his ideas to an expanding audience, which in turn boosted sales of his books. By the mid-1950s Orwell was, claims John Rodden, an 'ideological issue and cultural phenomenon'.[19]

Critical recognition attended upon popular success, with the devotion of a special issue of the journal *The World Review* to his writing, containing eulogistic contributions from eminent public figures such as Malcolm Muggeridge and Bertrand Russell. In the same year, E.M. Forster wrote of Orwell's achievements and of the paradoxically double-edged sword of his latest and, in Forster's opinion, greatest work:

■ There is not a monster in that hateful apocalypse which does not exist in embryo today. Behind the United Nations lurks Oceania, one of this [*sic*] three world-states. Behind Stalin lurks Big Brother, which seems appropriate, but Big Brother also lurks behind Churchill, Truman, Gandhi, and any leader whom propaganda utilizes or invents. Behind the North Koreans, who are so wicked, and the South Koreans, who are such heroes, lurk the wicked South Koreans and the heroic North Koreans, into which, at a turn of the kaleidoscope, they may be transformed. Orwell spent his life in foreseeing transformations and in stamping upon embryos. His strength went that way. *1984* crowned his work, and it is understandably a crown of thorns.[20] □

Orwell as a Christ-like figure, sacrificing himself through his desire to warn about the future, may appear an extreme image, but this is certainly not an isolated example of such idolatry. Much early criticism of his work gallantly maintains the iconography of a saintly and prophetic Orwell whose death resonates with the demise of an era of innocence and naïvety. The hyperbolic nature of many of these assessments may be ascribed to their authors' close friendships with Orwell, or their sense of dutiful homage to his memory. John Atkins produced the first full-length study in 1954, an encomium which lauds Orwell's perspicacity, while simultaneously claiming that 'all the useful things that can be said . . . have already been said'.[21] The implied interpretational exhaustion towards which this comment points is evidenced in Atkins' own study, which consists primarily of textual summaries and biographical information. The following extract from his discussion of *Nineteen Eighty-Four* illustrates Atkins' general approach and that of much early criticism:

■ *1984* is one of those books that overpower you as you read but which do not leave any strong conviction in the mind. After you have read it you find yourself discovering faults in retrospect. The imaginative effort which impresses the reader at first turns out to be not imagination at all but a painstaking pursuit of existing tendencies to what appear to be logical conclusions. There is no tension in the story, which weakens its appeal as art. We know, and Orwell always maintained, that totalitarianism can only be challenged by individual values. This Winston Smith was quite incapable of doing. He was a weak creature who was born to be victimised. There is truth in this but no drama, and great fiction requires drama. . . . The novel is internally consistent, except in one passage which jars on the alert reader. This is where an announcement is made that Oceania is not after all at war with Eurasia but with Eastasia. Eurasia was an ally. We know that such switches were common and we can believe in them. It is not easy to believe, however, in the automatic way in which the crowd receives and accepts the news. We know that they are mentally servile but this is more than servility, it is sheer mechanism. Orwell has not persuaded us that the citizens of Airstrip One have become quite so inhuman. We know that the possibility exists, but generations of indoctrination and probably drug injection are necessary before possibility could become actuality. In fact, for a few pages Orwell slides from his prevalent realism to satire, which is completely out of place. . . . . . .

My advice to old ladies is not to be too frightened by this book. Apart from the soothing syrup of 'It may never happen', even an aware and informed mind finds it hard to accept the world of *1984* after a little reflection. It is the kind of world many of us have feared but we have not had the skill to portray it. Now Orwell has done it for us and we immediately see (or rather sense) its flaws. At first we think that Orwell has expressed our own fears, but a little later we realise that he has spotlighted their improbabilities. I think our chief hope lies in the evident inefficiency of large-scale bureaucracy that we see all over the world. Neither bureaucracy nor its inefficiency is a product of social-ism or collectivism, as is so often asserted. Bureaucracy is a condition of large-scale enterprise, whether public or private. Administration in large-scale enterprise is always more inefficient and wasteful than in small-scale enterprise, and it always provides more loopholes for speculation, intrigue and even rebellion. It is possible that a foolproof bureaucratic system may be devised but I see no signs of it at present. Under modern conditions it is inconceivable that any Government could control, even with the most advanced technical resources avail-able, a population so completely as is done in *1984*. So far the highly efficient totalitarian systems have been much less successful in their search for security and longevity than the blundering, old-fashioned liberal systems. There is one exception, and periodically that pot appears to come near boiling over. The most thoroughgoing of all the modern dictatorships and the most contemptuous of the effete liberal democracies was to have lasted a thousand years, and collapsed in ruins after twelve.[22] □

Percolating this passage are two distinct strands of criticism: on the one hand, Atkins clearly admires the intellectual and imaginative architec-ture of the novel and seeks to praise Orwell's achievement; on the other hand, he is preoccupied with testing the solidity of the vision against an existing reality. He tracks the novel's 'faults' and inconsistencies in an attempt to challenge the validity of Orwell's satire. There is undeniably an undertone of an 'it couldn't happen here' mentality as he attempts to calm the anticipated fears of old ladies by assuring them of the inefficiency of large-scale corporate culture. As distanced readers, it is not difficult for us to dismiss Atkins' assessment as a slightly hysterical reaction, but what is clearly articulated here is both the genuine fear of totalitarianism which pervaded post-war British society, and an associated form of interpreta-tional paralysis in which the significance of Orwell's writing is problem-atised by its immediate and emotional impact. Atkins, like other early crit-ics, is uncertain how to categorise and rationalise the demons released by the texts, and falls back upon suspect systems of containment which provide understanding, but at the expense of the texts' multivalent constructions. Perhaps the most significant irony of Atkins' approach lies in his desire to countermand the potentiality of Orwell's 1984, thereby deliberately ignoring the warning against complacency that Orwell had so vehemently inscribed and publicly reiterated. *Nineteen Eighty-Four* may not hasten the conditions of Airstrip One in England, but to ignore its significance may be to allow the cancer of totalitarianism to grow. Such critical assessments as Atkins' reveal the extent to which Orwell's novels are tied to the historical moment of the early Cold War, but are also more broadly situated within a tradition of writing about the nature of politics and power-corruption. It is that tradition which the next chapter examines in order to establish not just the novels' contemporaneity, but also their places within generic parameters.

CHAPTER TWO

The Unmaking of Utopia: Experiments in Genre

GEORGE ORWELL was a professional writer who, throughout his career, tried his hand at many diverse areas of literary production, each of which demanded individual skills and a sensitivity to both form and genre. Primarily a journalist as we have seen, Orwell became an accomplished essayist, documentarist, novelist, broadcaster and editor. He was effectively a literary chameleon, prepared to extend his talents to varied literary forms; in the last months of the Second World War he became a war correspondent for the *Observer*, a job unsuited to a man wracked by ill-health. Nevertheless, his ability to switch between different modes of writing and to accommodate the shifting generic and semantic characteristics of these forms has led to a certain degree of confusion as to how to categorise Orwell as a writer. As some of the contemporary responses detailed in the last chapter demonstrate, Orwell's status as a first-class novelist has been questioned repeatedly and, almost certainly, if it had not been for his last two novels, his reputation would have been dictated by his journalistic, rather than his novelistic, output. Even in the contemporary academic world, literary critics and cultural historians are dubious about claims for his artistic skill; *Animal Farm* and *Nineteen Eighty-Four* are strikingly powerful works, but whether they artistically merit the attention they have received is a question that has remained posed, but largely unanswered, by critics.

Part of this critical prevarication stems from a generic fluidity around these texts which prevents the establishment of their place within a literary tradition of writing about politics, writing about the future and writing about utopia. This may not appear intrinsically to erect any significant barrier to interpretation, but on a critical level it does problematise the definite boundaries of genre, form and readerly expectation. This chapter of the Guide explores the disputed positions of *Animal Farm* and *Nineteen Eighty-Four* within several genres and investigates the traditions they inherit and influence. More importantly though, this chapter shows how Orwell deliberately writes across generic boundaries and, in doing so, parodies and destabilises his reader's expectations of his texts. The most frequently cited category within which Orwell's last works are positioned is that of utopian fiction, a genre which, though popular around the turn of the century had, by the 1940s, undergone radical transformation to proffer increasingly negative visions of future societies. *Animal Farm* and *Nineteen Eighty-Four* straddle the boundary lines between utopia and dystopia, revealing both Orwell's deep desire for a democratic socialist society and, at the same time, his ingrained scepticism about the possibility of its fulfilment.

Utopian Dreams: Dystopian Nightmares

Utopian fiction, or the imaginary projection of a perfect society in which all need and want have been removed and conflict is eliminated, has a long history in British literature. Sir Thomas More's *Utopia* (1516) is a focal point in the tradition of the genre, and More's contemplation of a society removed from daily struggle to a place of ease has had a powerful and lasting effect on subsequent visions of the future. Dystopian fiction is the natural correlative of this literary mode and presents visions of imaginary worlds in which the worst of all possible social conditions pertains and where all ethical, aesthetic and metaphysical judgements are consequently problematised. It is impossible to provide a full history of these genres in this space, but it is useful to consider some of the utopias and anti-utopias that most influenced Orwell. Before doing that, however, it is important to establish the anticipated generic parameters that Orwell would have been familiar with. The next two extracts (from Krishan Kumar's *Utopia and Anti-Utopia in Modern Times* and Vita Fortunati's '"It Makes No Difference": A Utopia of Simulation and Transparency') give some indication of the history of utopian fiction and what a utopia should resemble. Kumar comments:

■ [Thomas] **More shows himself, and his Utopia, to be the product of a new age. His Utopia has a rationalism and a realism that we associate typically with the classical revival of the Renaissance, and that are to be found equally in the architectural utopias of fifteenth and sixteenth-century Italy. We should remember that *Utopia* was published less than three years after Niccolò Machiavelli's *The Prince* (1513). More's urbane and witty style, his 'profound sense of political realities', constantly evoke the relentlessly de-mystified world of Machiavelli's notorious treatise (and, incidentally, remind us that utopia and anti-utopia shadow each other very closely). ... ...**

Not just the Renaissance but also the Reformation defines the modern utopia. Barely a year after the appearance of More's *Utopia*, Martin Luther nailed his Ninety-Five Theses to the church door at Wittenberg (1517). Luther's challenge to Rome of course initiated an era of intense religiosity in Europe. But it was a religiosity marked by bitter conflict, and it ended leaving Europe exhausted and divided. After that, Europe preferred to express its passions in non-religious terms, in the terms of secular revolutionism. The Protestant Reformation, in other words, launched Europe, and eventually the world, on the road to secularization. It broke up the unity of medieval Christendom, and gave rise to such a plurality of discordant voices that they ended up by silencing each other. ... ...

It cannot be accidental, then, that the birth of the modern utopia coincides with the break-up of the unified Christian world. More's *Utopia* ... emerged out of the turmoil of the wars and conflicts of religion in sixteenth and seventeenth-century Europe. These conflicts led eventually to a secularized world, a world of new possibilities which opened up new forms and objects for utopia. In much the same way, and at much the same time, the European voyages of exploration and discovery were literally discovering a New World, which was bound to stir the utopian imagination. ... ...

The Renaissance, the Reformation and the European voyages of discovery are one conventional and still persuasive line of division between the modern and the ancient and medieval worlds. Utopia is, on this view, a creation of the modern world. It is a modern European novelty. Thomas More did not just invent the word 'utopia', in a typically witty conflation of two Greek words (*eutopos* = 'good place', *outopos* = 'no place'): he invented the *thing*. Part of that new thing was a new literary form or genre; the other, more important, part was a novel and far-reaching conception of the possibilities of human and social transformation.

More said of his *Utopia* that it was 'a fiction whereby the truth, as if smeared with honey, might a little more pleasantly slide into men's minds'.[1] All utopias are of course fictions, by definition; and in choosing the utopia over other possible literary forms, later writers did so with much the same didactic intention as More. In one sense this simply expressed the common Aristotelian preference for the study of poetry over history, fiction over fact, as more effectively communicating moral and social truths. But the fictional form that More invented for his purpose differed radically from the standard poetic forms, just as it differed from the philosophical dialogue that had been the principal vehicle for social and political speculation. ... ...

The fiction of More's *Utopia* and its successors is of a very different kind. It shows the best society not as a normative or prescriptive model but as actually achieved, as already in existence. Utopia is a description of the best (or, in anti-utopia, the worst) society not as an abstract ideal, and not simply as a satirical foil to the existing society, but as a society in full operation in which we are invited vicariously to participate. A group of travellers happens upon a hitherto unknown society in a remote part of the globe; a spaceship lands on a planet whose inhabitants have radically different lives from earthlings; a time traveller journeys backwards and forwards to strange and astounding times: all give us a detailed account of what they see and do, of their adventures among the utopians, of the mixture of disbelief and admiration with which they contemplate utopian life. In the later utopian tradition, as in the anti-utopias of Zamyatin, Huxley and Orwell, the journey to utopia, whether in space or time, is dispensed with, and we are plunged straight into the daily lives of the utopians. The authors avail themselves of the full range of techniques, including characterization and plot, however rudimentary, that we associate with narrative fiction. Here it is made clear what is not so apparent in the earlier utopias: that the utopia is closer to the novel than to any other literary genre; *is* in fact a novel, though not necessarily of the kind that we have come to identify too exclusively with its nineteenth-century form and focus.

More, then, invented, more or less single-handedly, a new literary genre. But the literary form of utopia is not an important concern of this study; nor perhaps should it be in any serious treatment of utopia. Very few utopias stand out as great works of literature – More's *Utopia* and William Morris's *News From Nowhere* are among the best – and in many cases utopian authors are perfunctory in the extreme in their selection and use of the form. The didactic purpose overwhelms any literary aspiration . . . In any case, any attempt to define the boundaries of utopia by purely literary criteria speedily ends up in absurdity, and is best abandoned for a recognition of the diversity of literary forms that make up utopia. . . . . . .

As so often with concepts in the human sciences, it seems best not to insist on some 'essentialist' definition of utopia but to let a definition emerge: by use and context shall we know our utopias. Following Wittgenstein's discussion of these matters, we should also not expect to find more than 'family resemblances' between various instances of utopia. So nothing is to be gained by attempting to be too precise or exclusive. . . . . . .

The realm of utopia is wide but it is not boundless. Utopia is not some unchanging human archetype or universal human propensity. Distinctions have to be made and these must be largely historical. If utopia is not in one very obvious sense concerned with the here-and-now, for the most part it draws both its form and its content from the contemporary reality. . . . The modern utopia is egalitarian, affluent and dynamic. Such a conception emerged under unique historical conditions. As these changed so the content and even, to an extent, the form of utopia changed. So we should not be surprised to find ourselves dealing with utopias of many different kinds, and with many different purposes, in the more than four centuries since More's *Utopia*. A strict definition of utopia would serve no useful purpose; as Nietzsche says, 'only that which has no history can be defined.'[2] □

Krishan Kumar explores the historical development of the utopian tradition and the section extracted here relates to the modern incarnation of utopia. For Kumar this form is characterised by a flexibility in form and parameters, but descends fundamentally from the period of secularisation in the wake of the Renaissance. The movement towards a humanist vision of the universe, where human rather than divine influence is seen as central to the primary logic of existence, gradually moves the idea of utopia away from idealised conceptions of religious communities and towards a secularised paradise. The Reformation and the opening up of the 'new world' to Western eyes accelerated this transition and brought about an iconography of utopia as socially (rather than religiously) harmonious and guided by non-hierarchical and non-materialistic principles of justice and egalitarianism. It is this tradition which Orwell and many of the anti-utopians of the twentieth century have inherited and subverted, in Kumar's opinion; an opinion which is interesting to compare with that of Robert Elliott cited later in this chapter (p. 44). This is Vita Fortunati on the genre of utopia:

■ From the very beginning of the genre, utopia has had a ludic quality in that it is a speculative game with reality expressed in terms of a *political proposal* which is set up against reality. The *model suggests a possible reality which could substitute for the existing reality.* A utopia always maintains a close and specific relationship with the sociopolitical environment from which it stems. The alternative proposal which it represents in the form of a radically different society springs from a harsh criticism of the utopian writer's present reality of departure. The essence of utopia is to be found precisely in this shifting of position between a projected environment which is not reality and the actual reality to which the projected environment is in opposition. Utopia is thus a game played between the two poles of reality and fiction. Both the strength and the weakness of utopia rest in the basic underlying ambiguity of the genre. It is a strength in that a utopia represents a tension towards the elsewhere which reveals the ability to *think about the Other*, to go beyond the given facts and reality. It is a weakness because in utopia, in the model, there is the abstraction of the real and its *simplification*.

We have proposed the image of utopia as a game, but we must remember that every match of utopia versus reality reveals different characteristics from those of the preceding bouts since not only is any expression of utopia situated within a complex network of echoes of the preceding utopias, but it also sets up a specific relationship with the present which generates it. Each utopia is characterized by its identity with previous utopias and is distinguished by its diversity from these; thus the tradition of utopia is multiple and multifaceted. The march of utopias is a march of identical elements which are specific in their individual diversity.[3] □

As Vita Fortunati points out, utopian projection is fundamentally a game in which a possible world is constructed and set up against a 'real' world in order to comment negatively on that reality. In such a way is Thomas More's *Utopia* seen as a covert attack on the politics and government of Henry VIII. It is futile, Fortunati suggests, for the fantasy of a utopian world to be entirely divorced from the reality with which it is intended to contrast; there must be a recognisable relationship in order for the satire to be effective. The utopia is thus neither a completely alien construction, nor the mirror image of an existing reality, but a transfiguration of the familiar into the unfamiliar. Yet whilst a principal motivation of the fiction may be to criticise a governing regime, the form itself often mitigates against that critique. By reducing the real to an abstraction, Fortunati argues, there is an inevitable simplification which revolves around straightforward comparisons of real and ideal. In many ways this is a problem inherent in the genre of utopian fiction: the fictive element largely involves the initial projection of the utopia itself which, once fully imagined, customarily gives way to the intricate detailing of how that world operates: a process which can be seen to lack narrative drive and tension. As Robert C. Elliott argues, the utopia differs from the novel in that it depends less upon plot and narrative development than upon a series of set-piece discussions in which the parameters of the utopia are established:

■ The fictional conventions of the utopia are far more stereotyped than are those of the novel. Consider *Gulliver's Travels*. In each of the four books the central character embarks on a voyage, lands alone in a strange country, makes contact with the inhabitants, learns about the customs and institutions of their land, makes certain comparisons with Europe, returns home. This is the prescriptive pattern of the genre. It admits, of course, of a good deal of variation, particularly in the journey (whether in space or time) into and out of utopia, and it may be dressed up with love stories, strange adventures, complications of various kinds; but the central element – the exposition of utopian life – is notoriously invariant. ....

The pleasure palls, however, under this relentlessly mechanical approach to the necessary expository problem. Whereas Plato's dialogue in the *Republic* is a process of exploration and intellectual discovery, the creator of a fictional utopia presents us with a thing made – a new thing that must be explained. The technical problem has baffled even the best writers. William Morris, for example, clearly recognizes that old Hammond's long discourse in the middle of *News from Nowhere* is painfully wooden. It deals with the prescriptive materials: the customs, the mode of life, the politics ('we have none') of the new society and how these came about. The account of 'How the Change Came' reflects Morris's own shattering experience of 'Bloody Sunday' in Trafalgar Square (1887); but although his passion invigorates Hammond's discourse, the old man is allowed to go on far too long. . . . The dialogue is static, however, and to alter the format of the page temporarily is not enough to lighten the heavy expository load. Splendid work that it is, *News from Nowhere* is irretrievably swaybacked, overborne by old Hammond's garrulity.

Still, the difficulty with this section of Morris's book is quantitative rather than substantive, for at the heart of any literary utopia there must be detailed, serious discussion of political and sociological matters. This seems to be inescapable and constitutes a major difference from the novel. F.R. Leavis is surely right to insist on the 'elementary distinction to be made between the *discussion* of problems and ideas, and what we find in the great novelists.'[4] The novelist's art is to metamorphose ideas into the idiosyncratic experience of complex human beings. For reasons advanced throughout this chapter, the utopian writer has rarely been able to accomplish this translation. Instead of incarnating the good life dramatically, novelistically, the characters of utopia discuss it. In part, this is a consequence of the fact that the fictional utopia is a bastard form, answering to the claims of a number of disciplines. It purports to present a more or less detailed picture of a society significantly better than that in which the writer lives. The nature of the enterprise inevitably elicits from the reader a series of questions: is the society depicted just? does it answer to legitimate human needs? would it work? would we like to live there? is the writer's criticism of his own society well taken? Because they are subject to the laws of politics, morality, sociology, economics, and various other fields, the issues to which these questions and dozens like them apply require discursive treatment. They belong to a reality foreign to that enacted in a novel. They are not literary issues, nor can the work which elicits and tries to answer questions about them be judged in terms applicable to the work of Henry James.[5] □

Elliott's critique of utopian fiction distinguishes the genre from the novel by its overtly political intent which dictates certain formalistic criteria, most notably a discursive exposition. The slightly unwieldy structure and the didactic content may go some way to explaining why utopian fiction has often been seen to offer only limited artistic and aesthetic possibilities. Instead, it has tended to be categorised as a genre related to broader conventions of science-fiction, which has fewer obvious restrictions on content and plot-progression and is less explicitly concerned with the political or sociological.

William Morris's *News from Nowhere* (1890) and Jonathan Swift's *Gulliver's Travels* (1726), both mentioned by Elliott, are two texts frequently cited by scholars as literary antecedents of *Animal Farm* and *Nineteen Eighty-Four*. Writing of the parallels between Swift's satire and *Nineteen Eighty-Four*, Jeffrey Meyers suggests:

■ The major Augustan [i.e. relating to the literature of the seventeenth and eighteenth century in England] influence on *1984* is *Gulliver's Travels*, especially Book III which, Orwell says, is an attack on totalitarianism and 'an extraordinarily clear prevision of the spy-haunted 'police-State', with its endless heresy-hunts and treason trials'.[6] Julia's mechanical job on the novel-writing machines is clearly derived from the Engine in the Academy of Lagado, 'so contrived, that the Words shifted into new Places, as the square bits of Wood moved upside down'. The absurd scientific experiments described in Goldstein's book [*The Theory and Practice of Oligarchical Collectivism*] are very like those Swift used to mock the Royal Society; and the 'Floating Fortress' is reminiscent of Swift's 'Floating Island' that also reduces rebellious subjects to obedience. In *1984* 'Newspeak was designed not to extend but to *diminish* the range of thought, and this purpose was indirectly assisted by cutting the choice of words down to a minimum'; the Houyhnhnms have no word in their language to express lying, falsehood or anything evil. And State control of love, sex and marriage is similar in Houyhnhnmland and Oceania. Love is deliberately excluded from marriage, which is an objective and dispassionate conjunction for the sole purpose of propagation. It is arranged by the State or parents on a pragmatic basis, and adultery and fornication are forbidden or unknown.[7] □

Swift's attack on the oppressive institutions of his day influenced Orwell from a very early age[8] and in many ways the force of Orwell's animalistic analogies in *Animal Farm* is supplied by its comparisons with *Gulliver's Travels*, a point noted by T. S. Eliot in his reader's report on the novel.[9] Whether Swift's novel falls into the category of utopian fiction has been long debated. Whilst Swift does construct new models of existence to contrast with the 'real' world that he criticised, none of these models are utopian in the sense of harmonious and integrated systems of social order. Such niceties of definition are largely immaterial, however. Orwell clearly drew on Swift in his contemplations of *Animal Farm* and *Nineteen Eighty-Four*, and *Animal Farm* in particular conveys a similar sense of faux-naïveté which can beguile the reader into underestimating the import of the tale.

Orwell's debt to Morris's utopia is much more straightforward and falls within a broader late nineteenth- and early twentieth-century history of utopian romances. Krishan Kumar traces this debt through some significant and highly influential texts:

■ To see *Nineteen Eighty-Four* as both a warning and a prophecy, both a contemporary analysis and a vision of the future as totalitarianism triumphant, is also to place it squarely within the tradition of modern utopian and anti-utopian writing. This, too, is increasingly being denied, usually on the contention that the book is fundamentally a satire, and so belongs more with works like *Gulliver's Travels* than with what Orwell called 'the chain of Utopia books' – Wells's *When the Sleeper Wakes*, Jack London's *The Iron Heel*, Zamyatin's *We* and Huxley's *Brave New World*. *Nineteen Eighty-Four*, says Bernard Crick, is 'Swiftian satire in the disguise but not in the tradition of the Utopian or dystopian novel'. Elsewhere he refers to it as 'a mutant of social novel and satiric polemic', pointing here additionally to its place in the tradition of Orwell's own fictional and non-fictional works of 'documentary realism', which aimed to shock and stir the reader by showing how things 'really are'.[10]

Now it is true that to concentrate on *Nineteen Eighty-Four* as the product of a chain of purely literary influences is to obscure its relation to its own times, and hence its central meaning. So, for instance, referring to Orwell's undoubted debt to Wells's *When the Sleeper Wakes* and 'A Story of the Days to Come', David Lodge rightly says: 'When all the debts of Orwell to the early Wells have been totted up, the fact remains that *Nineteen Eighty-Four* derives most of its power and authenticity from Orwell's imaginative exploitation of facts, emotions, and iconography specifically associated with Stalinist Russia, Nazi Germany and World-War-II-devastated Europe.'[11] The same thing can no doubt also be said of the equally obvious influence of Zamyatin's We, which like 'A Story of the Days to Come' contains the basic narrative pattern of *Nineteen Eighty-Four*: the opposition between two lovers and a totalitarian state. But then of course precisely the same observation can be made of Zamyatin and Huxley in relation to Wells. Both of these writers clearly 'borrowed' from Wells, but in the writing of their anti-utopias they were strongly influenced by many social and political experiences – the First World War, the Russian Revolution – which had not occurred when Wells was in his anti-utopian phase. Their anti-utopian visions, as a result, were of a quite different character from his, whatever the superficial similarities of plot and detail. But in each case what they presented – with no less a satirical element than in Orwell – was the anatomy of what they considered the distinctive form and tendency of modern society, together with its projection, in magnified and grotesque proportions, into the future.

This is what Orwell also did, as he himself seemed quite happy to acknowledge. 'My new book is a Utopia in the form of a novel', he wrote to Julian Symons (*not* 'a novel in the form of a Utopia', as Crick and others would rather have him say). Earlier he had written to Fredric Warburg that he was working on 'a novel about the future – that is, it is in a sense a fantasy, but in the form of a naturalistic novel.'[12] Both of these remarks suggest that Orwell was consciously working in the tradition he knew so well, the utopian tradition of Wells, London, Zamyatin and Huxley. Like these, he drew as a matter of course on other than purely utopian writings . . . Like these, too, he used satire and parody to make his point: the Appendix on 'Newspeak' is a good example of this, as also his treatment of the proles. And for good measure he threw in the style and much of the content of his political essays and documentary works. Such a mixture was bound to flaw the finished work somewhat, and to leave several puzzles in the minds of his readers as to his precise intentions. But in most ways *Nineteen Eighty-Four* does function, as Orwell intended it to, as an anti-utopian novel: both a warning and a prophecy.[13] □

Of particular interest in this passage is Orwell's insistence on *Nineteen Eighty-Four* being 'a Utopia in the form of a novel'. Clearly Orwell sees the text as a conflation of distinct genres and implicitly makes the point, one that Elliott stressed, that each convention demands different representational techniques and reading strategies. That Crick and others have misread Orwell's comment is indicative of the confusion around both the parameters of the genres themselves and the nature of the intermingling of forms that exists in *Nineteen Eighty-Four*. The texts by Morris, Wells, London, Zamyatin and Huxley to which Kumar refers were all produced within the fifty years around the turn of the century. They provide an interesting context for Orwell's novel because they show a gradual movement from idealised and positive visions of the future to bleak and visceral projections. The development from utopian harmony to dystopian dissonance is a crucial one, as it provides us with a context not only within which to place the production of *Animal Farm* and *Nineteen Eighty-Four*, but also within which to read them. The turning of dream to nightmare coincides with a period of great social and scientific change, which impinged upon romantic idealisations of the future. Developments in the physical and biological sciences, which had their roots in the work of evolutionary theorists of the mid-nineteenth century, impacted upon new social sciences such as sociology and psychology, which were beginning to come to the fore by century's end. That Morris was able to write in *News from Nowhere* (1890) about the potential for positive human development, given the right ethical, political, aesthetic and environmental conditions, disguises the fact that such comforting notions were being seriously challenged by his contemporaries. Robert Louis Stevenson's *Dr Jekyll and Mr Hyde* (1886), Bram Stoker's *Dracula* (1897) and H.G. Wells's *The Time Machine* (1895) all question the inevitability of human evolutionary development, presenting instead retrogressive degeneration as a potential future for humanity. Meanwhile, Wells again, in *When the Sleeper Wakes* (1899), and Jack London, in *The Iron Heel* (1909), portrayed the State as the enemy of the people, whom it enslaved and manipulated in the interests of maintaining power. These are only a few indicative references, but they reflect the breach that had emerged between a philosophical idealism which contemplated the possibilities of human perfectibility and a scientific pragmatism which seemed to dismiss such notions as blind romanticism. Robert Elliott sums up this gradual disenchantment with utopianism very effectively:

■ By the nineteenth century Western man's fantastically successful command over Nature by means of science and his faith in the inevitability of progress made it seem that utopia – the good society, the good life for man – was a necessary consequence of present historical processes. The presses groaned under the weight of projects. 'We were all a little mad that winter,' wrote Emerson, recalling the year 1840. 'Not a man of us that did not have a plan for some new Utopia in his pocket.' Despite harrowing anxieties which underlay much of the speculation, life seemed to move inexorably toward a new Golden Age. ... ...

But today, instead of fictional renderings of these heady statements of confidence, we have Orwell's *1984* and science-fiction visions of the horrors that await us if we survive. Of course the reason for this radical shift is painfully obvious: to have faith in the possibility of utopia, one must believe in progress; but one looks back at our two great wars, our mass bombings, our attempts at genocide – our collective plunge into barbarism; one hears the Geiger counters of the world clicking away – and it is next to impossible for a rational man to believe in progress. To believe in utopia one must believe that through the exercise of their reason men can control and in major ways alter for the better their social environment; but few men outside some of the Communist countries any longer have faith in the power of reason to bring about desired political ends of large magnitude. To believe in utopia one must have faith of a kind that our history has made nearly inaccessible. This is one major form of the crisis of faith under which Western culture reels.[14] □

This disenchantment also coincides with the period of cultural modernism and of the First World War – two phenomena which had an enormous impact on the way in which people viewed their world. Notions of human perfectibility became increasingly untenable in the face of the annihilation of a generation of young men. The suspension of ethical and moral sensibility which was necessary to countenance the continuation of the War prompted serious philosophical questions about the limits to which human behaviour could be stretched. The memory of the War and the devastation that it had entailed rendered visions of future perfection insubstantial, if not entirely untenable. The pre-eminence of the machine and its destructive capabilities were brought firmly into focus by the War and suggested a potential nightmare future in which the human individual is subordinate to an efficient and emotionless machine culture. Such horrors had already been pre-figured by such novels as *The War of the Worlds* (1898) by H. G. Wells, but in Eugene Zamyatin's *We* (1920) and Aldous Huxley's *Brave New World* (1932) the prospect receives its fullest treatment.

These two dystopian visions of a future society honed through technological mastery and ethical simplification to the point of perfect 'happiness' are the two most evident precursors of Orwell's projection in *Nineteen Eighty-Four*. In Zamyatin's vision of the future, the struggles of life have been rationalised to the point where all problems are susceptible to a mathematical solution, where freedom of expression has been subsumed within discourses of containment, and where love of humanity is construed as a need to be inhuman. The main character, only ever referred to as D-503 and not dissimilar to Winston Smith in his rebellion against the repressive nature of the state, is finally relieved of his qualms about state practices by the expedient of a lobotomy operation which literally removes the 'malfunctioning' portion of his brain. The greatest crime in Zamyatin's dystopia is to be human – perfectibility is achievable, but only through the loss of identity. Zamyatin, a brilliant mathematician and revolutionary writer, composed *We* as a response to what he saw as a perversion of the aims of the 1917 revolution. His critique, extremely prescient in the light of what was to happen in the Soviet Union under Stalin, shows how the lust for power released by revolution can blind those in authority to the aims and objectives that were originally sought. Orwell clearly drew heavily on Zamyatin for both *Animal Farm* and *Nineteen Eighty-Four*. The theme of revolution betrayed is one which haunts *Animal Farm* as the pigs gradually turn a collective into an autocracy. In addition, the starkness of *We* and its emphasis on control of the mind, or the elimination of that mind, inevitably recalls Oceania.

Orwell's reaction to *Brave New World* was more equivocal. The state in Huxley's novel provides its citizens with happiness and stability, with protection, amusement, purpose and pleasure in return for submission to the Controller. In the pursuit of happiness, certain metaphysical variables have been lost: truth and beauty have become taboo, art has been abolished, belief in God outlawed. The individual has the ability to choose a form of happiness-induced narcosis but must, in return, forsake those things which define what it means to be human. The tension in the novel comes from the desire of the main rebel character, aptly named Savage, to choose unhappiness, and experience instead the full gamut of human emotions. His ousting from the protection of the State parodically mirrors that of Adam and Eve from Eden and his eventual suicide suggests that, like Zamyatin and later Orwell, Huxley felt that the individual who stands against or outside society is ultimately doomed. Yet Orwell did not agree with Huxley's presentation of a pristine, if artificial, happiness as the ultimate human panacea. In fact, he felt that the novel was fantastical and over-rated. As he points out in a letter to a *Tribune* reader:

■ I think you overestimate the danger of a 'Brave New World' – i.e. a completely materialistic vulgar civilization based on hedonism. I would say that the danger of that kind of thing is past and that we are in danger of quite a different kind of world, the centralized slave state, ruled over by a small clique who are in effect a new ruling class, though they might be adoptive rather than hereditary. Such a state would not be hedonistic, on the contrary its dynamic would come from some kind of rabid nationalism and leader-worship kept going by literally continuous war. . . . I see no safeguard against this except (a) war-weariness and distaste for authoritarianism which may follow the present war, and (b) the survival of democratic values among the intelligentsia.[15] □

So where exactly do Orwell's last novels fit into the genres of utopian and dystopian fiction? Clearly they seem to fall most comfortably into the tradition of dystopian writing canonised by Wells, Huxley and Zamyatin, but, at the same time, one must heed Orwell's statements that the future that is presented in *Nineteen Eighty-Four* is not an inevitability. His novel is intended as a warning against that future: to continue down the totalitarian path could lead to such a state as Oceania, but such an eventuality is not inevitable. Orwell does not suggest that a utopian future is either possible or impossible, but by the time he had come to write *Nineteen Eighty-Four* he was deeply sceptical about the workings of bureaucracy and about the will to power of the individual. His cynicism in the final years of his life contrasts strongly with the optimism he still retained during the writing of *Animal Farm*. This may seem an unusual statement, given that *Animal Farm* tells of a revolution betrayed by self-interest, and on one level this is undoubtedly the case. However, the actions of the pigs on *Animal Farm* do not negate the positive outcomes of the revolution. Orwell does not suggest, as some critics have inferred, that all revolutionary actions are bound to fail; only that those motivated by self-interest will invariably replicate the systems of oppression that were being overturned in the first instance. In many ways, the sentiment behind this novel is utopian; it does suggest that harmony and accord can be attained by collective responsibility and action. Only by a system of truly democratic socialism can such a utopia be achieved and although the Russian Revolution was socialist by name, the democracy that it should have instilled was, for Orwell, forgotten in a porcine tussle for pre-eminence at the trough.

More than a Fairy Story: Orwell's Use of Allegory and Fable

Whilst much of the foregoing has suggested that Orwell wrote with one eye firmly on the traditions of utopian literature, it is also important to consider other genres with which he experimented. This is particularly the case with *Animal Farm*, whose apparent simplicity belies a very complex structure of generic intertwining. This will be discussed in more depth later in the Guide, but at this juncture it is worth considering the traditions which Orwell manipulates in *Animal Farm*. Most prominent amongst those are the allegory and the fable – two very traditional modes of writing which are conventionally invested with moralistic or didactic significance, but in Orwell's case are utilised as a means of making political comment about the immanent will to power of human beings. Interestingly, whilst *Animal Farm* is commonly described as either an allegory or a fable, Orwell chose in his sub-title to indicate another tradition from which it may have derived: *Animal Farm: A Fairy Story*. Such a signposting of the way in which he wished the novel to be read may seem disingenuous. Whilst giving the story a child-like aura, the subtitle also indicates a frivolity and lack of serious intent that is not evidenced by the intricacies of the novel's structure. To have entitled the book *Animal Farm: An Allegory* or *Animal Farm: A Fable* would immediately have alerted the reader to the sub-textual content, and thereby firmly placed the text as a satire or a morality tale, a determinism which Orwell deprecated. Instead, by maintaining the ostensible façade of a children's story, Orwell is able to forestall such readings and point to the novel's apparently guileless simplicity. In the extracts which follow, the impact of this game with genres is explored and reveals an Orwell fully conscious of the traditions he is writing in and against.

Animal Farm's debt to the genre of the beast fable has been noted in numerous locations. The tradition of using animals as mouthpieces for human opinion has a long history, incorporating *Aesop's Fables* (sixth century BC), Chaucer's *The Parliament of Fowls* (1380–2) and *Gulliver's Travels* (1726). As Christopher Hollis points out, the fable form presents distinct difficulties of tone and balance:

■ The problems that are set by this peculiar form of art, which makes animals behave like human beings, are clear. The writer must throughout be successful in preserving a delicate and whimsical balance. As [Samuel] Johnson truly says in his criticism of Dryden's *Hind and the Panther*, there is an initial absurdity in making animals discuss complicated intellectual problems – the nature of the Church's authority in Dryden's case, the communist ideology in Orwell's. The absurdity can only be saved from ridicule if the author is able to couch his argument in very simple terms and to draw his illustrations from the facts of animal life. In this Orwell is as successful as he could be – a great deal more successful incidentally than Dryden, who in the excitement of the argument often forgets that it is animals who are supposed to be putting it forward. The practical difficulties of the conceit must either be ignored or apparently solved in some simple and striking – if possible, amusing – fashion. Since obviously they could not in reality be solved at all, the author merely makes himself ridiculous if he allows himself to get bogged down in tedious and detailed explanations which at the end of all cannot in the nature of things explain anything. Thus Orwell is quite right merely to ignore the difficulties of language, to assume that the animals can communicate with one another by speech – or to assume that the new ordinance which forbids any animal to take another animal's life could be applied with only the comparatively mild consequence of gradual increase in animal population. He is justified in telling us the stories of the two attacks by men for the recapture of the Farm but in refusing to spoil his story by allowing the men to take the full measures which obviously men would take if they found themselves in such an impossible situation. The means by which the animals rout the men are inevitably signally unconvincing if we are to consider them seriously at all. It would as obviously be ridiculous to delay for pages to describe how animals build windmills or how they write up commandments on a wall. It heightens the comedy to give a passing sentence of description to their hauling the stone up a hill so that it may be broken into manageable fractions when it falls over the precipice, or to Squealer, climbing a ladder to paint up his message.

The animal fable, if it is to succeed at all, ought clearly to carry with it a gay and light-hearted message. It must be full of comedy and laughter. The form is too far removed from reality to tolerate sustained bitterness. Both Chaucer and La Fontaine discovered this in their times, and the trouble with Orwell was that the lesson which he wished to teach was not ultimately a gay lesson. It was not the lesson that mankind had its foibles and its follies but that all would be well in the end. It was more nearly a lesson of despair – the lesson that anarchy was intolerable, that mankind could not be ruled without entrusting power somewhere or other and, to whomsoever power was entrusted, it was almost certain to be abused. For power was itself corrupting. But it was Orwell's twisted triumph that in the relief of the months immediately after the war mankind was probably not prepared to take such dark medicine if it had been offered to it undiluted. It accepted it because it came in this gay and coloured and fanciful form.

The film version [Bacheler and Halas, 1955] gives to *Animal Farm* a happy ending. The animals all the world over, hearing how Napoleon has betrayed the animal cause, rise up against him at the end and in a second revolution expel him. After this second revolution, we are left to believe, a rule of freedom and equality is established and survives. But of course this ending makes nonsense of the whole thesis. It was the Orwellian thesis, right or wrong, that power inevitably corrupts and that revolutions therefore inevitably fail of their purpose. The new masters are necessarily corrupted by their new power. The second revolution would necessarily have failed of its purpose just as the first had failed. It would merely have set up a second vicious circle.

Animal Farm possesses two essential qualities of a successful animal fable. On the one hand the author of such a fable must have the Swift-like capacity of ascribing with solemn face to the animals idiotic but easily recognized human qualities, decking them out in aptly changed phraseology to suit the animal life – ascribe the quality and then pass quickly on before the reader has begun to find the point overlaboured. ... ...

But what is also essential – and this is often overlooked – is that the writer should have himself a genuine love of animals – should be able to create here and there, in the midst of all his absurdity, scenes of animal life, in themselves realistic and lovable. In that Chaucer, the first and greatest of Orwell's masters in this form of art, pre-eminently excelled. It was in that that Orwell himself excelled. He had always been himself a lover of animals, intimate with their ways. 'Most of the good memories of my childhood, and up to the age of about twenty,' he wrote in *Such, Such were the Joys*, 'are in some way connected with animals', and it was the work with animals which attracted him in maturer years to agricultural life.[16] □

As Hollis intimates, part of the difficulty of employing a form such as the fable lies in the inevitable negotiation of the suspension of disbelief which must be in place to enable readers to accept the ability of animals to talk, rationalise and, above all, conceptualise complex ideological theories. To succeed in this, Hollis suggests, the author paradoxically needs to forget that the main characters are animals, but never to lose sight of their animality. This is an intriguing idea and perhaps points towards Orwell's decision to use this particular form. The essentially ludicrous notion of politically motivated animals would seem to work against the sharp distinction of the satire against the betrayed revolution and yet it is this fundamentally unconvincing quality of the novel which gives it much of its power. The simplicity of form demands of the reader both a willed suspension of disbelief and simultaneously, an active political and historical consciousness. The novel, therefore, never becomes weighted down with its own seriousness, or insubstantial because of its child-like formula. It is this inherent self-contradictoriness that has led many critics either to underestimate the text or over-deterministically to impose readings. Patrick Reilly touches on some of these issues of construction in the next passage:

■ The artistic triumph is inseparable from the chosen form; its good humour and equanimity stem from its status as animal fable. It was initially rejected by American publishers on the ground that there was no market for animal stories.[17] We smile at a judgement so childishly blind to the allegorical import, yet this in itself is a tribute to the art. There is, in any case, something decisive about the Aesopian base: the choice of animals rather than human beings gave Orwell for the first time a certain latitude, release from that sense of moral constraint that otherwise held him captive, driving him to violate knowingly the unity of *Homage to Catalonia*, soliciting his own intervention throughout other books. The liberating secret lay in making animals behave like men.

Men behaving like animals, if comic at all, makes for a comedy verging on nightmare, that of [Ben Jonson's] *Volpone* or *Gulliver's Travels* – the Yahoos alarm us not as beasts but as brothers, for Gulliver's shocking discovery is that beneath his European disguise he is a 'perfect Yahoo'. Animals behaving like men are, by contrast, inherently funny, the fact so assiduously exploited by Walt Disney – even the villainous tiger of *The Jungle Book* has proved irresistible to generations of delighted children. . . . *Animal Farm* is so exuberantly successful because one cannot hate an animal, not even when the animal is Napoleon, a nasty pig who is farmyard stand-in for a monstrous dictator.

The very style of the fable tames catastrophe through levity, resolves terror in comedy. In life Orwell dreaded totalitarian propaganda as the supreme iniquity of our time, the throttling of truth even as a theoretic possibility; in the art of *Animal Farm* the image of a pig up a ladder with a paintbrush alchemises the horror into humour, putting Orwell and the reader in serene control of the situation. If the other animals are taken in by Squealer's impudent trickery, so much the worse for them – the reader isn't such a fool, and when he laughs at the bungled cheat he simultaneously proclaims his happy superiority to it. Material unbearable in life becomes in art a source of comic delight. When the newly liberated animals, obedient to the first duties of the victors, bring out the hams from Jones's kitchen to enact the solemn ritual of interment, the reader is invited to smile rather than mourn (p. 14). Orwell's burial of the dead has nothing in common with T. S. Eliot's.

In a book where comedy rules, it is fitting that Jones should be chased off the farm with no more than a few butts and kicks, that, after his pride, his backside is the most serious casualty of the Battle of the Cowshed. Admittedly, his eventual death in alcoholic delirium is horrific enough, but it is self-inflicted, and, like the catastrophes of classical drama, occurs off-stage. The fable is inhospitable to anything resembling the ghastly conclusion in the cellar at Ekaterinburg – the reader would be revolted at the Joneses trampled to death under the horses' hooves or devoured by the dogs. We only hear that Jones has children because of the old discarded spelling-book which the pigs rescue from the rubbish heap in order to learn to read. In fact the Czar's children, not their primer, were flung on the rubbish heap, but the fable softens reality. Orwell insists on a victimless revolution. When, later, the men invade the farm, Orwell will not allow any of them to be killed in the successful counterattack. ... ...

Nevertheless, the form of the fable reprieves the reader from the sense of chill disillusion he must otherwise surely feel – we need only contrast it with its successor to see the truth of this. Moving from *Animal Farm* to *Nineteen Eighty-Four* is like leaving Lilliput for Brobdingnag, passing from a situation of control to one of helplessness: Gulliver the man mountain is shockingly reduced to the most impotent of creatures. *Animal Farm* diminishes, *Nineteen Eighty-Four* magnifies, and, while the diminution is a delight, the magnification is a nightmare. In the fable Stalin becomes Napoleon, and, however fearful on the farm, Napoleon cannot terrify us; like Jack at the end of *Lord of the Flies*, he dwindles in the presence of the adult human being, becomes, at worst, an unpleasant nuisance, never, what he is for his fellows, lord of life and death. However successful against the men in the fable, we know he could never take the farm away from *us*. In the prophecy Stalin becomes Big Brother, the tyrant in the most teleologically perfect scnsc, invincible, undeceivable, inescapable, god rather than man.

When Europe dwindles to a farm and twentieth-century history to a record of barnyard chicaneries, the effect is similar to that achieved by Swift when he presents the history of *his* times as the squabbles of Big- and Little-Endians, the rivalries of low heels and high. Becoming smaller, things become less menacing and more manageable. By contrast, the institutions and rulers of *Nineteen Eighty-Four* are monstrously and appallingly enlarged. The whole world is dominated by three super-powers, and even Big Brother's acolyte, O'Brien, seems to the helpless Winston a kind of superman. The diminution is done to *us*, for it is Winston, the individual, the human representative, our spokesman, the last man in Europe, who shrivels into insignificance and, beyond that, to unpersonhood. On the farm the reader is like Swift in Lilliput, surveying, whether with amusement or exasperation the antics of inferior beings, men and animals alike: we are not *in* but *above* the story, and it is this Olympian security that finally makes it a comedy in Aristotle's sense. But, in the dystopia, the reader, as entrapped as Gulliver in Brobdingnag, is made painfully aware through Winston of their shared nullity, and, in his enforced identification with the mined 'hero', feels as impotent as Gulliver in the hands of the giants. Orwell's readers should fear the worst when he invites them to leave today's farm and accompany him on a journey to tomorrow's nightmare.[18] □

Like Hollis, Reilly points towards the reader's expectations of the fable genre as central to the power of the novel. The apparent conformity to the conventions of the form and the unwillingness to break the (albeit bleakly) comic spell by introducing the more appalling acts of the revolution renders the satire more forcefully. The reader is more prepared to accept the seriousness of the criticism because the form is not intrinsically undermined; the integrity of the form complements the asperity of the satire.

To say that Orwell respects the formalistic qualities of genres is not to suggest that he does not manipulate or destabilise the borders of those genres. In the final two passages of this chapter we see how, in both *Animal Farm* and *Nineteen Eighty-Four*, Orwell challenges the generic conventions of utopian fiction and allegory in order to subvert them. On *Animal Farm*, Lynette Hunter writes:

■ While *Animal Farm* is not utopian it does contain the twin elements of satire and allegory which Orwell thought of as the basis for the genre, and the consequent doubleness of reading has resulted in much critical controversy. Constructing the simple satire of the story is a plot line of similarity with actual events, specifically with those of the Russian Revolution and its immediate consequences. There are inescapable one-to-one associations between the animal figures and specific human characters which are established by direct linear connections. These direct comparisons are didactic, and from a defining authoritarian stance that designates one figure to one character.

Such naïve satire is not only resented because of its tone, but is at a fundamental disadvantage because of its logic of direct one-to-one connections. No figure or image can provide an adequate representation of an actual human being. The attempt to do so leaves the reader dissatisfied and encourages him to find fault with the work. Naïve representational satire raises objections not only because its definitive manner appears to dominate over the reader leaving him no personal involvement, but also because many readers will disagree with the narrow definitions it is imposing upon the situation it discusses.

Many readers are tempted to think of allegory as a similar associative process, which would differ from satire only by reinforcing instead of criticizing the standards being presented. But the word allegory has as its root 'allos' or 'other', and 'other' does not just imply the one thing standing for the other, which is the word as emblem or even as a restricted coded sign for the object. . . . allegory attempts to communicate by admitting that it cannot express what it wants to say adequately. This does not leave its technique as a negative dismissal of the ability to communicate. Instead it tries to involve the reader by alerting him to the radical difference between what is being said and of what it is speaking, of the impossibility of conveying any identity absolutely, and of the consequent need to interact with the words to achieve any communication.

The concept is not new. The stance of allegory recognizes that the external world exists outwith the control of human beings. It exercises a rhetoric or a persuasion that is positive because of its willingness to step outside often restrictive and isolating man-made definitions, in order to recognize the external. Whether that externality be theological, spiritual, material or mystical, the primary human response to the world through allegory is one of attempted interaction with it, all the while perceiving that it cannot be fully controlled. Allegory provides a counterpoise to those stances which respond to the world by attempting to control and define it within their own terms. As Orwell suggested, fantasy is an important contemporary rhetorical stance which tries to control by creating an isolated world of its own within which the inventor rules supreme. To isolate itself successfully, it needs the strategies of a negative rhetoric. Depending upon which medium it realizes itself in – the literary, the political, the historical, the scientific – its generic features will change. In literature for example the image of the island is particularly important to a fantasy stance because it provides a natural isolation from actual life. . . . .

Allegory like fantasy is a rhetorical stance. As such it is not a theory of knowledge nor a specific generic mode of expression. Although current attitudes to perception or to media affect its manifestations, it is primarily concerned with realizing a belief about the relationship between human beings and their world. For example, the generic confusion surrounding the many different kinds of literature that make use of alternative, non-actual worlds within their techniques, arises from failing to perceive the ways in which different stances structure the same generic aspects. Orwell's separation between the contrasting use of similar alternative worlds that opposes the genre of fantasy to utopia, satire and 'allegory', is based on whether they attempt to exercise power or to stimulate involvement. The distinction indicates his understanding of a rhetorical, rather than generic or epistemological, basis for the stances. It also places him in the forefront of critical studies in this area. ... ...

But further, because the root of allegory is interaction rather than imposition, specific definitions and enumerated theories are difficult to provide. Guides to strategies that adapt and change in particular practical circumstances are about as far as the criticism can go. But fiction, which is more clearly recognized as a particular case, can present its context more fully in the activity or stance of its text. It can more easily avoid domination and control over other examples or situations because it is recognized as an analogy for them rather than a set of definitions about them. In all cases, not just in the literary, allegory establishes a process in which a human being admits that he cannot fully know the 'other', the external world. He not only admits but makes that admission the source of his experience or expressiveness. It is a process opposite to the establishing of private identities for actual things and events external to one. What allegory effects and is concerned to realize is the activity of one's lack of knowledge. It is often frightening because it throws us back on the things we do know and these are shown to be limited. Because it is frightening it is often resisted, avoided and denied.

Human beings crave and appear to need group certainties, some escapes, delusions of knowledge and authority that allow us to abdicate activity. Without them people create their own, and because these are private and not shared they are thought abnormal, insane. Societies could be said to be bound together on common grounds of escape. The catch is that without a coincident pursuit of the 'other', the escapes become rigid, unsatisfactory and technically decadent. Imagination could be described as the faculty which allows us to deal with the concept of the 'other'. If, as Orwell suggests, words and worlds fossilize through historical accretions, allegory is a device for stripping away those accretions. Allegory also strips away the accretions of the self, but in doing so it allows us to see again differently and with intensity the things other than ourselves that surround and place us.

Once allegory engages the reader or writer in activity with the 'other' or the external, it assumes the position of a positive rhetorical stance. The stance not only involves the writer in self-examination but also involves the reader in self-discovery. It does not try to lay down the exact representations of figures, events or reactions which emblematic, one-to-one definitions attempt. Instead it suggests parallel and divergent activities that often indicate directions of involvement through interpretation; and it does so by presenting the difference and radical separation which the text overtly establishes between the figure or image, and the actuality.

It is helpful to recall the different strategies that satire and genres informed by allegory employ in their use of alternative worlds. Where genres of fantasy, such as romance, need the alternative to ensure the isolation necessary for the completeness of their desires, satire establishes an alternative world which is similar enough to actuality to propose criticisms in the contrast and comparison of the two. The problem for satire is that because its structure is dependent upon the actual it may become too tied to the very things it attacks. It may acquire a stance like that of fantasy and begin to protect and isolate the grounds it initially sought to cut away.

Allegory goes further and tries to juxtapose a radically different alternative with the accepted perception of the world. The allegorical stance challenges both writer and reader to interact with the external rather than control it by imposing upon it. Genres employing an alternative world through an allegorical stance will use its difference from the conventional to encourage a fundamental change in the way human beings participate in the world. These genres cannot help but guide the reader, but their stance attempts to stimulate him to involve himself rather than dictate his response.

As an allegory *Animal Farm* does provide a didactic element but it is actively educative rather than authoritarian; it raises questions about itself and its processes at the same time as it questions its concerns. The allegory reforms a naïve satire into a complex satirical presentation of party politics and propaganda that is based on metaphorical not associative figures, and involves difference as well as similarity. But the novel also functions as straight allegory, discussing the interaction between personal and party politics and the communication that that interaction depends on, by establishing a fundamental separation between the strategies involved within the text itself. The interaction of those strategies provides a guide to or an active analogy for the communication it is discussing. To read the work as a complex satire is rewarding. It provides a sound education in the rhetoric of politics, but its conclusion appears cynical and negative. Only if read simultaneously as allegory does it proffer a positive conclusion.[19] □

As well as providing a very perceptive insight into the ways that allegory functions as a mode of literary expression, Hunter's extract shows how *Animal Farm* goes beyond the limits of the genre in order to extend them. As she says, although Orwell's novel can be read as a straight allegory, working within that architecture are micro-structures based around the difference rather than the similarity between the Russian Revolution and the mutiny on *Animal Farm*. It is this distinction between metaphorical and associative allegory which takes the novel beyond naïvety and into astute satire. We will come back to Hunter's work later in this Guide to see how that satire is dependent upon the shifting tone of the narratorial voice and its interaction with implied reader and implied author.

On *Nineteen Eighty-Four*'s subversion of utopian fiction's conventions of representation, Vita Fortunati argues:

■ In *1984*, Orwell takes the ideas and images with which the utopian imagination had worked in the past and turns them upside down. He makes the language of utopia his own and rewrites it in terms of parody. *1984* sets up an intertextual dialogue with the utopias which precede it and inverts the values of these models using characteristic techniques of parody such as amplification and grotesque.

It is not within the scope of this present study to analyze in detail the many parts of the novel where Orwell may be seen to be rewriting the utopias of the past. However, I shall here concentrate on two of three of the most important *topoi* [plural of topos; 'a stock theme in literature', *COD*] of utopian literature which Orwell systematically inverts or turns inside out. In this way, the anti-utopia explodes the whole genre of utopia.

The typical utopian city, well-ordered, harmonious and perfect in all its parts, the very layout of which reflects the sociopolitical ideals of the utopian writer, in *1984* is represented by a decaying, bomb-shocked London of ruins and skull-like houses denuded of windows. In the standard utopia there ruled a harmonious relationship between both man and his environment and man and the State. The constant watchful regard of power in Oceania does not unite its people, but rather isolates and separates them.

As O'Brien says, 'It is the exact opposite of the stupid hedonistic Utopias that the old reformers imagined.' It is thus in no way a utopia founded on love and justice. 'A world of fear and treachery and torment, a world of trampling and being trampled upon. . . . The old civilizations claimed that they were founded on love or justice. Ours is founded upon hatred. In our world there will be no emotions except fear, rage, triumph, and self-abasement.' (p. 279)

The total transparency of the standard utopian place which hides nothing of its workings and leaves no shadow of doubt or uncertainty of its motives and functions under the all-pervading light of rationality, honesty and truth becomes in Oceania total invisibility. In Oceania, mirrors do not reflect; glass is opaque. As C.S. Lewis said, a totally transparent world is an invisible world.

The appendix giving details of Newspeak may also be read as a sort of parody of the utopian principle that everything should be apparent at a single glance, including the language (pp. 312–26). With Newspeak, Orwell ridicules the various different attempts (for example, new alphabets) by earlier creators of utopias to invent a pure, simple language which would be transparent in all its parts. Newspeak is thus a parody of pure and simple language, a language mutilated and homogenized.

Even O'Brien the dictator may be seen as a parody of the creator of utopias, a moralist, censor, and pedagogue who wants to reform humanity, as represented in Winston Smith, 'the last man' of a generation which is in the process of becoming extinct. O'Brien represents future humanity, the new man, man uprooted from his past culture and history, man with no memory, stripped of his own individual identity and his own past.[20] □

According to Fortunati, Orwell's version of utopia in *Nineteen Eighty-Four* is essentially parodic – it deliberately calls to mind those utopias that have preceded it in order to deconstruct them. Admittedly Fortunati's arguments are slightly too generalised and curtailed to be utterly convincing, but the key point that is being made is that in the dystopic world of *Nineteen Eighty-Four* Orwell has not simply envisioned all the worst eventualities, but has effectively inverted many of the cornerstones of a utopian society. This is a reflection of the ideal and, as much as the novel incorporates a sense of a post-1945 austerity, it also challenges many of the notional principles fundamental to the construction of a utopian community.

Although *Animal Farm* and *Nineteen Eighty-Four* sit firmly within generic traditions and make demands upon readers based around those traditions, they also seek to exploit the assumptions and presumptions that are implied by those forms. Orwell was a master of different journalistic discourses and in the construction of his final novels he installs and then subverts fictive discourses in order to heighten the reader's awareness of the parameters and limitations of those discourses. In a process often termed defamiliarisation, Orwell takes genres to which reader have become accustomed and manoeuvres them in such ways as to make them appear new and unfamiliar. Consequently, we are always simultaneously reading with and against the generic grain of the text. In many ways this conflictual reading process reflects broader contradictions within Orwell's writing generally and, partly, at least, accounts for some of the confusion that has dogged critical assessment of the last works. It is this battle for critical ownership of Orwell that the next chapter examines.

CHAPTER THREE

Modes of Criticism 1

Political Paradoxes, Psychobiographical Investigations and Feminist Demythologies

CHAPTERS THREE and Four of this Guide seek to provide a broad overview of the dominant schools of thought in Orwellian criticism from the 1950s to the present day. By distilling this critical output into generalised categories of response, it becomes clear that study of Orwell has tended to follow well-worn lines of inquiry based largely upon issues of political, biographical and ideological import. This is not to suggest that alternative critical perspectives do not exist; merely that they are overshadowed by the weight of material which locates Orwell firmly within an historicised and overtly politicised context. In the present chapter, therefore, the intention is to explore three key modes of critical response to *Animal Farm* and *Nineteen Eighty-Four*, namely: readings which address the ambiguous nature of the texts' politics; psychobiographical readings which revolve around the man/book dichotomy; and feminist reinterpretations of both the man and his work which became increasingly popular through the 1970s and 1980s and coincided with the rise of feminist schools of theory in Anglo-American academic institutions. Whereas Modes of Criticism 1 may be seen to focus on the macrostructure of Orwell's reputation, Modes of Criticism 2 will explore specific clusters of critical inquiry which have repeatedly emerged in studies of *Animal Farm* and *Nineteen Eighty-Four*. The extracts in these chapters are not arranged by order of date, nor by their authors' political affiliations or nationalities. Instead, they are guided by common critical concerns and reflect upon each other as much as upon the work they address. Ironically, given the depth of criticism on him, the following survey reveals a telling stagnation in Orwell studies. Even recent criticism has chosen to focus on established aspects of Orwell's politics and personality, whilst contemporary theoretical readings, along poststructuralist or postmodernist lines, are virtually non-existent. This reluctance to approach Orwell through theories which have dominated late twentieth-century literary critical discourse reiterates Orwell's contested position within a canon of British literature, but also evinces the often personal and identificatory relationship that critics have with both the man and his texts. As we shall see, Orwell's reputation amongst critics has been subject to frequent reappraisal and readjustment in the light of the critic's own changing politics. The case study of Raymond Williams, for instance, evidences the ambiguous reactions of the British political Left to Orwell's work, but also shows how closely Williams' own political education is linked to Orwell's writings. Such personal association between writer and critic is unusual and indicates the complex matrix of emotions inspired by Orwell's last novels.

Political Paradoxes

Orwell's writing has fascinated readers and critics alike and few would suggest that his influence on twentieth-century culture has been anything less than highly significant. Yet he remains an enigmatic figure, emblematic of a mid-century ideological fluidity that endorsed and then rejected Communism within a relatively short period. Orwell's shifting political associations, whilst relatively uncomplicated in themselves, have given rise to an enduring confusion as to his suitability as an icon of either Right or Left. As we see from the following two extracts, the first by Alaric Jacobs, a writer and schoolboy peer of Orwell, and the second from *Harper's* magazine by Norman Podhoretz, Orwell's rejection of hard-line Stalinist Communism had, by the 1980s, transformed him into both a hate-figure for the Left and an idol of the conservative Right. This is what Jacobs has to say:

■ For me *Nineteen Eighty-Four* is one of the most disgusting books ever written – a book smelling of fear, hatred, lies and self-disgust by comparison with which the works of the Marquis de Sade are no more than the bad dreams of a sick mind. Only a very sick man could have written it, and six months after it appeared Orwell was dead. Apologists for *Nineteen Eighty-Four* maintain that it is not only a prophecy of what is bound to happen if socialism is misdirected, but an attack on fascism and Nazism as well. We know that neither Hitler nor Mussolini abolished the capitalist system; on the contrary, private wealth continued to accumulate. But in *Nineteen Eighty-Four* Ingsoc has triumphed, the old system of private enterprise has gone for ever, Big Brother rules over a squalid, poverty-stricken society in which only the Party bosses retain some semblance of what had once been the good life. Ingsoc is in fact no more than a projection of the kind of regime which extreme anti-Communists have always envisaged as existing in the USSR since 1917 and which anyone who has lived in that country, as I have done, knows to be a travesty of the truth. Despite all the stupidities, errors and crimes that have been committed in the name of Marx it is absurd to suggest that the millions who live in the Communist world are universally downtrodden and depressed. Aspiration, ambition, love and the pursuit of happiness are as common in Moscow as they are in Manchester.

The history of socialism in England is a history of betrayal. The Labour Chancellor of the Exchequer who observed in recent days that 'Socialism is a word I haven't used for many years' typifies generations of working-class politicians who, beginning as revolutionaries who never bothered to read Marx, ended up in the House of Lords. But a socialist of Orwell's presumed integrity must be judged by higher standards. To write a book like *Nineteen Eighty-Four* is to present a gift of inestimable value to those who hate socialism and who would wish, as Churchill once did, to 'strangle it at birth'. In the thirty years and more since Orwell died several generations have been indoctrinated with the idea that socialism leads inexorably to the horrors described in that book. This is a lie but it is widely believed, and the man who launched it is the same wretched little boy who was so unhappy at St Cyprian's School.

Orwell's basic defect is that although he produced convincing reasons for hating the world he knew, he was quite unable to put forward any ideas for the future happiness of mankind – save for a sentimental vision of rural working life before the 1914 war from which most real workers have been only too eager to escape. ... ...

Orwell owed his rise to fame not to fellow socialists but to the conservative establishment in Britain and America who seized upon his last two books with delight. Forty years ago they first heard Orwell's voice telling them just what they wanted to hear, and they were overjoyed. In their eyes, here was a truly honest socialist who had come to hate socialism – not just Russian socialism but socialism of any kind. Because Orwell concentrated on the dangers that are certainly inherent in socialism, rather than the benefits such a form of government can bring, it was possible to read him in this light. And of course, from *Animal Farm* onward, the time was absolutely ripe.[1] □

Here is Podhoretz's view:

■ ... there can be no doubt that Orwell did belong in 'the camp of the Cold War' while he was still alive. Nor can there be much doubt that if he were alive today he would have felt a greater kinship with the neo-conservatives who are calling for resistance to Soviet imperialism than with either the socialist supporters of détente or the coalition of neutralists and pacifists who dominate the 'peace movement' in Europe and their neoisolationist allies in the United States.

For consider: Orwell's ruling passion was the fear and hatred of totalitarianism. Unlike so many on the Left today, who angrily deny that there is any difference between totalitarianism and authoritarianism, he was among the first to insist on the distinction. Totalitarianism, he said, was a new and higher stage in the history of despotism and tyranny – a system in which every area of life, not merely (as in authoritarian regimes) the political sphere, was subjected to the control of the state. Only in Nazi Germany and the Soviet Union had totalitarianism thus far established itself, and of the two the Soviet variety clearly seemed to Orwell to be the more dangerous.

Indeed, Orwell's loathing for Nazi Germany was mild by comparison with his feeling about the Soviet Union. He was sufficiently serious in his opposition to fascism to risk his life in struggling against it in Spain (where as a soldier he was very nearly killed by a bullet through the neck). Yet he showed surprisingly little awareness of how evil Nazism actually was. Not only did he never write anything like *Animal Farm* about the Nazi regime; there is scarcely a mention in all his writings of the death camps. (Two of his closest friends, Arthur Koestler and T.R. Fyvel, saw a relation between this curious 'blind spot' about Nazism and his equally curious hostility to Zionism.)

When Orwell wrote about the dangers of totalitarianism, then, whether in his essays or in *Nineteen Eighty-Four*, it was mainly the communist version he had in mind. To be sure, he followed no party line, not even his own, and he could always be relied on to contradict himself when the impulse seized him. At one moment he would denounce any move to establish good relations with the Russians, and at another moment, he might insist on the necessity of such relations.

But these were transient political judgments of the kind that, as he himself ruefully acknowledged, were never his strongest suit. What he most cared about was resisting the spread of Soviet-style totalitarianism. Consequently he 'used a lot of ink' and did himself 'a lot of harm by attacking' the successive literary cliques that had denied or tried to play down the brutal truth about the Soviet Union, to appease it, or otherwise to undermine the Western will to resist the spread of its power and influence.

If he were alive today, he would find the very ideas and attitudes against which he so fearlessly argued more influential than ever in left-wing centers of opinion (and not in them alone): that the freedoms of the West are relatively unimportant as compared with other values; that war is the greatest of all evils; that nothing is worth fighting or dying for; and that the Soviet Union is basically defensive and peaceful. It is impossible to imagine that he would have joined in parroting the latest expressions of this orthodoxy if he had lived to see it return in even fuller and more dangerous force. ... ...

Orwell was never much of a Marxist and (beyond a generalized faith in 'planning') he never showed much interest in the practical arrangements involved in the building of socialism. He was a socialist because he hated the class system and the great discrepancies of wealth that went with it. Yet he also feared that the establishment of socialism would mean the destruction of liberty. In an amazingly sympathetic review of F. A. Hayek's *The Road to Serfdom* Orwell acknowledged that there was 'a great deal of truth' in Hayek's thesis that 'socialism inevitably leads to despotism,' and that the collectivism entailed by socialism brings with it 'concentration camps, leader worship, and war.' The trouble is that capitalism, which 'leads to dole queues, the scramble for markets, and war,' is probably doomed. (It is indeed largely as a result of the failure of capitalism that the totalitarian world of *Nineteen Eighty-Four* comes into being.)

Suppose, however, that Orwell had lived to see this prediction about capitalism refuted by the success of the capitalist countries in creating enough wealth to provide the vast majority of their citizens not merely with the decent minimum of food and housing that Orwell believed only socialism could deliver, but with a wide range of what to his rather Spartan tastes would have seemed unnecessary luxuries. Suppose further that he had lived to see all this accomplished – and with the year 1984 already in sight! – while 'the freedom of the intellect,' for whose future under socialism he increasingly trembled, was if anything being expanded. And suppose, on the other side, he had lived to see the wreckage through planning and centralization of one socialist economy after another, so that not even at the sacrifice of liberty could economic security be assured.

Suppose, in short, that *he* had lived to see the aims of what he meant by socialism realized to a very great extent under capitalism, and without either the concentration camps or the economic miseries that have been the invariable companions of socialism in practice. Would he still have gone on mouthing socialist pieties and shouting with the anticapitalist mob?

Perhaps. Nothing has been more difficult for intellectuals in this century than giving up on socialism, and it is possible that even Orwell, who so prided himself on his 'power of facing unpleasant facts,' would have been unwilling or unable to face what to most literary intellectuals is the most unpleasant fact of all: that the values both of liberty and equality fare better under capitalism than under socialism.

And yet I find it hard to believe that Orwell would have allowed an orthodoxy to blind him on this question any more than he allowed other 'smelly little orthodoxies' to blind him to the truth about the particular issues involved in the struggle between totalitarianism and democracy: Spain, World War II, and communism.

In Orwell's time, it was the left-wing intelligentsia that made it so difficult for these truths to prevail. And so it is too with the particular issues generated by the struggle between totalitarianism and democracy in our own time, which is why I am convinced that if Orwell were alive today, he would be taking his stand with the neoconservatives and against the Left.[2] □

The polarised Orwells that are constructed in the assessments of Jacobs and Podhoretz bear little relation to Orwell's own protestations over his political vacillations. Instead, they reveal a significant manipulation of the popular perception of Orwell and perhaps reflect more accurately the prejudices and political predispositions of Jacobs and Podhoretz. The reader of Orwellian criticism is consistently confronted with such a paradox; Orwell's own persuasions are endlessly recast as supporting or refuting disparate political locations. Podhoretz's central premise to his article – what would Orwell's politics be if he were alive in 1983 – is a curious, compelling and yet strangely irrelevant basis for a reassessment. Orwell's political views, forged in the maelstrom of 1930s international brinkmanship and reconsidered in the event of world war, are historically specific to the conditions that gave rise to them. To extrapolate those views into political and ideological contexts about which Orwell could have no knowledge is an arbitrary gesture which reveals a great deal about the ways that the Orwell mystique has been perpetuated in his absence, but little about his actual political beliefs. Whether or not Orwell would have tended towards the Right in the wake of the Cold War, as Podhoretz suggests, is an immaterial projection which ironically does not take account of the vacillations in political affiliation that he frequently underwent, and would presumably have continued to undergo, and which the article uses as the basis of claim for Orwell as a neoconservative. What is interesting in both these polemical pieces is that they demand of Orwell a political foresight which would in some way predict the conditions of ideological fluctuation in the aftermath of his death. Expectations of Orwell, as presented in these extracts, are exceptionally high in that both Jacob and Podhoretz challenge his attitudes towards the Soviet Union from their position of 1980s hindsight, a perspective which Orwell never achieved. This expectation is intriguing in itself because it suggests the ways in which Orwell's predictive skills actually work against his reputation. Criticism such as the above threatens to decontextualise Orwell and construct him instead as an ahistorical visionary, capable of comment on the most divergent of issues. Orwell as prophet comes very close in these cases to outgrowing Orwell as writer.

Questions of Orwell's political fidelity go far deeper than the establishment of his anti-Communist, pro-socialist democracy credentials. For Jacobs and Podhoretz the issue is clear: Orwell is a socialist apostate whose flirtation with Soviet ideology ultimately gave way to disillusion, allowing the residue of an imperial self to be revitalised. Orwell is the arch-conservative and a precious object to the Right; a convert who has seen the absolute justice and righteousness of the capitalist, individualistic state. From opposing ideological positions, both construct an image of Orwell that is some distance from the revolutionary radical polemicist that earlier critics envisaged. Yet as Isaac Deutscher suggests in the next extract, Orwell's last fictions were of such monumental significance in a period of ideological self-consciousness that they were always destined to signify in widely disparate ways, and would always become instruments of political propaganda:

■ The novel has served as a sort of an ideological super-weapon in the cold war. As in no other book or document, the convulsive fear of communism, which has swept the West since the end of the Second World War, has been reflected and focused in *1984*. The cold war has created a 'social demand' for such an ideological weapon just as it creates the demand for physical super-weapons. But the super-weapons are genuine feats of technology; and there can be no discrepancy between the uses to which they may be put and the intention of their producers: they are meant to spread death or at least to threaten utter destruction. A book like *1984* may be used without much regard for the author's intention. Some of its features may be torn out of their context, while others, which do not suit the political purpose which the book is made to serve, are ignored or virtually suppressed. Nor need a book like *1984* be a literary masterpiece or even an important and original work to make its impact. Indeed a work of great literary merit is usually too rich in its texture and too subtle in thought and form to lend itself to adventitious exploitation. As a rule, its symbols cannot easily be transformed into hypnotizing bogies, or its ideas turned into slogans. The words of a great poet when they enter the political vocabulary do so by a process of slow, almost imperceptible infiltration, not by a frantic incursion. The literary masterpiece influences the political mind by fertilizing and enriching it from the inside, not by stunning it.[3] □

Taken from Deutscher's highly influential essay '*1984* – The Mysticism of Cruelty', this passage perfectly illustrates the manner in which history had outstripped Orwell's prognostications even by 1954. Part of Orwell's cultural mystique in the years before 1984 was drawn from his apparently prophetic ability to predict the future conditions of Cold War politics, and yet his reputation simultaneously became ensnared in the very process he described. The repeated recyclings of history that the Party demands in *Nineteen Eighty-Four*, the 'perfecting' of language into a single system of truth and the ability of doublespeak to juxtapose contradictory concepts, have all been brought to bear upon Orwell's legacy to such an extent that *Nineteen Eighty-Four* is capable of simultaneously signifying numerous contradictory 'truths'. For Deutscher, Orwell's importance lay not in the accuracy of his prediction but in his position as a conduit for broader feelings of insecurity. *Nineteen Eighty-Four* is the canvas upon which a nervous public paints its own demons and, because there is sufficient flexibility in Orwell's portrayal of the perpetrators of Ingsoc to allow numerous readings, a single, stable interpretation becomes increasingly untenable. Consider, for example, the Soviet interpretation of *Nineteen Eighty-Four*, common in the late 1950s, in which Orwell is considered to have portrayed life in present day America, under the pernicious aegis of a Big Brother surrogate, J. Edgar Hoover and his ubiquitous FBI.[4] Such interpretations fly in the face of Western anti-Stalinist readings but reflect the text's multivalency. *Nineteen Eighty-Four* was to become a totem of Cold War antipathies; a novel indicative of collective rather than individual consciousness, and as such increasingly tangential to Orwell himself.

Questions about Orwell's political identity crisis have dominated studies of Orwell's politics. Was he a socialist, a conservative, or a bizarre mixture of both? Are his novels fundamentally revolutionary or do they assert that class action will always result in failure? How do we account for Orwell's ambiguous attitude towards the proletariat? These questions continually appear in criticism, as the following extracts show. Writing in 1961, John Mander drew parallels between Orwell's own political views and those enshrined in his final work:

■ We have arrived at the fundamental contradiction in Orwell: that he was both a revolutionary and a conservative. It would be over-simplifying the case to call him a revolutionary by instinct and a conservative by intellect. He was rather, as Goldstein's Testament shows, both at once. Even in *1984*, in a moment of utter despair, he still looks forward to the day of revolution: 'If there is hope, it lies in the proles' (p. 72) can mean nothing else; it is the only way out. Yet, equally, it is no way out at all; for the Low will lose their battle, and the Middle and the High re-establish themselves (pp. 209–12). It is thus wrong to say, as some critics have done, that Orwell had no theory of history. He had a surprisingly well-developed one. It is essentially, as I have suggested, a Devil's parody of the Historical Dialectic. 'There must always be revolutions' is its first premiss; and its second 'all revolutions are entirely useless' [see *The Theory and Practice of Oligarchical Collectivism* (pp. 191–226)]. It is a theory that contrives to be revolutionary and conservative at one and the same time. And it shows also, I think, that Orwell had more of the Marxist in him than is usually recognised.[5] □

Mander constitutes Orwell as janus-faced, at once conservative *and* revolutionary, a man who longs for the social upheaval of revolution but with the desperate knowledge that revolution is bound to fail. This Orwell, ostensibly Marxist in outlook, nevertheless leans towards a form of conservative quietism in the face of inevitable hierarchies of class and power. A distinctly fatalistic Orwell emerges here, one that hopes for change but only with an abstract expectation of its fulfillment. This pessimistic vision of Orwell in his later days is a recurring trope in criticism and has enjoyed a popular cultural currency, casting Orwell as a failed prophet figure, capable of seeing a potentially bright future but always knowing its unavailability.

A more straightforwardly conservative reading is provided by Christopher Hollis:

■ Orwell's complaint was not so much against an ideal philosophy of Conservatism, for which, when he found it, he had a reasonable respect, as against those who called themselves Conservatives and had captured the Conservative machine. His complaint against them was that they were at once too arrogant and too compromising. They were too arrogant in so far as they tended to claim their privileges as something which they had deserved and to arrogate to themselves the airs of superior people. These very claims obscured the true case for Conservatism which was that society had to be arranged, that there was little reason to think that it would ever be arranged ideally well, that it was fatally easy for men to fritter away all their energies in agitation and scheming for its rearrangement and that therefore there was always something to be said, within limits, for accepting society broadly as it is and getting on with the business of living. It may very well turn out that there would be more liberty that way than down a more revolutionary, more ideally perfectionist, road – and liberty was what really mattered. Even in his most revolutionary moods – as in 'England, Your England' – he was, if we analyse his argument, primarily concerned with the proclamation of a libertarian and egalitarian purpose. Once the purpose was proclaimed he was quite content in practice to let things move forward at a slow and conservative pace. Willing to impose drastic sufferings upon himself, he never, save in moments of special exaltation, imagined that it would be possible to impose such drastic sufferings on society at large and to preserve freedom.

But a more important complaint against the Conservatives was that they were too compromising. While the case for Conservatism was that it stood for traditional ways and ancient liberties against the menace of the new philosophies, the Conservatives in practice, he complained, had shown themselves always only too ready to do a deal with the new philosophies and 'the stream-lined men', as Pilkington did his deal with Napoleon, as soon as the 'stream-lined men' had shown themselves to be in the least tough and strong. They did a deal with the Fascists before the war and with the Communists in the Anglo-Russian alliance during the war. Orwell despaired of the Conservatives because the Conservatives despaired of Conservatism. They were without principle.[6] □

Here we are presented with a purely conservative Orwell whose flirtations with the Left are broadsides against the intractability of modern conservatism. For Hollis, Orwell's fundamental concern is the pursuit of liberty and to that end more can be achieved by a conscious acceptance of society's implicit hierarchies than by dissipating one's energies on dreams of revolution. Hollis's interpretations are interesting but limited and have received much condemnation from other critics. They do, however, represent an approach to Orwell which became increasingly popular during the 1960s and 1970s, when the Left began seriously to question his relevance to a changed political and ideological Europe. One prominent figure of the Left who engaged consistently with Orwell's work and whose critical appraisal of that work turned from admiration to scepticism was Raymond Williams. An important critic amongst the British Left in the aftermath of the War, Williams initially hailed Orwell as a guiding light for socialist sympathisers, but as the following passage shows, he came to readdress that opinion and considerably to qualify his previous enthusiasm. The passage is from John Rodden's book on Orwell's literary reputation and provides an excellent case study which is worth quoting at length:

■ As the twenty-six-year-old co-editor of the Cambridge University journal *Politics and Letters*, Williams had some slight contact with Orwell. . . . Williams' 1955 article in *Essays in Criticism* reflects his and the young Left's still strong and affectionate attachment to Orwell. The Orwell chapter in *Culture and Society* (1958) is obviously the same essay revised. The difference in the first two stages of Williams' response to Orwell can be seen by contrasting the first and last paragraphs of the two pieces:

'It is not so much a series of books, it is more like a world.' This is Orwell, on Dickens. 'It is not so much a series of books, it is more like a hero.' This, today, is Orwell himself. . . . We look elsewhere [than to bravery in war] for a different mode of virtue; we emphasize one of the alternative definitions of hero – 'a clear-seeing, self-reliant, valiant man.' Orwell is our most common illustration. (1955)

'It is not so much a series of books, it is more like a world.' This is Orwell, on Dickens. 'It is not so much a series of books, it is more like a case.' This, today, is Orwell himself. . . . It is not that he was an important thinker. . . . It is not that he was a great artist. . . . His interest lies almost wholly in his frankness. (1958)

If . . . [conservative Laurence Brander's *George Orwell*] introduces new readers to Orwell's work, it will have served a useful purpose. And it may be seen also as a kind of memorial to the man; to one who was kindly, brave, frank and good, and whom we should long remember. (1955)

I maintain, against others who have criticized Orwell, that as a man he was brave, generous, frank and good, and that the paradox of his work is not to be understood solely in personal terms, but in terms of the pressures of a whole situation. . . . His conclusions have no kind of general validity, but the fact is . . . that good men are driven again and again into this kind of paradox. . . . We have to try to understand . . . how the instincts of humanity can break down under pressure into an inhuman paradox; how a great and humane tradition can seem at times . . . to disintegrate into a caustic dust. (1958)[7]

Williams' 'hero' worth remembering in 1955 became his 'case' worth 'understanding' in 1958. His clear-sighted 'hero as exile' became 'the good man' caught in an historical paradox. . . . in *Culture and Society*, Williams lauded Orwell's character while delicately knocking his judgment, thus patronizing his work with faint praise as 'frank' and well intentioned even as he dismissed it as naive and misguided. . . . . . .

The Orwell chapter in *Culture and Society* reflects the tension between Williams' official Communist reading of Orwell and his still-deep attraction to his heroic image of Orwell as a hater of orthodoxy and the intellectual's Common Man. Looking more critically and less admiringly at Orwell than in 1955, Williams felt torn in 1958 between affection for Orwell the man and distaste for Orwell 'the propagandist.' Now in his mid-30s and from a generation once-removed from Orwell's, Williams split 'the man' and 'the writer' as a way of preserving his attachment to Orwell. He sought in *Culture and Society* a middle course between acceptance and condemnation of Orwell, striving instead to sympathetically 'understand' Orwell's 'situation.' Orwell saw the working classes as 'not yet conscious,' Williams argued. 'One day they will be so, and meanwhile [Orwell] keeps the truth alive.'[8] . . . . . .

By the late 1950s, Williams . . . had shifted Left attention away from *Animal Farm* and *Nineteen Eighty-Four* and toward Orwell's popular culture essays on boys' newspapers, crime thrillers, and penny postcards. A depoliticized 'cultural' Orwell thus replaced the 'ideological' Orwell of the Cold War in this second stage of postwar Left reception. During what became known as the 'cultural' phase of the New Left (1957–62), Orwell seemed, Williams later wrote, the one intellectual from an older generation who had 'tried to live and feel where the majority of English people were living and feeling, reporting, understanding, respecting, beyond the range of Establishment culture.'[9] .. ...

Williams says he disagreed with the young Left's inflated image of Orwell in the 1950s. Nevertheless he felt fascinated by it. He realized that his and Orwell's careers had crisscrossed even as their interests had dovetailed. Williams, son of a railway signalman, was the lower-class Welsh boy moving up into Cambridge circles and the 'snooty' journals (as editor of the *Cambridge University Journal* and *Outlook*) which Orwell derided; Orwell was the lower-upper-middle-class Etonian plunging (temporarily) into the world of the tramps and miners. Both Williams and Orwell would spend much of their careers looking over their shoulders at the classes which they left. .. ...

By the time of the . . . escalation of the Vietnam War, many Left intellectuals had concluded that 'reading their Orwell' had led to political passivity and resignation. . . . Williams . . . in *George Orwell* . . . constructed an admirable 'young' Orwell, the tramp and Catalonia militiaman, and a disillusioned 'mature' Orwell of *Animal Farm* and *Nineteen Eighty-Four*. .. ...

But Orwell's maudlin myth of England as a 'family' and his Trotskyist notion of a People's Revolution won via wartime social transformations perverted his thinking during the early 1940s, said Williams. These illusions gave rise to a 'stale revolutionary romanticism' and then to reaction and 'despair' when the expected revolution failed to occur. The 'older' Orwell of *Animal Farm* and *Nineteen Eighty-Four* thus became, Williams agreed with Thompson, the fatalistic archetype for their generation: 'We can write Berlin, Algiers, Aden, Watts, Prague in the margins of Orwell's passivity. . . . What in Orwell was a last, desperate throw became for many others, absurdly, a way of life.'[10] .. ...

Williams himself by 1971 had become a model for younger radicals; and one can observe in the tensions of his response to Orwell hereafter a subtle feature of the dynamics of the reputation process: how the audience which the authoritative voice represents not only influences him and is influenced by him in more obvious senses, but how he may also begin to shape his message and identity in accord with what he believes his constituency wants him to say. In a very real sense he can become captive to his followers, for the model is drawn to scrutinize their responses to him, and the more he watches their responses, the more likely he in turn begins to model himself on them – or to feel paralyzed, the victim of his own fame. . . . . . .

By the close of Williams' 1971 monograph, Orwell's individuality has evaporated in Williams' ideological categories. Orwell the India-born 'exile,' public school boy from a 'lost class,' and Burma police-man embraces the 'illusion' that 'capitalist democracy' was becoming 'social democracy' during the war and inevitably slips into a period of 'radical pessimism' after it. *Animal Farm* and *Nineteen Eighty-Four* con-stitute an 'overadjustment' to capitalism's wartime 'contradictions.'[11] The overadjustment, however, seems more like Williams' own. *Culture and Society* sought to 'understand' Orwell's historical 'situation'; the monograph makes Orwell's historical situation and social structure the determinants of his work. And so the 'paradox' motif of 1958 becomes the thesis of 1971. Paradox and contradiction are 'paramount' in Orwell's history; the Marxist categories leave us here, with Orwell himself a vexing 'paradox.' Williams, however, stopped short of draw-ing the conclusion to which his own analysis had driven him: that ideology cannot provide a total explanation of Orwell, no more than it could, say, for 'working-class,' 'Cambridge-educated' 'Professor' Raymond Williams. The fact is that 'Eric Blair' and 'George Orwell' transcend ideological categories; the individual residue – that which finally made *this* India-born Etonian and policeman into 'Orwell' – remains. . . . Williams' attempts to disengage himself from Orwell were obviously part of a longer and even more traumatic process of dissociating himself from the Labour Party and 'pragmatic' leftism altogether, a lengthy divorce whose 'final break' took place in 1966, when his 'long-looked-for' Labour Party parliamentary majority turned Britain not toward socialism or social democracy but 'into an actual and necessary agency of the mutation of capitalism by the repre-sentative incorporation of the working class.' . . . . . .

Williams' estrangement from Orwell finally erupted into open hos-tility in the late '70s. In this fourth stage of reception, which was also reflected in the increasingly hostile attitude of the *New Left Review* toward Orwell, Williams concluded that what had originally drawn him to the heroic Common Man Orwell – his sense of Orwell's plain-ness, decency, and honesty – was a sham. Orwell's style was widely 'received as wisdom, achievement, and maturity,' Williams said in his Orwell interview in *Politics and Letters*, obliquely referring to his own response, 'although it was false to the core.' Williams felt duped; Orwell's deceit, rather than the exaggeratedly heroic image of Orwell projected by his younger self, was to blame. Prodded throughout the interview by the editors of the *New Left Review*, Williams admitted that

Orwell's 'impression of consistent decency and honesty was an invention.' *Animal Farm* and *Nineteen Eighty-Four* could only have been written
by 'an ex-socialist.' Because of his new awareness of Orwell's false plain-
man persona and 'defeatism,' Williams said, he could not even affirm
his reserved judgment of 1971. *George Orwell* had been 'the last stage of
working through a sense of questioning respect' for Orwell and now a
very much harder assessment was due. But even this task seemed
overburdening. 'I am bound to say, I cannot read him now.' ... ...

In Williams' attempt to find a road around Orwell is reflected the
entire postwar Left's frustrated struggle to forge a program and vision
beyond the first Labour government under Attlee: the achievements
and large personalities of the 1940s still tower before socialists of the
1980s as a standard and judgment. Orwell, the young Left's intellectual
model in the 1950s, is now often perceived as its obstacle and foe.
And, for some, one suspects that Orwell as Enemy of The People
became a personal enemy. For by dislodging Orwell, Williams could
clear space for himself – and for his own reputation – and so 'move on'
in more than one sense. His history of response to Orwell was reception as anguish and displacement; it illustrates what happens when a
reader tries to salvage a hero who has become increasingly objection-
able. First Williams took Orwell whole, seeing his weaknesses as the
price of his strengths, then he carved him up to minimize the 'late'
Orwell of *Animal Farm* and *Nineteen Eighty-Four* but finally he judged
him 'false to the core' and rejected him as unbearable. Thus does the
inspiration of the heroic become the anxiety of influence.[12] □

The above is an abbreviated version of Rodden's analysis of Williams's
disaffection with Orwell, but it does reveal the complex responses that
Orwell induced, particularly in the British Left, which sought in vain for
a consistent and consensual line to such an important popular symbol of
Socialism. Admittedly Williams's reactions constitute a special case and
writers of the Left such as Richard Hoggart and E.P. Thompson maintained a more consistently sceptical attitude towards Orwell. Williams is
fascinating for the emotionality of his response and for what it reveals
about the position of Left-wing politics within post-War Britain. As Rodden
details, that position demanded constant renegotiation throughout the
period of the Cold War and the prominence of Orwell's memory
throughout the 1950s and 1960s necessitated either the accommodation
or rejection of his views within the ideological make-up of the British
Left. Williams's vacillations suggest both his own ambivalence towards
the ambitions of the Left-wing in British society and the curiously inde-
finable position of Orwell within the political spectrum as a whole. By
trying to constrain him within a specific historicised agenda, Williams's
work reveals the extent to which Orwell has outgrown parochial politics

and has instead become a symbol of the fluidity of the ideological landscape of the period.

Evident in much of Williams's mature writing on Orwell, and indeed in many of the critical texts which deal with Orwell's political views, is the assumption that Orwell is a man in political crisis, one who cannot effectively make a firm decision about his allegiances. Some (such as Stephen Greenblatt) see him as caught in a moral bind – intellectually conservative and emotionally revolutionary.[13] From this it is frequently extrapolated that Orwell suffered from a deep-seated identity crisis that remained unsolved throughout his life. But is this in fact the case? Orwell's letters, essays and journalism make clear a political position which has shifted from an endorsement of Soviet Socialism to a hatred of the methods of Stalinist control. Orwell's time in Spain convinced him of the iniquity of Communism without undermining his fundamental faith in the potential for democratic Socialism. Both *Animal Farm* and *Nineteen Eighty-Four* illustrate a political consciousness at odds with orthodox politics and it is this refusal to accept the party line of either Right or Left that seals Orwell's reputation as an outsider. Because he is a critic of both political flanks in a time of radical polarisation, he is claimed and condemned by diverse parties, and his status is akin to that of a loose cannon. The lengths to which some critics have gone therefore to pinpoint Orwell's affiliations tends to reflect more upon the critics' own political predispositions than upon their subject's. Deutscher's comment about Orwell as an ideological weapon constitutes an important critical intervention, for much of the confusion that has surrounded the figure of Orwell and his final texts derives from a tendency in the discourse of literary criticism to construct rather than to deconstruct Orwell.

Psychobiographical Investigations

Such ambivalences of interpretation are evident in the following passage from John Mander's chapter on Orwell in *The Writer and Commitment*:

■ What was the essence of this literary personality? I suggest: his inability to wear a mask.[14] Orwell's whole work is a kind of didactic monologue, vividly documentary at times and never introspective, but spoken always in his own voice. He had a peculiarly direct relationship to his work and to his imagined reader which constitute, I think, the 'honesty' for which he is so often praised. In one sense Orwell's 'honesty' is, of course, undeniable and wholly admirable: the man had courage. But it can have the unfortunate secondary effect of disarming serious criticism. Orwell is like the public speaker whose wrongheaded and contradictory views tend to be overlooked because he is 'so obviously sincere'. Mr. Philip Toynbee, for instance, in an article in

Encounter (August 1959) remarks: 'Orwell was a much better man than most of us.' Yet Mr. Toynbee goes on to point out that Orwell cannot possibly be allowed to get away with some of the judgments he makes in *The Road to Wigan Pier*. Orwell's 'honesty' then, must be regarded with a certain scepticism; we have to be careful not to be intimidated by it. Orwell was a man who always spoke his mind: that was the essence of his literary personality. But the mind he spoke was more wayward and contradictory than is often realised.[15] □

The transformation of Eric Blair into George Orwell has consistently been a focus of critical attention. The adoption of a pseudonym has always been a common device for writers wishing to disguise their identities but, with Orwell, the taking of a *nom de plume* had implications far beyond the mere masking of a true identity. Critics have consistently returned to the metamorphosis as a locus of ideological crisis in Orwell's life and have repeatedly viewed the creation of the 'George Orwell' persona as a deliberate renunciation of a position in society which he found contradictory to his political views. The name change has become, in some Orwell criticism, the fulcrum upon which are pivoted the two sides of the Blair/Orwell personality – the middle-class Etonian who became an imperial policeman and the socialist fellow-traveller who rejected his own past in favour of an empathetic working-class world-view. It is a desire to reconcile these two contradictory positions within the image of one man that has driven much critical appraisal of Orwell. For Raymond Williams, the paradox of personality is always at the root of the writings and, as we saw in the above extract, John Mander's Orwell is quintessentially double-voiced.

Neatly circumventing the Blair/Orwell duality by the suggestion that such interrogation of personality is the sphere of the psychoanalyst and not the literary critic, Mander asserts that Orwell's unique skill is his inability to construct a discrete authorial persona through which he can project the 'true' feelings of Eric Blair. Moreover 'Orwell' is deemed preternaturally honest and sincere, naïvely so for it inhibits his ability to express his own feelings vicariously through an implied authorial presence. Because of this undisguisable honesty, Orwell is incapable of the dissembling required of an author and fails to establish sufficient distance between his own sentiments and those expressed through the narratorial figures of his novels. Such criticism is distinctly spurious and ignores the constructed personality of 'Orwell' to mask Blair. Its principal failing, however, is in the assumption that the ostensibly sincere, open and straightforward style is a guileless, unmediated transcription of Blair/ Orwell's true feelings. It is an assumption that we as critics have no right to make and yet it does not stop Mander from dismissing the literary quality of Orwell's work:

■ Few critics would be prepared to defend Orwell's novels on their literary merits today; their faults are exactly those we would expect of a writer who can only speak naturally in his own voice. Whole passages can be lifted from them and put alongside similar passages from the documentary writings without the reader being able to distinguish one from the other. Many of the documentary passages in the novels are excellent: the descriptions of London, for instance, and the evocations of English or Burmese countryside. But at these moments it is unmistakably Orwell's voice we are hearing. And this is true of the reflective passages as well: we are hearing Orwell's prejudices.[16] □

The construction of Orwell as a simple and clear voice is interesting because it points towards a mask that was created for the author and which he has been forced to wear in public and academic circles ever since. Orwell as the common man, plainly spoken and direct, confrontational and clear-sighted, have all become familiar tropes within criticism, thereby interpellating Orwell into a host of different ideological positions which ultimately serve the critic's cause as much as Orwell's.

Following swiftly upon his death, Orwell began to be constituted within criticism as a 'decent', 'good', 'honest', 'sincere', even 'saintly' man who, whatever one felt about the merits of his writing, was indubitably worthy for the intensity and complexity of his emotional responses. Much of this criticism was biographical in tenor and sought an accommodation of the novels within a complex and contradictory life. Written, in many cases, by friends and admirers of Orwell, this criticism tends towards the adulatory and emphasises the deep personal impact of the man on the work. The intensity of his convictions becomes a location for critical entrance into his work, leaving some critics with very little to say about the literary qualities on display. In the two following extracts – the first by Laurence Brander, the second by Frederick R. Karl – we see how effectively this mask was fitted over the image of Blair/Orwell:

■ All these books were written by a man who was very intelligent and quite simple. His intelligence indicated which were the real problems at issue in our society; and he was able to reduce an apparently baffling and complex problem to a simple issue. . . . His beliefs, the criteria on which he based his diagnosis of society, are simple and homespun. He believed in decency, justice and liberty. He had the preacher's faculty for making these familiar words shine again with meaning. He reached them, not through academic training, but by the exercise of his native intelligence and much personal suffering in Burma and Europe. . . . Homespun thinking of this fine order comes from a lonely and persistent examination of what is going on. Orwell became an original thinker for his generation, matching simple and necessary truths against the contemporary situation, indicating solutions.

It is the vocation of the preacher; and a study of George Orwell's works will show us how the preacher fulfils his vocation today. He addresses a generation which has listened to talks by professors on the air, reads popular science and seeks sense on politics from the weeklies. Orwell assessed the various media. He was not a broadcaster. He did not have the academic background of the professor or the training of the scientist. He worked through the Sunday newspapers, the weeklies and the periodicals. He was at pains to try to bring back the pamphlet to favour because it is the most natural vehicle for the perfervid proselytizing individualist. He used fiction. He used autobiography. He used satire. He used all these forms expertly and successfully, and always with the attitude of one ordinary person talking colloquially to another.

He retained his independence with scrupulous care. Independence was a dogma in his religion. When he came back from Burma, and made the decision to be a writer, he allowed himself to sink and be submerged among the hopelessly poor and outcast for considerable periods. He knew poverty; he knew semi-starvation; he tasted starvation. . . . When it was necessary to earn, he never compromised his writing. He dug the good earth of Essex to grow his own vegetables. He kept a village shop; he kept a pub with his wife. Earlier, he even undertook the most exhausting and self-sacrificing of all jobs, school-teaching. It was an essential part of George Orwell's freedom that he was always ready to do the next thing necessary in his vocation.[17] □

Karl's perspective is:

■ No single work predominates, no single idea is clearly remembered, no theory has been set up for future expansion or discussion. What cannot be doubted is the sense of decency of this man who was often wrong, often unjustifiably opinionated, but who in his anger tried to become the moral conscience of his generation. Orwell lived through one of the most chaotic periods in history, and he saw radical changes occurring in the world, unprecedented ones, but he chose to retain hard-gained truths and human dignity. Perhaps more than any of his contemporaries, Orwell has to be read as a whole, or else the keenness of a mind which saw through the falsity of his day will ultimately be forgotten, or at best remembered by over-praised works like *Animal Farm* and *1984*. Possibly, he was better as a man than as a novelist.[18] □

Both Karl and Brander present Orwells who are fundamentally straightforward: intellectual without being detached from people's lived realities;

morally upright without being priggish; and philosophical without being passive. All these early critics are comfortable in making the distinction between Orwell as man and Orwell as writer. As with Mander, Karl finds the personality behind the books much more attractive than the books themselves and elsewhere he condemns Orwell for an inability to portray realistic characters, to distinguish sufficiently between history and fiction, and fully to integrate political comment into a tightly plotted narrative. Emerging throughout the 1950s, therefore, is a distinction between the unimpeachable ethical and intellectual Orwell and the technically limited Orwell of the novels.

This dichotomy has an enduring attraction for critics who have consistently sought connections between Orwell's biographical history and the emergence of his writing. Even with the development of linguistically based theories of criticism during the 1960s and 1970s, Orwell studies have continued to produce psychobiographical readings. The writings of the man seem inextricably entwined with the mythology which surrounds his personality. This interdependence is also partly formalistic in that the principal genres within which Orwell wrote tended towards the 'openness' of journalistic reportage and thus can be seen to create a similar expectation within the fictional production. His documentary writings of the 1930s – *Down and Out in Paris and London* (1933), and *The Road to Wigan Pier* (1937) – along with the ostensibly autobiographical account of his Spanish Civil War experiences – *Homage to Catalonia* (1938) – have inscribed on a reading public's consciousness the journalistic nature of much of Orwell's writing. This has certainly impacted upon interpretation of his novels and in particular *Nineteen Eighty-Four*, as we see in the next extracts from George Woodcock's *The Crystal Spirit: A Study of George Orwell* and Keith Alldritt's *The Making of George Orwell: An Essay in Literary History*. In the first piece, Woodcock attempts to locate the thinly veiled sadism of *Nineteen Eighty-Four* within Orwell's own experiences as a child:

■ . . . when he presents his own thoughts on the subject of guilt at the age of eight, these appear not only exceptionally mature for a child of such an age, but also suspiciously near to the speculations about the awakening of feelings of guilt which he was pursuing at the time in connection with *Nineteen Eighty-Four*, and which were much influenced by Koestler's *Darkness at Noon*. . . . Far from such thoughts being 'peculiar to childhood', they had been the stock-in-trade of sophisticated Continental writers for many years before Orwell wrote *Such, Such Were the Joys*, and I suggest that they are more important for what they tell us about Orwell's preoccupations with sin during the later 1940s than for anything they may reveal about an early 'hidden wound'. The same, I think, applies to the accounts of headmaster Sim's methods of impressing fragments of knowledge on his pupils' minds by frequent applications of physical punishment; such methods, of course, resemble the elaborate forms of mental conditioning by torture which are used in the Ministry of Love in *Nineteen Eighty-Four*. But I think that here again Orwell recollected them and gave them prominence in *Such, Such Were the Joys* precisely because in writing *Nineteen Eighty-Four* he was concerned with the techniques of teaching by painful experience, and it was natural that he should think back, as all of us do, to incidents within his own experience. The fact that we can find other parallels between Winston Smith's experiences and those of Orwell's childhood does not mean that the incidents in *Nineteen Eighty-Four* are, as Anthony West suggests, 'of an infantile character'; it merely shows that just as Orwell earlier saw the resemblance between the condition of animals and that of oppressed people, so now he saw the resemblance between the child facing the arbitrary rules of an adult world and the bewildered individual locked in the equally arbitrary system of a totalitarian society.[19] □

In the following piece, Alldritt argues that:

■ There is one further and final aspect of the book which is of special significance in terms of the approach to Orwell's writings that has been emphasised in this essay, and that is its very pronounced autobiographical element. We cannot but remark again that one of the things which the book involves is a recapitulation of the major experiences and phases of Orwell's own life. The story of Winston Smith is also very much a resumé of Orwell's own history. Thus in Winston Smith's act of rebellion, in his attempt to escape the dehumanising influences of his native environment, we have a representation of the major act of Orwell's own life. Smith's search for a relationship and alliance with the oppressed is also his author's. And his slogan, 'If there is hope it lies with the proles' (p. 72), is also obviously an expression of Orwell's own outlook during the thirties. Furthermore, neither character nor author has his faith easily shaken by the difficulties of making such contact. For both, the working class serves as the objectification of the good life, even if only in terms of images and memories. Both commit themselves to fight for the valuable feelings which these images evoke, and commit themselves to essays in constructive autobiography. And most important of all, author as well as character come at the very end to doubt these commitments and to feel forced to regard them as a futile, forc-doomed and (most terrible of all) deluded lyricism.

Such an estimate can only seem shocking in the depth and intensity of its pessimism. This is because there is nothing in Orwell's preceding writings to prepare us for the vehemence of the despair in this final statement. And we are quick, perhaps anxious, to recall Orwell's own suggestion of the influence of illness on the writing of it. But even if we are able to some extent to regard the book as an aberration, as the expression of an only temporary state of mind, its inevitable effect is to make us view Orwell's history from a new perspective. Above all, it serves to remind us of the extreme precariousness of the Orwellian vision. We are made to recall that neither his idea of the egalitarian society nor his commitment to democratic feeling were easy to his nature and background. Both were created consciously and with difficulty. They were an ideal that was confirmed only on rare occasions by actual experience. His vision was not something innate; it was created by imagination and sustained by will and moral energy. And *Nineteen Eighty-Four* makes it all too clear how aware he was of the challenge to his commitments presented by that alternative view of life which was the more familiar one for the articulate consciousness of the time. Indeed, the book shows how Orwell was able, at moments at least, to become convinced of the inevitability of this more conventional set of feelings. The Orwellian commitment, the book suggests (and in view of the social nature of his commitments, this is the greatest of the many paradoxes in his life), cannot finally prevent the isolation, the solipsism, the despairing sense of unreality that constitute the standard version of the modern condition. *Nineteen Eighty-Four* is the most important evidence of the perpetual tension in Orwell's mind between two opposing attitudes to experience. It makes clear the continuing and obdurate difficulties involved in the commitment to George Orwell and the renunciation of Eric Blair. It shows the contradictions and the pain underlying the often bluff Orwellian persona. It emphasises the complexity of what was in modern times a rare moral endeavour.[20] □

Both Woodcock's and Alldritt's assessments of *Nineteen Eighty-Four* situate Orwell at a retrospective distance in his life during the writing of his final novel. Both explicitly point towards the transposition of biographical events into fictional materials and both implicitly infer that the novel's pessimistic vision of the future derives from Orwell's ill-health and consequent introspection. Both also acknowledge, however, the difficulties that Orwell struggled with in the negotiation of the transformation from Blair to Orwell and how that necessitated a reassessment of past experiences. They are therefore more astute than some earlier critics who confused the constructed persona of Orwell with a 'real' Orwell in an attempt to persuade the reader of the 'honesty' of his political responses. These passages typify a certain mode of response to *Nineteen Eighty-Four* which ultimately sees the novel as the disillusioned culmination of Orwell's contemplation of the individual's relationship to the social body. Such critiques do, however, run the risk of inverted readings of Orwell; they interpret Orwell and his early work in the light of the novels he was to produce in his last years. As a result, Orwell's oeuvre becomes a neatly progressive movement towards the final epiphanies of *Nineteen Eighty-Four*, which are frequently seen as Orwell's last and considered words on the dynamics of power. Such a teleological method of criticism enables the form of generalised biographical correspondence in Woodcock and Alldritt, where events in Orwell's fiction are casually extrapolated from life incidents. The dangers of reading *Animal Farm* and *Nineteen Eighty-Four* as projections of childhood angst, as Woodcock attempts, or as reflective of internalised identity crises, as Alldritt proposes, are that such readings assume the uncomplicated mediation of life into art. Orwell's traumatic experiences at school thus inevitably become prefigurations of the inflexible authority of Big Brother's minions.

Whilst such correspondences are undoubtedly possible, they do tend to render interpretation a closed system of cause and effect and can lead to problematical assumptions. One such assumption made by critics, and implied in Woodcock's analysis, is that the pessimistic tenor of *Nineteen Eighty-Four* derives from Orwell's consciousness of his failing health and impending death. In many ways such an interpretation is attractive; the dying author prophesying the doom to come. Much criticism of the last novel is predicated upon the premise that Orwell was aware of his nearing demise and the mythological status of the novel has grown in no small part from a perception of its origins in the pain-wracked imagination of a dying man. Yet biographical accounts of the final years suggest that, far from seeing *Nineteen Eighty-Four* as his final broadside against totalitarianism, Orwell was already planning a new fiction on the assumption that he would survive. Furthermore, as Bernard Crick has pointed out, given that he had drawn up an outline for the novel by 1943, conclusions that the vision was born out of the misery of illness are somewhat debatable.[21] This is not to discount theories of correspondence, which certainly offer insightful openings into criticism, merely to contend that this tendency can be vulnerable to reductive reasoning which, through an adherence to empirical evidence, privileges modes of interpretation based on biographical readings of an author.

That meditation upon the 'true' Orwell abounded in early criticism is not entirely surprising. Critics such as Brander and Woodcock knew Orwell personally and could therefore be excused for projecting memories of him onto their writing. That the contemplations on identity continued throughout the 1970s and 1980s (and even to some extent in the 1990s) suggests an abiding and intriguing force to the cultural significance of Orwell's constructed persona. Writing in 1971, Raymond Williams considers crisis of identity to be the predominant theme of Orwell's fiction, stemming from the emotional and psychological ambivalence surrounding the conscious rejection of one self and the adoption of a distinct and writerly persona:

■ It would be easy to say that almost all Orwell's important writing is about someone who gets away from an oppressive normality. From the central characters of *The Clergyman's Daughter* and *Keep the Aspidistra Flying* to those of *Coming Up For Air* and *Nineteen Eighty-Four*, this experience of awareness, rejection and flight is repeatedly enacted. Yet it would be truer to say that most of Orwell's important writing is about someone who tries to get away but fails. That failure, that reabsorption, happens, in the end, in all the novels mentioned, though of course the experience of awareness, rejection, and flight has made its important mark.

The real paradox of Orwell may, then, be more clearly seen. Without the act of awareness and rejection he would not, probably, have been a writer at all. Most of his emphasis, understandably, is on that. But what if he felt, all the time, that in just this movement he was destined to fail? What if he felt, simultaneously, that the flight was necessary but also useless?

This would explain a good deal. For Orwell is then not only the man and the writer setting out on a new path, but also, could it not be, the man and the writer whose 'nature' has been invaded by an unwelcome reality, who has to live and write in these ways but who would have preferred other ways? An image of what he might have been under some other name (the renaming is crucial) is there and persists while what he is and has chosen to be is very different. And the stress falls, necessarily, on 'chosen'. What Orwell consciously made of himself under very real pressures can be seen as an invasion of his nature: not only because of the difficulty of the choice and its break from what he has been intended to be; but also because he felt, against much of the evidence, that he would in any case fail; that he would be dragged back, reabsorbed, into the powerful orthodox world. 'Being a writer', in one definition, had been a possible way out. But being the writer he was, the real writer, led him into every kind of difficulty, every tension that the choice had seemed to offer to avoid.[22] □

For Williams, the name change is a determined step towards the construction of an artistic self which would exist outside and independently of the class and ideological imperatives of Eric Blair. The making of 'George Orwell' is therefore a renunciation of a limiting self and the creation of a new voice with which to speak. Something similar is argued in the next extract from Richard Filloy's 'Orwell's Political Persuasion: A Rhetoric of Personality':

■ The temptation to equate the historical Orwell with his literary persona is strong. Few writers have done more to experience what they wrote about, and Orwell's rhetoric of personality was greatly aided by his breadth of experience. Indeed Orwell the writer and Orwell the man can be exceedingly hard to separate. After Eric Blair adopted the pen-name George Orwell, he increasingly abandoned his original identity in favour of the invented one. His second wife, Sonia, uses Orwell as her surname and always refers to him in her writing as Orwell. She notes that although he never legally changed his name, 'new friends and acquaintances knew him and addressed him as George Orwell.'[23] Once he determined to become a writer, he seems to have lived his life largely for that purpose. Much of what he did was done in order to write about it, and still more was turned to literary account as an afterthought. Yet it is not these facts of time, place, and action nor the deliberate attempt to recreate himself as the political being whose experiences he reported that mark Orwell's persona as a construct; it is the way in which they are reported. This essay has repeatedly pointed out that the pose of ordinariness is an effective persuasive strategy. Incidentally it has shown how unreal that pose was. Orwell was not the average Anglo-Indian official, schoolboy, soldier, or reporter. His feelings and actions are made to seem commonplace, but they were not. They were the result of an exceptionally astute and sensitive observer of wide experience bringing a sophisticated intellect to bear on his situation. His very determination to experience the 'ordinary' lives of those he wrote about was exceptional – and sometimes mocked as an affectation. Those who knew Orwell and have remembered him in print, Cyril Connolly, Richard Rees, and Malcolm Muggeridge among others, do not recall an ordinary man but an extraordinary one who had exaggerated sensibilities and a morbid sense of class consciousness. It took all of Orwell's literary craftsmanship to bury his Eton education and his intellectualism and to render his perceptions and thoughts ordinary.[24] □

Filloy's essay argues that the dual personae of Eric Blair/George Orwell are central to any interpretation of Orwell's canon because the constructed persona of Orwell has a rhetorically persuasive effect. The transformation, Filloy suggests, may have resulted from Blair's ambivalence towards his background, but it is also fundamental to the construction of a persuasive political discourse. By reconstituting himself as Orwell, a talisman for the oppressed factions of society, Blair, in Filloy's view, stood to gain moral high ground and a rhetorical platform from which to castigate the negligent political establishment and a middle class from which he himself originated. The name change is not therefore so much an act of ideological disguise, but the adoption of a vicarious mouthpiece through which Blair can initially express and ultimately reinvent himself.

As Filloy's account shows, psychobiographical approaches to Orwell continue to form a significant mode of criticism. John Rodden's monumental *The Politics of Literary Reputation: The Making and Claiming of 'St. George' Orwell* (1989) locates itself at the crossroads of critical discourses around Orwell and focuses on the numerous faces that have been applied to him, each in some way reflecting the ambiguous relationship between the man and his books. The ongoing publication of Orwell's collected writings by Secker and Warburg will continue to problematise this distinction, as more of Orwell's letters and journalism appear to interrogate the space between private and public individuality. Undoubtedly the image of Orwell as a politically committed man of action still has a notable cultural currency, as does the image of Orwell as class traitor and political apostate. It is the apparently irreconcilable nature of these extremes of perception that continue to focus critical attention on the search for a stable Orwellian persona.

Feminist Demythologisations

The final section of this triptych of critical discourses focuses upon feminist readings of Orwell's work which came to prominence in the late 1970s and 1980s. For our purposes, their interrogations constitute a significant mode of criticism because they foreground *Nineteen Eighty-Four* principally as a text of unreconstructed chauvinism and misogyny. As we shall see, Orwell's own self-confessed anti-feminism has attracted both robust criticism and trenchant support, split largely along gender lines, and arguments between those camps have frequently centred on the validity of applying contemporary debates on gender to a writer from a cultural and ideological context at a significant remove from the terms of those debates. Whilst the aim of this section is to reflect both views, the principal focus will be on the feminist readings which attempt to demythologise a masculinist Orwell.

Orwell's portrayal of women in both his fiction and documentary writing has excited heated debate, as we see in the following denunciation by Deidre Beddoe:

■ . . . a pervasive anti-feminism is evident in Orwell's writing. In 1934 he wrote to a friend, Brenda Salkeld:

> I had lunch yesterday with Dr Ede. He is a bit of a feminist and thinks that if a woman was brought up exactly like a man she would be able to throw a stone, construct a syllogism, keep a secret etc. He tells me that my anti-feminist views are probably due to Sadism! I have never read the Marquis de Sade's novels – they are unfortunately very hard to get hold of.[25]

Brenda Salkeld, a friend of Orwell from Southwold days, described his attitude to women in general very succinctly. 'He didn't really like women', she said in a Third Programme broadcast in 1960.[26] But one does not need other people to testify to Orwell's anti-feminism and to his contempt for women: he does a splendid job quite unaided. He cannot mention feminism and the women's suffrage movement without scorn. Writing of the period following the First World War he states,

> England was full of half-baked antinomian opinions. Pacifism, internationalism, humanitarianism of all kinds, feminism, free love, divorce reform, atheism, birth control – things like these were getting a better hearing than they would get in normal times.[27]

Writing on socialism, he expressed his fear that it was a refuge for every 'fruit juice drinker, nudist, sandal wearer, sex maniac, Quaker, Nature-Cure quack, pacifist and feminist in England'.[28] . . . Orwell was not only anti-feminist but he was totally blind to the role women were and are forced to play in the order of things. His prejudice severely hampered his analysis of capitalism and its workings. He saw capitalism as the exploitation of a male working class by a male ruling class. Women were just men's wives – middle-class nags and working-class housekeepers, to be judged simply as good or bad in keeping a 'decent' home. He failed to see how capitalism manipulated both men and women, middle class and working class, alike. He seems to have been totally unaware of the integral role played by the family unit in capitalist production, i.e. male bread-winner with dependent wife (who serviced the male bread-winner and produced the next generation of workers) and dependent children. He was unaware too – or chose to ignore – the role women played in the waged work-force, either as poorly paid workers who could depress wages or as a reserve army of labour, to be brought in and out of the work-force to suit the changing needs of capitalism.

In short, Orwell as an Eton-educated, middle-class man, had little or no understanding of the role and predicament of women in the society in which he lived. His fiction presents us with a series of nagging middle-class wives whom he saw as a brake on the radicalism of their husbands: 'you cannot have an effective trade union of middle-class workers, because in times of strikes almost every middle-class wife would be egging her husband on to blackleg and get the other fellow's job.'[29] While there may be an element of truth in this, Orwell did not see the reasons for it, i.e. the dependency of middle-class wives, lack of employment opportunities for women, the operation of marriage-bars in many professions. His non-fiction ignores women workers and judges working-class wives by their abilities as home-makers. Orwell's awareness of class divisions in society went alongside his lack of understanding of gender divisions, and is summed up in his discussion of women's magazines. He was perceptively aware that these magazines project a fantasy of 'pretending to be richer than you are'[30] for the bored factory-girl or worn-out mother of five, but totally unaware of how these magazines reinforced gender divisions in society and promoted the dominant female stereotype of the interwar years – the housewife.[31] □

Deidre Beddoe's critique of Orwell appears to emanate from a deep antipathy towards a reactionary bent in his attitude to women. As is common amongst gender-related re-readings, Beddoe highlights Orwell's reduction of feminist concerns to mere side-issues, to be considered only as the ramblings of the non-conformist and the alienated. Ironically, however, Beddoe's dismissal of Orwell stems largely from her perception of his generalisations about women, generalisations which she promptly reverses as a critique of Orwell's masculinity. Also of interest in Beddoe's approach is the directly biographical tenor of her criticism; Orwell's worth as a writer is implicitly undermined by his attitudes towards women as far as Beddoe is concerned. This is a stance not distantly removed from the naïvety of the early psychobiographical critics. For feminist critics like Beddoe, Orwell's dismissive attitude towards feminist issues is unacceptable for its flippancy and cynicism, but is more significantly damaging to Orwell's credentials as friend of the common person. With justification, critics have argued that Orwell's self-proclaimed egalitarianism should have extended beyond the plight of the working-class man to a consideration of the working-class woman. That it does not is seen as an indictment of his hypocrisy, but also of the superficiality of his identity change. His attitudes towards women display, so some critics contend, his deeply entrenched middle-class conservatism which explodes the fragile persona created in empathy with a working-class perspective. This is a point which Beddoe raises: Orwell's socialism may consist of a hatred of capitalist exploitation, but if that hatred is only for the exploitation of the working-class man, then it amounts to little more than a shallow gesture towards a notion of equality and freedom from oppression, in the opinion of Beddoe. Orwell's ignorance of the role of women within an exploited workforce, or his construction of them as nagging wives and hindrances to male self-determination, undermine his claims to speak for the oppressed.

Like Beddoe, Daphne Patai has examined Orwell's representation of women, and while she too finds his casual assumptions about femininity hard to reconcile with his iconic status as a socialist hero, she perceives, within his novels, structures of patriarchy which inevitably constitute women as gender-inferior beings. Patai, furthermore, argues that Orwell supports a paradigm of representation that 'polarizes human beings according to sex roles and gender identity and legitimizes male displays of dominance and aggression'.[32] In such a paradigm, women feature purely as a comparative group against which men can define and root themselves. Applying these notions to *Animal Farm*, Patai explores, in the following extract, the implicit gender-stereotyping amongst the animals:

■ Although *Animal Farm* is mentioned in scores of studies of Orwell, no critic has thought it worth a comment that the pigs who betray the revolution, like the pig who starts it, are not just pigs but boars, that is, uncastrated male pigs kept for breeding purposes. Old Major, the 'prize Middle White boar' (p. 1) who has called a meeting to tell the other animals about his dream, is initially described in terms that establish him as patriarch of this world: 'He was twelve years old and had lately grown rather stout, but he was still a majestic-looking pig, with a wise and benevolent appearance in spite of the fact that his tushes had never been cut' (p. 1). In contrasting his life with those of the less fortunate animals on the farm, Major says: 'I am one of the lucky ones. I am twelve years old and have had over four hundred children. Such is the natural life of a pig' (p. 5). Orwell here repeats the pattern we have seen in his other fiction, of stressing paternity as if the actual labour of reproduction were done by males. Authority comes from the phallus and fatherhood, and the sows, in fact, are hardly mentioned in the book; when they are, as we shall see, it is solely to illustrate the patriarchal control of the ruling pig, Napoleon. Leaders, then, may be good (Major) or bad (Napoleon) – but they must be male and 'potent.'

Contrasting with the paternal principle embodied in Major is the maternal, embodied in Clover, 'a stout motherly mare approaching middle life, who had never quite got her figure back after her fourth foal' (p. 2). Clover is characterized above all by her nurturing concern for the other animals. When a brood of ducklings that had lost their mother come into the barn, Clover 'made a sort of wall round them with her great foreleg,' and they nestled down inside it (p. 2). Though Clover works along with Boxer – the enormous cart horse 'as strong as any two ordinary horses put together' (p. 2) whom Orwell uses to represent the working class, unintelligent but ever-faithful, to judge by this image – she is admired not for her hard labour but rather for her caring role as protector of the weaker animals.'[33] Orwell here attributes to the maternal female dominion over the moral sphere but without any power to implement her values. As in *Nineteen Eighty-Four*, this 'feminine' characteristic, though admirable, is shown to be utterly helpless and of no avail. In addition, this conventional (human) division of reality restricts the female animal to the affective and expressive sphere and the male to the instrumental. ... ...

Clover stands at one of the poles of Orwell's conventional representation of female character.[34] The other pole is represented by Mollie, 'the foolish, pretty white mare who drew Mr Jones's trap' (p.2) and is shown, early in the book, to have a link with human females. When the animals wander through the farmhouse, Mollie lingers in the best bedroom: 'She had taken a piece of blue ribbon from Mrs Jones's dressing-table, and was holding it against her shoulder and admiring herself in the glass in a very foolish manner' (p.14). A less important female character is the cat who, during Major's speech, finds the warmest place to settle down in and does not listen to a word he says (p.3). Both Mollie and the cat, we later learn, avoid work; and Mollie is the first defector from the farm after the revolution, seduced by a neighboring farmer's offerings of ribbons for her white mane and sugar.

Orwell's characterizations of old Major, Boxer, Clover, Mollie, and the cat all appear, clearly packaged and labeled, in the book's first three pages. The animal community thus forms a recognizable social world, divided by gender. This world is presented to us complete with stereotypes of patriarchal power, in the form of male wisdom, virility, or sheer strength, and female subordination, in the form of a conventional dichotomy between 'good' maternal females and 'bad' non-maternal females. It is difficult to gauge Orwell's intentions in making use of gender stereotypes in *Animal Farm*. Given the evidence of his other texts, however, it seems unlikely that the possibility of a critical, even satirical, account of gender divisions ever crossed his mind. Perhaps he simply incorporated the familiar into his animal fable as part of the 'natural human' traits needed to gain plausibility for his drama of a revolution betrayed. But in so doing he inadvertently reveals something very important about this barnyard revolution: like its human counterparts it invariably re-creates the institution of patriarchy. ... ...

The animals are differentiated not only according to gender but also by intelligence, the pigs being described as both intelligent and piggish even at an early stage in the revolution, when they appropriate the cows' milk for their own use. The other animals, with only a few exceptions, are generous, hardworking, and stupid by contrast. It is not power that corrupts the pigs, power simply provides them with the means to realize their 'nature.' The betrayal of the revolution in *Animal Farm*, though it occurs over a period of time, is not, in fact, described as a process. This is why *Animal Farm*, beyond what it has to say concerning Stalin and the Soviet Union, has a profoundly dispiriting message. Orwell presents a static picture of a static universe in which the notion of the pigs' animal nature explains what happens. The final tableau, with the pigs and the men indistinguishable, is the actualization of the potential inherent in the pigs from the beginning. Unlike what he does in *Nineteen Eighty-Four* however, Orwell gives the pigs specific material motives for the exploitation of the other animals: better food, more leisure, and a privileged life, all acquired partly by terrorizing and partly by gulling the others into thinking that because the pigs are more intelligent they alone can manage the farm. The question of intelligence is a problematic one in this book, for Orwell associates this characteristic with exploitation. There is a suggestion here that generosity, cooperation, devotion are somehow incompatible with intelligence. The deeper question, of what power hunger is really about, is avoided, and the apparent answers Orwell provides in his animal fable are inconsistent and unsatisfying, for even among the pigs not all are shown to be corrupted by greed and the desire for power.

As the pigs duplicate the human model of social organization, they not only reproduce the pattern of patriarchy already familiar to the animals (judging by Major's status early in the book) but add to it those human characteristics that Orwell found most reprehensible – especially softness. They slowly adopt Mr. Jones's manner of living, complete with cushy bed and booze. This is contrasted with the heroic labor of the immensely strong Boxer, who literally works himself to death. Relations between the pigs and the other animals follow the patriarchal model also in that they are hierarchical and discipline-oriented; submission and obedience are extracted from the worker animals as the price of the supposedly indispensable pig leadership.

In addition to the touching solidarity evident among the worker animals, some individual relationships also emerge. One of these is the nonverbal 'masculine' friendship between Boxer and Benjamin, who look forward to their retirement together. There is no female version of this friendship, however. Instead, Clover plays the role not only of maternal mare to the other animals but also of 'wife' . . . in that she has a heart-to-heart talk with Mollie. Cast in the role of the rebellious 'daughter' who refuses to adhere to the farm's values, Mollie disbelieves in the communal cause and prefers to ally herself with powerful human males outside the farm, thus assuring her easier life as a kept and well-decorated mare. Orwell signals his disapproval of Mollie by showing her cowardice (pp.30–1) as well as her vanity and sloth. Given the revolution's eventual outcome, however, Mollie's behavior, though egocentric, is not as misguided as it may seem. Orwell makes it explicit that under the rule of Napoleon the animals (except the pigs and Moses, the raven, who represents the church) have an even more arduous work life than animals on the neighboring (i.e., capitalist) farms. Mollie might better be viewed as having some spontaneous understanding of the rules of patriarchy . . . .

With astonishing ease and aptness, *Animal Farm* can be read as a feminist critique of socialist revolutions which, through their failure to challenge patriarchy, have reproduced patriarchal values in the postrevolutionary period. In this reading of the fable, the pigs would be the sole male animals, while most of the other animals are stereo-typed females: compliant, hardworking drones brainwashed with the illusion that their work is done for themselves, surrendering the fruits of their productive and reproductive labor to their masters, who tell them that there never was hope of a different future.[35] □

Patai's controversial but extremely influential study seeks to reveal Orwell's inherently male-centred world view which situates masculinity as the gender norm and from which women are always therefore viewed as deviations and implicitly inferior because less manly. By taking apart the apparently classless and genderless cast of *Animal Farm* and arguing that Orwell constructs the fable according to a strongly masculinist ideo-logy, Patai can contend that a fundamentally male-oriented vision of the world is presented. Whilst she, like Beddoe, reads Orwell as sexist and misogynistic, these qualities do not preclude a feminist reading of his texts, which as she states can be done with 'astonishing ease'. Unlike Beddoe, Patai does not choose the easy target of Orwell's own expressions of antipathy towards some women, but instead constructs an interesting thesis based upon what she sees as the inherent structures of power evident in the novel.

Time and again feminist critics have argued that women have very little importance in Orwell's fiction, and debates, particularly amongst American scholars, have focused primarily on *Nineteen Eighty-Four* and on the two principal female characters – Julia and the prole washer-woman. A typical early response to Julia is presented in the next passage, taken from Richard Rees's short study *George Orwell: Fugitive from the Camp of Victory*:

■ As opposed to the depressing emphasis upon the monstrousness of the prole woman (p.228), the figure of Julia is the one point of relief and contrast against the nightmarish horror of the book. Not that she would be remarkable in the work of a more subtle and sensitive novel-ist; but in Orwell's work she stands out as his liveliest and most perceptive study of a woman. The shallow and frigid Elizabeth of *Burmese Days* and the warm, generous Rosemary of *Keep the Aspidistra Flying* (based upon the character of his wife Eileen) are well described; but they are no more than sketches of features in the human landscape surrounding the hero. Julia is something more. If, as is possible, she can be taken as representing Orwell's idea of essential femininity, it is a somewhat 'reactionary' portrait, although not really very different from the 'progressive' Bernard Shaw's typical woman. Julia is intelligent but completely unintellectual, determined, practical, unscrupulous, capable of generosity but rather narrowly single-minded. Above all, she is realistic and a vigorous puncturer of hypocrisy and cant. She is brilliantly successful in deceit . . . but prepared to take extraordinary risks to gain her ends.

The middle-aged Winston is astonished at the coarseness of her language, but is rather pleased by it. 'It was merely one symptom of her revolt against the Party and all its ways, and somehow it seemed natural and healthy, like the sneeze of a horse that smells bad hay.' (pp.128–9) With her tough vitality and ability to survive and even enjoy life against overwhelming odds, her self-absorption and total indifference to the wider issues of truth and justice, and her lack of interest in the past and the future, she strikes a poignant note in the book and makes a dramatic contrast to the tormented, far-seeing Winston. The essential difference between them, and Orwell probably meant it to illustrate the difference between men and women, is hinted at when they visit the enigmatic and formidable O'Brien to offer their services to the underground organisation against the Party, which they believe exists; and of which they believe, or at least hope, rashly and mistakenly, that he is a leader. O'Brien asks them to what lengths they are prepared to go. Will they commit murder, treason, blackmail, forgery, disseminate venereal diseases, give their lives, and so on? They answer 'Yes' (p.179). Then are they prepared to separate and never see one another again?

'No!' broke in Julia.

It appeared to Winston that a long time passed before he answered. For a moment he seemed even to have been deprived of the power of speech. His tongue worked soundlessly, forming the opening syllables first of one word, then of the other, over and over again. Until he had said it, he did not know which word he was going to say. 'No', he said finally (p.180).[36] □

Rees strives to portray a very positive version of Julia, but only in contrast to the 'monstrousness' of the washerwoman. In his estimation she is an intelligent, pragmatic, clear-sighted and romantic individual who complements the intellectual rebellion of Winston with its physical correlative, but will not contemplate the emotional detachment and ideological submission necessary for wholesale revolution. The passage is revealing for its assumption of an 'essential femininity' which Rees reads into Orwell's depiction of Julia, but which could equally have been gleaned from the nature of Rees's interpretation. An 'essential femininity' is a concept which gender theory has argued to be a cultural construct but acknowledges as a powerful weapon in the male armoury against any deviation from female 'norms'. It is against this construct of gender conformity that the following extracts on Julia, from Beddoe and Patai, position themselves. Here is Beddoe:

■ Julia, Winston's mistress in *Nineteen Eighty-Four*, is distinguished from Orwell's other female characters in that she shows courage. She flouts the minor and then the major rules of this future totalitarian society. It is she who initiates contact with Winston: she has the enterprise and experience to arrange liaisons with him. She is prepared too to follow Winston in joining the Brotherhood, the opposition to Big Brother. But the protests of Winston and Julia against the regime are inspired by totally different motives. Whereas Winston is inspired by intellectual concepts like the integrity of history and the notion of freedom, Julia is only 'a rebel from the waist downwards' (p. 163). The sexually attractive and sexually active Julia objects to the regime because it stops her having a good time. She is totally incapable of understanding the motives which drive Winston to revolt. 'Any kind of organized revolt against the Party, which was bound to be a failure, struck her as stupid. The clever thing was to break the rules and stay alive all the same.' (p. 138) When Winston talks to her of the Party and its doctrines, she invariably falls asleep (pp. 163; 226). Her response to his reading of Goldstein's subversive text is the same. Julia is as brainless as Elizabeth Lackersteen [*Burmese Days*] or Hilda Bowling [*Coming Up for Air*].[37] □

This is Patai:

■ The women in Orwell's narrative by and large appear as caricatures: they are Party secretaries, Party fanatics, Party wives like Katharine or the stereotypically helpless housewife Mrs. Parsons. They are also antisex freaks or prole prostitutes. There is no woman character in the novel comparable to Syme or Charrington or O'Brien. Although Goldstein's book explains that the Inner Party is not linked by blood and that no racial discrimination is practiced – 'Jews, Negroes, South Americans of pure Indian blood are to be found in the highest ranks of the Party' (p. 217) – no female Inner Party members are mentioned. When Winston sees a man and a woman in the canteen, he assumes that the woman is the man's secretary. In describing Julia's work in Pornosec (which churns out machine-produced pornographic literature for prole consumption), work that is assigned to unmarried girls because they are thought to be less vulnerable than men to the corrupting influences of pornography, Orwell includes the detail that 'all the workers in Pornosec, except the heads of the departments, were girls' (p. 137). Although Orwell reveals male dominance to be a continuing feature of life in Oceania, he does not treat this as worthy of analysis and does not raise the issue of its role in a totalitarian society. Women's options in a given society, what access they have to earning their own living and what kind of living that would be compared, for example, to becoming a man's economic dependent in exchange for housework and child-care services; how, in general, society structures women's life paths in comparison with men's – all this has everything to do with the shape of life in that society. But Orwell does not realize this, judging by his lack of attention to this problem in *Nineteen Eighty-Four*. Even Julia is a largely unexplored character, seen only in terms of her relationship with Winston.

In charting Julia's character, Orwell introduced an important deviation from several of the novels that are known to have influenced his composition of *Nineteen Eighty-Four*. Both Jack London's Iron Heel and Zamiatin's [*sic*] We have heroic female protagonists. But Julia, the only major female character in *Nineteen Eighty-Four*, though also a rebel, evokes yet another female stereotype. She is a rebel only 'from the waist downwards' (p. 163), as Winston comments; she is motivated by love of pleasure – sexual pleasure – and is totally uninterested in the political dynamics of the society that oppresses her. Orwell invites the reader to view Julia in a largely negative way and to contrast her lack of seriousness with Winston's heroic attempt to understand his society. And, indeed, most critics have faithfully echoed this view of Julia, so that in comments on the novel she is routinely described as egocentric and unintelligent. A slight variation of this criticism is the condescension of Irving Howe, who refers to Julia's 'charming indifference to all ideologies.'[38] Yet there are grounds for a more positive understanding of Julia's character: she does not take the Two Minutes Hate seriously, unlike Winston who gets genuinely caught up in it. She falls asleep while Winston reads to her from Goldstein's book and is skeptical about all official pronouncements. But these positive aspects of Julia's character emerge more despite Orwell's conception of her than because of it. Significantly, Julia, who is also opposing the Party, receives no attention from O'Brien. Her rebellion against the Party does not have an ideological or theoretical foundation; rather, it is grounded in her desire for pleasure and for the pursuit of a personal life. The three central characters in Orwell's novel form an interesting group, and the ways Orwell names them reflect their status within the novel. Julia has only a first name, she is an insignificant female, and Orwell in this respect follows his society's convention of considering a woman's last name a disposable, because changeable, element in an uncertain social identity. O'Brien, at the opposite pole, has only a last name, in typical masculine style. And Winston Smith, halfway between the powerless personal feminine and the powerful impersonal masculine, has a complete name albeit an ironic one in that it combines the legendary with the commonplace.

Julia's aim is to have as much pleasure as she possibly can, which, given the oppressive world in which she must function, is no small feat. And she harms no one. O'Brien, in the key scene in his apartment, assumes that Winston speaks for both himself and Julia as he questions them about their willingness to commit all sorts of atrocities for the sake of destroying the Party. While Winston agrees to everything, Julia says nothing (she must find all this talk about throwing acid in the face of a child ridiculous [p. 180]) – until O'Brien asks if she and Winston are willing to be separated for the sake of destroying the Party. Only now does she break into the conversation, to say no (p. 180). Here it is Julia who is revealing the commitment to purely private values that Winston so admires in the idealized maternal figures of the prole woman (pp. 144–5) and his own mother (p. 32), yet she is not held up for our admiration. In fact, Julia becomes yet another source of misogynistic comments. She hates her living arrangements in the hostel where she lives with thirty other women (Winston, for reasons unknown, has his own flat) and complains to Winston: 'Always in the stink of women! How I hate women!' (p. 136).

Throughout the novel the contrast is drawn between Winston's attempt to understand his society and Julia's purely practical orientation: she is cunning, capable, mechanically oriented (she works on the machines in Pornosec) – and hedonistic, unanalytical, opportunistic. Winston's strenuous resistance to O'Brien's torture is depicted in great detail, but we are told in passing that Julia had capitulated at once to O'Brien's methods: 'She betrayed you, Winston. Immediately – unreservedly. I have seldom seen anyone come over to us so promptly. You would hardly recognize her if you saw her. All her rebelliousness, her deceit, her folly, her dirty-mindedness – everything has been burned out of her. It was a perfect conversion, a textbook case' (p. 271), hence not worthy of either admiration or pity, unlike the tougher, more heroic (given the values of the novel) Winston. The Party's aim is to destroy men – and the more they resist, the greater the thrill of power for the Party. Julia obviously does not play this game.[39] □

The accounts of both Patai and Beddoe foreground the negative portrayal of Julia. For Beddoe and Patai, Orwell creates a partner for Winston who is defined by her limitations rather than by her potentiality. She represents physical rebellion, whilst Winston contemplates the moral and ethical consequences of their actions. Yet, as these critics suggest, her non-conformity is motivated solely by her desire for sex and for no greater ideological reason. Julia is constituted fundamentally as a sensory shadow to Winston's mutiny, an inferior, because less intellectual, form of insurrection. As both critics point out, Julia is portrayed as incapable of staying awake during Winston's reading of Goldstein's manifesto, but their conclusion is far more damning than Rees's implicit judgement that this is a charming response. Julia's anti-intellectualism is instead construed as a condescending critique of female intelligence; Orwell seems incapable of conceiving that a woman would ever be able to match a masculine grasp of political or economic affairs. So whilst many critics acknowledge Julia as Orwell's most rounded and sympathetic female character, there remains the conviction that she is ultimately insignificant within the text and a mere vehicle for Orwell's anti-female sentiments. Such criticism again shows the clear association of Orwell's own personal antipathies with the credibility of his work. Therefore, whilst feminist criticism seeks to question Orwell's artistic integrity from a more dispassionate position than the early psychobiographical critics, their approaches are complementary rather than contradictory, and analysis of Orwell becomes once more mired in the man/work duality.

In contrast to Julia, the prole washerwoman is commonly seen as an encapsulation of Orwell's minimal hope for future relief from the totalitarian state. She represents a femininity which is essentially passive and unchanging; fecund and yet asexual, maternal and indefatigable. Yet even this representation of women is deeply ambivalent, as we see in Beatrix Campbell's analysis which compares the portrayal of the washerwoman with that of the miners in *The Road to Wigan Pier:*

■ Part of the problem is that Orwell's eye never comes to rest on the culture of women, their concerns, their history, their movements. He only holds women to the filter of his own desire – or distaste. ... In his avowedly political work the snarling innuendo he reserves for his 'Brighton ladies' and 'birth control' fanatics is rarely directed towards the figures of *real* power in capitalist societies – the judges, the parliamentarians and the capitalists. In fact, you are left with a sense of a society run, not only by the national family's old buffers, but of a society run by a febrile femininity, an army of doddering dowagers.

The point is that given his own centrality, and that of masculinity in Orwell's work, women are congratulated only when they stick to their men. The sexual filter surrounds all his female personae.

In *Nineteen Eighty-Four* we have working-class women represented by poor Mrs Parsons and a prole washerwoman. Mrs Parsons is a 'woman with a lined face and wispy hair, fiddling helplessly with the waste pipe' (p. 77), an infuriating person, always in the slough of a housewife's ruinous mess. And then there is the washerwoman whom

Winston discovers during his fugitive flights into proletaria. He only begins to reflect on her with any respect when he inexplicably discovers the revolutionary potential of the proles. Her 'indefatigable voice' sings on, as she endlessly hangs out her washing. He watches her 'solid, contourless body, like a block of granite', quietly admiring 'her thick arms reaching up for the line, her powerful mare-like buttocks protruded.' (p.228) She's as strong as a horse, an image which has echoes in *Animal Farm*, where as Raymond Williams reminds us, 'the speed of his figurative transition from animals to the proletariat is interesting – showing as it does a residue of thinking of the poor as animals: powerful but stupid.'

As Orwell's Winston watches the 'over-ripe turnip' of a washerwoman reach for the line 'it struck him for the first time that she was beautiful.' Her 'rasping red skin, bore the same relation to the body of a girl as the rose-hip to the rose. Why should the fruit be held inferior to the flower?' (p.228)

So we start with the strong but stupid work-horse and move to a vision of a woman in labour: both as she labours solitarily and stoically, and as a symbol of fertility. As Winston muses on how he and his lover Julia will never bear children he reflects on this washerwoman-mother: 'The woman down there had no mind, she had only strong arms, a warm heart and a fertile belly.' (p.228) Just like Orwell's panegyric on the miners, all brawn and no brain, this quintessential proletarian woman is all belly and no brain. She has no culture and no consciousness worth contemplating. ... ...

Women are akin to the proletarian man in Orwell's work, they are rendered natural rather than skilful, almost infantile in their unconsciousness rather than alert and organised.[40] □

Campbell's implicit suggestion here is that Orwell's portrayal of women reveals not only a troublingly misogynistic consciousness, but also a deeply entrenched class bias to that misogyny. In constructing the working-class woman as the unthinking corporeal correlative to the miner's brawn, Orwell's vision of the working classes is, Campbell implies, dominated by notions of essentialised identity growing from nature. The normalisation of class hierarchies that is implicated by this vision are, for Campbell at least, indicative of Orwell's ideologically dubious romanticisation of the working classes. Such sentimentalisation is seen by Campbell throughout Orwell's fictional and documentary writing and relegates women (and particularly lower-class women) to the infantile and the unconscious.

Despite the trenchant criticisms of Orwell's work put forward by feminist readings, Orwell has inspired equally vigorous defensive protestations. The final extracts in this chapter present spirited rebuttals to the work of Campbell and Patai. John Rodden and John Newsinger contend that such feminist reappraisals of Orwell inevitably decontextualise and therefore depoliticise the import of the novels before artificially repoliticising them in the terms of debates on gender. Rodden writes:

■ *The Orwell Mystique* warrants considerable, and critical, attention not only because it fairly represents Orwell's left-wing feminist reception and has been well-received by feminist academics,[41] but also because it stands as the most substantial feminist critique of his work to date. Moreover, like many readers in the 1980s, I find Orwell's conventional attitudes toward gender and his uninterest in, even condescension toward, women's rights issues a notable deficiency in his work. The special contribution of the feminist response is to make us more gender-conscious about Orwell's writings; their unfavorable reception is, however, also an excellent example of the difference between taking a 'hard' versus 'sympathetic' stance toward a subject, between judging him by the present or trying to understand him in his own historical moment.

And so one pauses at the very phrasing of one feminist's question, 'Is . . . Orwell . . . a sexist after all?'[42] Its scholastic, verbal nature – much like the onetime Soviet obsession with the epithets 'naturalist' and 'formalist' – gives a hint of the schematized approach dictated when one sifts a writer's work through the ideologically orthodox filter of what could be termed 'feminist realism.' Whatever the wording, however, the question of Orwell's attitude toward women cannot be answered merely within the terms of present-day critical ideologies, or by textual and autobiographical readings of his work.

What is disheartening about the radical and Marxist feminist critique of Orwell is how a genuine insight of restricted scope is magnified into an *idée fixe* and then applied like a blanket to an author's work. Some feminist critiques present Orwell in a new light, but they often focus down too narrowly, ultimately falsifying his sexual politics. It is hard to see the value of conclusions such as, 'Orwell altered the record of the past, so far as women are concerned, as efficiently as if he had been in the employ of Minitrue.'[43] Likewise, though *The Orwell Mystique* fairly insists on judging a moral critic like Orwell 'by the standards he proclaimed – honesty, decency, egalitarianism, [and] justice' – Patai doesn't finally judge Orwell in those terms. Instead she hypostatizes 'honesty,' 'decency,' 'egalitarianism,' and 'justice' according to a 1980s feminist standard which swamps the political complexities and historical situation in which he found himself.[44] Certainly, Orwell was not sensitive to women's rights (or gay rights or the special needs of the aged either), but relative to the issues of race and class which gripped literary London in the 1930s and '40s – and despite his mild lifelong antipathy toward Catholics, Irishmen, and Scotsmen (and his early prejudice toward Jews, reflected in *Down and Out*) – he is, on the whole, a witness to his time.

Verdicts like those above reflect disdain (most ironic from Marxists) for the (admittedly laborious) task of gathering historical and biographical data, through which one might partly recover the social conditions of an author's writing and reception. In their rush to label Orwell a 'sexist,' some feminists have been blind to the extent to which Orwell's attitudes toward femininity and social roles were conventional for his time, among socialists as well as non-socialists. Although Patai denies in passing that her approach is anachronistic, she in effect concedes it when she admits that Orwell's 'identification of the male with the human norm is among the conventions of an androcentric society that is only now being seriously challenged.' She seems not to have considered that the 'neglect' of Orwell's 'exceptional' sexism might be due precisely to the fact that it was not 'exceptional' for his time.[45] . . . . . .

To contextualize, however, is not – and should not be – to radically historicize. Historians must walk the fine, unmarked line between contextualizing to understand and historicizing to whitewash. As we strive to understand the past, we need not – and should not – renounce the task of historical judgment, only maintain a keen awareness of the implications and responsibilities of judicial criticism. This entails neither rationalizing nor condoning the newly perceived shortcomings (sexism, racism, imperialism) of figures of the past, only the injunction to see their limitations and achievements in the light of their situation and that of their contemporaries. Interestingly, the situation of Orwell's reception by feminist radicals presents an analogous challenge: to appreciate the complicated context of *their* criticism and yet not recoil from noting its tendencies toward anachronism and essentialism.

Such sensitivity to Orwell's and his readers' historical situations is especially necessary given that his chilly reception by the feminist Left exemplifies the role of the history of ideas in shaping reputations, i.e., what happens to an established reputation when it collides with a belief system in direct conflict with the values which helped enshrine and sustain it. Orwell's reputation ascended in the non-feminist '50s; the feminist revisionism of the '80s represents not only the newest but also the strongest challenge to his reputation, at least in the academy and among intellectuals.

How can one be a truly 'popular' hero and not stand as the champion of half of humanity? Feminists across the political spectrum ask, justly, about Orwell. . . . A real champion of 'decency and democracy' should recognize that 'the people' include women too! His egalitarian call should extend to everyone; feminism, after all, is humanism.

In one sense, however, the impulse behind the 'feminist Orwell' represents yet another ideal image of Common Man Orwell. Fairly or not, feminists have expected more of Orwell than of his contemporaries; they have wanted him to be Trilling's and Spender's 'extraordinary ordinary man' on women's issues too. In effect they have wished that The Common Man were The Prophet, a feminist trailblazer. 'If Orwell were alive today,' some feminists dream, he might be different; and yet they hold him to his past: he should have been different *then* too. The case of Orwell and the feminists indicates how history can overtake an author, so that he becomes judged by standards he could not have anticipated in his own day. He must, therefore, not be merely a man of his time if he is to remain a figure; subsequent generations of readers must be able to project *their* bedrock values as *his*. When a figure can no longer accommodate his readers' idealized self-images, his status is in jeopardy. For most readers seem to feel that a figure must somehow guide them; when they sense that they have 'overtaken' him or her, their responses often turn from gratitude to contempt.

Indeed Orwell's exalted status only increases the urge to make him an 'extraordinary' ordinary man on all issues, which in turn heightens the frustration when he cannot finally be remolded into the figure one desires. And there *is* recalcitrance: the gender gap is there. Many women cannot 'read themselves into' Orwell very easily. They come to him with the expectation that he speaks to 'the common reader,' only to find the dialogue virtually closed. His reader seems to be the common *male* reader, and the disappointment is keen. His defaced 'anti-woman' image held by some feminists thus arises partly from the pain of seeking to identify with a figure, only to be deflected. Their feeling of letdown, which their high expectations deepen and sharpen, points to the large problem of heroic identification across gender. This process of heightened anticipation and painful disenchantment suggests the dynamics of what might be called *figural recalcitrance* – and the spectrum of response available when one encounters it. The range of Orwell's fractured reception within the radical/liberal feminist audience reflects variously the urge for a heroism that transcends gender modeling, the longing for intellectual heroes who are heroines too, the acquiescence to gradual social change, and the recognition or evasion of the differences between present and past.

In part 'the Orwell cult' *is* a 'cult of masculinity.' . . . the images of Orwell as The Rebel and The Common Man – especially as iconoclast, plain speaker, and tough-minded pragmatist – have even been portrayed on the covers of popular men's magazines. The masculine voice of Orwell's prose, his association of moral courage with physical courage, his own 'manly' example that socialism is something to fight and die for, his railing against the 'softness' of a machine civilization, his emphasis on 'hard' experience rather than theory and jargon, his conviction that one could be a socialist and yet be an 'ordinary' man, his Quixotic capacity to act: Orwell the man and writer projected a virile image, especially attractive to radical male intellectuals of a generation naively worshipful of 'common' men of action. Indeed part of his appeal has always been his capacity to make intellectual life seem manly, not effeminate, a calling of unusual adventure, larger than life. Male intellectuals have therefore projected their own dreams onto him, romanticizing his life as the saga of a world-historical individual somehow managing to touch all the major currents of his age, from poverty to imperialism to fascism. In all this Orwell has seemed the quintessential public writer – and the public sphere is the one to which men have traditionally felt called and compelled. Patai is wrong to suggest that Orwell has appealed especially to 'British males of his own class';[46] as this study makes clear, his attractiveness to readers has transcended class and nationality, if not gender.[47] □

Rodden's riposte to the feminist critical position cuts to the heart of its dismissal of Orwell and in many ways draws together the three key modes of criticism established in this chapter. For Rodden, the feminist objection to Orwell is a reflection of the stagnation of criticism around his work because it functions most effectively within the context of biographical critiques of his work, which are themselves extremely limited. The criticisms that are proffered by feminists as to the generalised nature of Orwell's view of women become, for Rodden, stale reiterations of single, and often partial, perspectives. To focus on Orwell's personal sexism, or on the patriarchal structures of his texts, is to render his sexual politics one-dimensional and decontextualised. In order to understand Orwell's complex attitudes towards women, Rodden suggests, one must extricate oneself from the political bind of criticism and read those attitudes within the broad cultural-historical context from which they emerged. The intellectual and political contexts of 1980s American academia encouraged such narrow dismissive opinions in Rodden's view, and it is only through the acknowledgement of this partiality that a workable and suitable historicised relationship with the original context of Orwell's comments can be achieved. Rodden's argument is articulate and persuasive, and contained, as it is, in a study about the relationship between the author and her/his reputation, shows the problems manifest in the negotiation of cultural memory.

John Newsinger bases his repudiation of feminist critiques on an analysis of Julia, refuting the suggestion that she is a weak and intellectually ineffective character and recasting her instead as a symbol of self-determination and political independence:

■ Those critics, both feminist and non-feminist, who regard Orwell as denigrating Julia are, in fact, misreading the book or rather, are only reading half of it. *Nineteen Eighty-Four* is not just a portrayal of a totalitarian regime that is terroristic politically, but of one that is terroristic sexually as well. This is an absolutely crucial dimension to the novel and yet its importance is so often missed. The Anti-Sex League is a vital part of the Party's apparatus of control over Oceania's population and has, we are told, as its undeclared purpose the elimination of all pleasure from the sexual act (pp. 68–9). It wanted to suppress not just love, which might lead to the establishment of loyalties outside Party control, but eroticism as well. All marriages had to be approved by the Party and permission was always refused 'if the couple concerned gave the impression of being physically attracted to one another' (p. 68). The Party, O'Brien tells Smith during his interrogation, is going to kill the sex instinct. Procreation will become an annual formality like the renewal of a ration card. 'We shall,' O'Brien proclaims, 'abolish the orgasm' (p. 280).

With the Party determined to eradicate sexual desire, Smith concludes that 'the sexual act, successfully performed, was rebellion. Desire was thought crime.' (p. 71) From this point of view, his relationship with Julia is his first (only) successful act of defiance. What is sometimes overlooked is that it is Julia who initiates the relationship, it is she who confidently and with practised ease breaks a capital law by declaring her love for him, while he is considering ways to murder her for fear she is a member of the Thought Police (p. 113). She is portrayed as a strong, determined character, by far the more experienced and practical rebel. Daphne Patai acknowledges some of this but argues quite astonishingly that this is 'despite Orwell's conception of her rather than because of it'.[48]

If the sexual act, successfully performed, is rebellion, then Julia is a rebel *par excellence*. Smith is enthused by her promiscuity: 'His heart leapt. Scores of times she had done it; he wished it had been hundreds – thousands. Anything that hinted at corruption always filled him with a wild hope.' (p. 131) 'Listen,' he tells her, 'the more men you've had, the more I love you.' (p. 132) The double standard is here dramatically overthrown. Their embrace was 'a battle. The climax a victory. It was a blow struck against the Party. It was a political act.' (p. 133) Orwell makes through Julia a powerful declaration for sexual liberation.

While Julia is a sexual rebel, she is at the same time sturdily non-political in the conventional sense. She hates the Party with a ferocity that even shocks Smith but does not regard it as possible to organise against it. Instead she contrives to regularly break the law without being caught. 'In some ways,' we are told, 'she was far more acute than

Winston, and far less susceptible to Party propaganda.' (p. 139) The remark that she is a rebel from the waist down is admiring and affectionate rather than denigratory in the context of the novel and serves to emphasise the importance of the theme of sexual rebellion; its offensiveness outside of that context is, of course, undisputed (p.163). When Julia falls asleep while Smith is reading Goldstein's book out loud it is not because she is stupid or shallow, it is because she is not interested in politics, because the book does not address her concerns (she is, of course, at one with the many readers who skip the extracts from *The Theory and Practice*) (p.226). This is not to say that Orwell does not make use of sexist stereotypes in *Nineteen Eighty-Four*, but is rather to argue that these have to be placed in the context of a thematic claim for sexual liberation that is centred on the book's principal female character. The feminist critique of *Nineteen Eighty-Four* misses its target.[49] □

Both Rodden and Newsinger provide interesting and nuanced responses to the criticisms made by feminist readers of Orwell's work. In so doing they raise important issues not only about the reception of Orwell's novels, but also about the political uses of criticism. A curiosity of Orwell criticism is its domination by male critics, and the 'cult of masculinity' that Rodden sees as intrinsic to an Orwellian mythology has undoubtedly led to an overtly identificatory relationship in some cases of criticism. However, the feminist broadsides against Orwell's patronising and dismissive attitudes to women and their implicit assumption that androcentric writers will inevitably attract androcentric critics is wholly inadequate. The gendered response to Orwell that has increasingly emerged perhaps reveals more about the nature of critical practice than it does about the author himself, but it also shows again the malleability of his writings to divergent ideological and political causes. Having established the broad architecture of Orwellian criticism, it is now appropriate to consider some of the more intricate thematic structures that support that edifice.

CHAPTER FOUR

Modes of Criticism 2

Subjecting the Form – Forming the Subject

HAVING EXPLORED some of the macro-criticism of Orwell's writing in the previous chapter, it is important now to focus on more specific sites of critical engagement with *Animal Farm* and *Nineteen Eighty-Four*. This chapter of the Guide therefore examines some of the key issues that have dominated analysis of the final novels and in doing so will show their interdependence but also their strikingly different critical histories. In particular, this chapter engages with the critical interrogation of formalistic issues in the last novels and with theoretical approaches to the formation of the individual subject. Contained within these analyses are contemplations on the dynamics of power, the corruptibility of language and the disintegration of selfhood under totalitarian regimes.

Animal Farm

There is little doubt that *Animal Farm* is one of the most famous books in the English language. Yet despite its elevation to the status of cultural icon, the text's critical history is far more limited than one might reasonably anticipate. Undoubtedly, part of the reason for this is that it has been consistently overshadowed by its successor; *Nineteen Eighty-Four*. The prophetic qualities of the dystopic vision of the future during the Cold War and particularly in the run-up to 1984 itself have resulted in the fable of *Animal Farm* being relegated to a position of inferiority. *Nineteen Eighty-Four* has garnered much of the critical attention that Orwell has received and whereas *Animal Farm* is seen as a text appropriate for secondary level teaching, *Nineteen Eighty-Four* has always been viewed as the counterpart for grown-ups. Raymond Williams has also pointed towards the effacement of *Animal Farm* in critical terms as the product of a process of 'reading Orwell backwards'.[1] Williams implies that critics are inclined to read Orwell's career retrospectively as a way of accounting for the final masterwork. By this token, all his previous writings become not individual and independent works of art, but preparation for the last novel. Williams's point is an astute one and goes some way to explaining why *Animal Farm* is frequently seen as a lesser achievement – a shadow of the magnum opus, experimenting with similar themes but without the same depth of intellectual exploration.

A Story for Children? *Animal Farm*'s 'Simplicity'

Without doubt, a further reason for the relative sidelining of *Animal Farm* has been its own linguistic and stylistic simplicity. Critics have been consistently divided over the literary merit of the text, as is shown in the following extracts from Keith Alldritt's *The Making of George Orwell* and Laraine Fergenson's 'George Orwell's *Animal Farm*: A Twentieth Century Beast Fable'. This is Alldritt's assessment:

■ *Animal Farm* is subtitled 'A Fairy Story'. Since the book does not tell of fairies, nor yet of the magical, this description seems hardly appropriate. Still it does suggest one intention of the book, which is to tell a story directly and simply. In this respect Orwell's purpose is a characteristic one, namely the vigorous sweeping aside of jargon, cant and hypocrisy and the presenting of issues clearly and intelligibly. But this sort of intention always has its attendant dangers and, in the telling of his fairy story Orwell has succumbed to them. His account of revolution is greatly oversimplified; it is too obvious, too facile, too easy. For whatever we may think of the Russian revolution or, for that matter of any revolution, we cannot but be aware that the crises of a society are much more complex than Orwell is here able to suggest. And the feelings about revolution which the book elicits are as unsophisticated as the narrative itself. Take, for instance, the emotional climax of the book which comes when Boxer, the loyal and hard-working but unintelligent work horse, emblematic of 'the common people', is sold to the knackers by the pig-commissars when he becomes too ill to work any more (pp. 81–3). The feelings of simple compassion and absolutely righteous indignation which this incident is calculated to evoke may be tolerable in a nursery tale that has no pretentions to being anything other than a nursery tale. But in one which lays claim to offer the adult intelligence some feeling for the realities of modern social and political life, they cannot, because of their crudity and sentimentality, merit serious attention. At the cost of this sort of oversimplification the sustained poise of the narrative is purchased. Clearly Orwell enjoys the easy confidence to which the position of a teller of nursery tales entitles him. The avuncular security and the poker-faced humour bestowed by the conventions of the form solve completely the difficult problem of the author-reader relationship which in the past had proved so troublesome. But in order to enjoy writing in this way, Orwell has made himself oblivious of the complexity of the experience with which his story purports to deal. He has here found a form which is easy and pleasing to him, but which is a means for turning away from the disturbing complexities of experience rather than from confronting them. It allows only of simple ideas, easy responses and obvious conclusions.

This particular form of the nursery story has been borrowed from that cosy world prior to the first World War [*sic*] upon which, as we have seen, Orwell was so ready to dwell. *Animal Farm* especially reminds us of Kipling's stories for children. The laws of the revolution that are painted on the wall of the cowshed and chanted by the animals clearly owe something to 'The Law of the Jungle' in Kipling's *Second Jungle Book*. Indeed the central device of *Animal Farm*, the convention of humanised animals, may also derive most immediately from Kipling's *Jungle Book*. And Orwell's narrative tone is obviously modelled on that of the *Just So Stories*. And of course there is the Dickensian element, that traditional element which endures beneath the experimentalism in every one of Orwell's novels and shows the strength of the premodern and the unmodern in his literary sensibility. The humour of the book, when it is not 'just so' humour, is Dickensian, achieved by the use of 'the unnecessary detail' which Orwell in his critical essay had identified and given examples of and relished as 'the unmistakable mark of Dickens's writing'. For instance, an important stage in Comrade Napoleon's gradual abandonment of the principles of animalism occurs when he sits down at table to eat. But in relating this, Orwell tells just a little bit more; he 'always ate', he tells us, 'from the crown Derby dinner service which had been in the glass cupboard in the drawing room.' (p.62) This comic surface of the prose is the major effect of *Animal Farm*. The book is, in fact, a piece of literary self-indulgence. As a writer Orwell has here taken refuge in a simple, comfortable Edwardian form which allows him a perspective upon the modern world and a relationship with his reader which, however relaxed they may be, are neither engaging nor illuminating.[2] □

Here is Laraine Fergenson's perspective on *Animal Farm*:

■ What is *Animal Farm*'s true message? Actually, as long as one keeps carefully to certain generalities or to certain specifics, there seems to be really no problem in answering this question.

Despite *Animal Farm*'s ambiguities, certain general messages seem clear: Power corrupts; Passivity is dangerous; Freedom, dearly won, may be lost; Political movements with just goals that attract idealistic people may turn evil. We might also find fairly clear a few specific points: the Russian Revolution, noble in its inception, was a revolution

betrayed by the greed, cruelty, and lust for power of its leaders, specifically Stalin, and also by the inability of the Russian people and
communist insiders to oppose him effectively; Socialism, which had
held out the promise of a better life for the great majority of people,
and had lured many idealists, had degenerated in the particular case of
Russian Communism into a means of oppression. These 'meanings' –
elaborations of those we began with – are all seemingly unarguable,
but they did not, and do not, satisfy the interpreters of this work. Why
do we seek more?

I would like to suggest two reasons, and these are related to each
other. One is that the above interpretations are static. To paraphrase
Orwell from *Nineteen Eighty-Four*, they explain to some extent the *how* –
but not the *why*. They may offer a reading, a *how* to read the work. But
Why, the critics, kept – and keep – asking, *did this happen, or does it happen?* Is it inevitable that socialist revolutions will be betrayed, as the
Soviet one was because of some innate human defect or some innate
flaw in socialism? The second reason for the discontent with the messages above relates to the genre of the work – the beast fable. . . .
although *Animal Farm* can be considered a 'beast epic,' the term 'fable'
more clearly illuminates the interpretive problems it presents. A fable
may be defined as 'a short tale, usually epigrammatic, with animals,
men, or gods . . . as characters. The action of a fable illustrates a moral
which is usually (but not always) explicitly stated at the end. This
moral often attains the force of a proverb'. We know . . . that *Animal
Farm* certainly does not have one clear moral, but there is, in fact, a
proverb near its conclusion. When the animals, totally disillusioned at
seeing the pigs on two legs and indistinguishable from the human
masters they thought had been overthrown, return to the wall that
once contained the Seven Commandments of Animalism, all of which
have been subverted, they find instead just one sentence – the chilling
'ALL ANIMALS ARE EQUAL BUT SOME ANIMALS ARE MORE
EQUAL THAN OTHERS' (p. 90). This motto is what the pigs have
written in place of the Seven Commandments, and we, of course, need
not take it as Orwell's final statement. It is, nevertheless, this basic
inequality that has subverted the revolution. . . . . . .

Orwell, despite a lifetime of writing, working, and fighting for
equality, had grave doubts about it as a political force. He never totally
overcame the early indoctrination in snobbery that he acquired from
his 'lower-upper-middle class' background[3] and his upper-class education. Thus, the not so hidden message of *Animal Farm* is not that
human beings are not capable of great kindness, nobility, and sacrifice, but that basic inequalities may make these virtues insufficient to
guarantee freedom.

The beast fable has often been a means of veiling social and political criticism. Certainly Orwell's use of the genre to cloak an attack on Stalin was motivated by the necessity of not directly assailing him as he was playing a crucial role in the world's struggle against Nazism. But the allegory did not hide Orwell's anti-Stalinism: the satire's application to the Soviet Union was so obvious that one might well ask whether Orwell had another motive for choosing this form. Perhaps it was to hide – even from himself – a more subversive message, one that undermined not just the Anglo–Soviet alliance, but the nature of democracy itself.

This unique work seems to imply that the masses cannot save themselves from would-be exploiters: they need the leadership of intellectuals. But intellectuals, unfortunately, can be cowed and defeated, like some of the pigs; bribed and corrupted like most of the pigs; or hopelessly cynical, and hence uninvolved and irresponsible, like Benjamin the donkey. The beast fable medium allows Orwell to put forth this pessimistic message in a veiled and engaging way, but it has troubled commentators since the work's publication and no doubt will continue to do so.[4] □

For both Laraine Fergenson and Keith Alldritt, the simplicity of *Animal Farm*'s themes and the uncomplicated style are problematic. The problems they generate revolve around the anticipated reader's response which, interestingly, neither of them is sure about. Both see potential for misinterpretation in the straightforwardness of the allegory and yet at the root of their respective critiques seems to lie the question: is this anything more than a clever, but limited, children's story? Alldritt clearly concludes that the simplicity of the form and writing and the transparency of the allegory render the text over-determined and inflexible to diverse readings. The engagingly child-like qualities of the novel enable Orwell to obviate any serious questions about the human condition, allowing instead only 'simple ideas, easy responses and obvious conclusions'. The whole is trivial, unsophisticated and naïve as far as Alldritt is concerned. It has to be stated that such excoriating attacks on the novel have been rare but in Fergenson's article we see a similar concern with the weightiness of the themes of the text. Fergenson argues that the novel is beguilingly simple and this simplicity has led to a catalogue of misreadings. Intellectual argument, she suggests, has sought a greater depth of insight in the novel than actually exists and, unable to locate sophisticated meanings, has manufactured spurious lines of criticism. *Animal Farm* is as straightforward as it appears, according to Fergenson, its message being that revolution will always be corrupted by self-interest and that the masses will always be duped into subservience.

These two critics in many ways restate in more sophisticated terms the cases made by the earliest commentators on *Animal Farm* who concluded that there was little worth saying about a text which seems so readily to offer up its meaning. It is certainly ironic and perhaps indicative of literary criticism's own self-reflexivity that a seemingly uncomplicated text must be meticulously deconstructed in the search for latent structures, whilst ignoring the fact that its force and enduring appeal undoubtedly derive from its lack of complexity. Having said that, many critics have looked beyond the obvious moral didacticism of the text and explored its wider-ranging engagement with issues of form and genre. The following passages by critics Patrick Reilly and Lynette Hunter present sophisticated analyses of the novel which take us beyond its ostensible simplicity. The first extract is by Reilly:

■ In *Animal Farm*, apart from a possible irritation at being forced to choose between Napoleon and Boxer . . . the reader is always in control of the fable. The villain of *Animal Farm*, unlike those of *Othello* or *Nineteen Eighty-Four*, is always pellucidly open, often derisively so – we never *fear* Napoleon as we do Iago and Big Brother. The reader is in the superior position of a sophisticated onlooker at a country fair watching a bunch of yokels being taken in by a third-rate charlatan. Orwell castrates terror in the comic spectacle of an allegedly teetotal pig suffering from a hangover and swearing, like the rest of us, never to do it again (p. 72). It is a scene not from the world of totalitarian terror, of Hitler and Stalin, purges and camps, but from that of Donald McGill, of mothers-in-law, dirty weekends and marital squabbles.

Naturally, the animals take a very different view of things, but the reader sees Napoleon less as a ferocious tyrant than as a comic cheat whose inept attempts at duplicity provoke laughter rather than indignation. When human tyrants suffer hangovers, they presumably become more fearful as the executions mount with the migraines. In Orwell's *Nineteen Eighty-Four*, we are forced to identify with Winston, the main character, and we fear Big Brother, and rightly, for our lives hang upon his whims. In *Nineteen Eighty-Four* the reader is included *in* the diminishing-technique, which makes him an insignificant bug like Winston, liable at any instant to be squashed into unpersonhood. In *Animal Farm*, by contrast, the reader is serenely above the diminution, watching with amused immunity the terrifying tale of contemporary history scaled to Lilliputian proportions, tamed to the level of barnyard fable. The prophecy magnifies the tyrant and diminishes the reader: the allegory magnifies the reader and diminishes the tyrant. . . . . . .

All the events are deliberately diminished. The suppression of the kulaks in the Ukraine is reduced to a rebellion of hens at the sale of their eggs; it ends with nine hens starved to death – the fable's equivalent of the millions of peasants who died in the aftermath of Stalin's victory. Swift in Lilliput similarly trivialises the wars of the Reformation to an absurd wrangle between Big- and Little-Endians. Orwell employs the same technique to exchange the harrowing emotions provoked by twentieth-century history for an Olympian pose, so making the events easier to handle. The allegations of industrial sabotage which issued in the Moscow showcase trials dwindle into a broken window and a blocked drain, while treason to the Revolution finds its appropriate image in a sheep urinating in a drinking-pool.

The most amusingly 'domestic' of these substitutions is the account of Mollie's defection. We hear that she is becoming 'more and more troublesome,' and there are rumors of 'something more serious' than her habitual giddiness. What Marxist and social philosopher Herbert Marcuse deplores as the seduction of large sections of the Western working class, bribed by the titbits of consumerism, is here depicted in terms of a fallen woman of Victorian melodrama, as Mollie goes down the well-worn road of Little Em'ly and Hetty Sorrel. The matronly Clover does her best to save the wanton – she is accepting sugar and ribbons from the men, has even been caught *in flagrante delicto* allowing her nose to be stroked (p. 34) – but the attempted rescue is as futile as Mrs Poyser's remonstrations. The last the scandalised animals hear is that Mollie is traipsing about town with a vulgar publican; after this, 'none of the animals ever mentioned Mollie again.' (p. 31) The shame of the lapse is emphasized in the best Victorian tradition. When the animals metaphorically turn Mollie's face to the wall, the reader applauds the reductive wit, and, in his amusement, necessarily neglects the seriousness of the defection as viewed from Marcuse's perspective. ... ...

Orwell's purpose is to control a material which, taken at its everyday estimate and customary magnification, would cause the writer pain, alarm and indignation. Small is masterable; when Stalin becomes a pig and Europe a farmyard, the nightmare of contemporary history is transmuted, through the power of art, into a blithe and inspired fantasy.

Thus to criticise Orwell for allegedly demeaning the common people by depicting them as moronically credulous brutes is to misread the book. The animal fable is devised not to insult the ordinary man but to distance Orwell from the terror: existence becomes endurable as an aesthetic phenomenon. Philosopher Schiller argues that only in art is man free. German novelist Thomas Mann described his Joseph tetralogy, written between 1926 and 1943 (the period covered by Orwell's fable), as his attempt to escape the horror by burying himself in an innocent and serene creation of the Spirit. Simplicity is an essential part of Orwell's disarming strategy. *Animal Farm*, as its subtitle 'A Fairy Tale' makes plain, is a convenient simplification, yet its simplicity came hard: 'the only one of my books I really sweated over,' he wrote.[5] □

The second extract is from Lynette Hunter:

■ The complex satire of *Animal Farm* is built upon an awareness of the power that language wields. The interaction between politics and language does not just establish one-to-one relationships between animal characters and historical figures but creates an understanding of a particular set of rhetorical techniques that have a broad political application. Further, it does not simply criticise certain forms of government but suggests reasons for why they occur and what contributes to their success. However, what limits the tale to satire, no matter how constructive it is in its suggestions, is the sense of inevitability, of describing an insoluble problem, ending on a note of negativity and cynicism. At the same time though the reader cannot ignore the coincident tongue-in-cheek humour of the narrating voice. The melodramatised character of the elderly Clover, the formal dance of speeches with their all-too-neat structure, the final exaggerated irony, all belie the negative pattern of the satire.

What turns the writing into positive allegory is the establishing of genre conventions that are shifted and reversed. In these changes the narrator takes a positive stance that contrasts sharply with the satirical voice; and the primary and most obvious reversal is that to which we are alerted in the subtitle of the book, 'A Fairy Story'. The function of allegory depends on differences. Yet . . . what is commonly termed 'allegory' is one-to-one use of representational emblems, similarities: hardly a subtle genre. The dissatisfaction with it comes from the limited and reduced nature of stance. If acted well the movements can afford a similar pleasure to that of chess, but as with chess the more significant aspects of the game lie in the battle between the players not that between the pieces on the board. Restricting themselves to those pieces and what they are capable of, the players limit the scope of their interaction and the involvement of their audience. The supposed author of this kind of reduced generic 'allegory' is limited by the overtly representational nature of his structure. It takes great skill to maintain the grounds of his alternative world and to avoid the sense of inevitability that arises from the associative links and habitual connotations that are established. At the same time simple destruction of those links can be just as reductive; something positive needs to be suggested to open out the dialogue and make interaction possible. The complex satire of *Animal Farm* is generated by the process of allegory out of a reductive satire about events in Russian history. Its positive nature is found in its broad applicability to politics and language. But it is still limited to the criticism and exposure of weaknesses, to saying what not to do rather than what to do.

However, there is also the broader, interactive allegorical stance of

Animal Farm which removes itself one step further from the representational, by turning to literary conventions which establish the bases for difference. The writer spends much of the first chapter getting the narrator to set up the genre conventions that surround fairy stories. Yet from the beginning there is a counter-element which indicates why this particular genre has been chosen. Elements to note are the simple phrasing and the repetition of grammatical structures which create a formal rhythm in the prose. There is also use of specific constructions such as 'there was a stirring and a fluttering' (p. 1) or the literal use of common expressions like 'chewing the cud' (p. 2) that are traditionally allied to the genre. Especially distinctive is the formal and detached quality of the narrator generated by these elements. It is as if he has a specific recognised role as tale-teller, because individual style is played down. Even before the more personalised descriptions of the animals begin, these details alert and orientate the reader to a genre.

For several reasons, the convention is immediately effective. The form is instantly recognised as non-novelistic. The reader does not expect the naturalism of psychological exploration or 'round characters'. What he does look for is a formal structure for teaching and knowing, by way of a conventional and non-representational mode. From the beginning, we are involved in an expected manner, alerted to certain rules. The narrator has the freedom to state, and present 'types', without appearing to dictate or over-control. He also has a convention that encourages detachment because its formality states his stance for him. However, at the same time he is part of the narration in a manner that a tale-teller would not be. He throws forward the convention he is using with the addition of extraneous comment, such as Major's alternative name being 'Willingdon Beauty' (p. 1). The use of brackets at this particular point in itself indicates a grammatical 'aside' different from his formal role. The use of fairy story is further highlighted by the humour which emerges in applying human description to animals, which is unusual for the genre. The mare Clover 'had never quite got her figure back after her fourth foal' (p. 2), and Benjamin's cynicism is undercut by a devotion to Boxer. Neither character will regain the formal distance of a fairy story figure after such description.

These effects are generated by the unusual use of animals as the main elements in the fairy story. The effect for the reader is that he can identify with the animals because they fit recognisable types, but the humour in their human description allows one to remain detached. We see the humanity in them because of their lack of it. The two views are the key to the allegory. The fairy story genre conditions one to certain expectations, an inevitability, a certain and set ethical development of specific issues in which the 'good' get rewarded and the 'bad' punished, according to the terms of the society they are written for.

Excitement, adventure and apparent change occur only to reaffirm the basis of the society. Working against this all the way through is the fact that the characters are animals not humans. As a result many incongruous and ludicrous comparisons surface which detract from the formality of the fairy story and call into question its ethical inevitability.

Over and above the interconnection of these two is the interplay of the narrative allegory with the satire. After all Major's speech dominates the first chapter. It is an example of a rhetoric containing within it the seeds of negative persuasion. The premises of that speech establish a power-wielding, knowledgeable, acceptable identity; they evidence total control over the development of the logic; and they encourage acceptance and group participation in agreed custom. The fairy story elements of the first chapter also do this. If we are aware of the manipulation involved in Major's speech we should be doubly aware of the negative rhetorical elements in the fairy story. In this interplay and in the interaction of fairy story and humour, the allegory of the writing may be discerned. However, on first reading the dominant note is that of the fairy story not its disruption. Similarly, it is difficult to be immediately aware of the implications of Major's speech. Yet I would suggest that this is a positive aspect of the writer's stance. The reader's gradual learning about the negative use of language parallels his gradual recognition of the subversion of the fairy story convention. The process of learning involves the active participation of the reader, draws him into a personal assessment necessary to the positive rhetoric of the writing.[6] □

Both Hunter and Reilly take the discussion of genre further than Fergenson and Alldritt, and cite the relationships between narrator, reader and narrative as central to the novel's affective force. Reilly contends that a certain narratorial self-effacement throws control of the text onto the reader and by this procedure distances us from the terror of *Animal Farm*'s slide towards despotism. Far more thoughtfully than Alldritt, Hunter examines the interplay of generic expectation and narratorial voice to show the ways in which Orwell uses the limitations of the genres of fairy story, fable and allegory to satirical ends. For Hunter the genius of the text is its ability to manipulate the reader's response through an increasingly detached narratorial position. This process lends the tale an impersonal tone consistent with the rhetorical status of the satirical observer rather than the engaged teller of the fairy story.

Language and Power on the Farm
One significant area of interest for Hunter is the importance of language use and in particular how that is distinctively different between the animals. It is a field of criticism that has borne fruit in some fascinating work

on the power of language and its potential for corruption, as we see in the next group of extracts. The first of these is from Robert Lee's 1969 book *Orwell's Fiction*:

■ Power inevitably corrupts the best of intentions, apparently no matter who possesses the power: At the end, all the representatives of the various ideologies are indistinguishable – they are all pigs, all pigs are humans. Communism is no better and no worse than capitalism or fascism; the ideals of socialism were long ago lost in Clover's uncomprehending gaze over the farm. Religion is merely a toy for the corrupters, neither offensive nor helpful to master or slave. But perhaps more distressing yet is the realization that everyone, the good and the bad, the deserving and the wicked, are not only contributors to the tyranny, are not only powerless before it, but are unable to understand it. Boxer thinks that whatever Napoleon says is right; Clover can only vaguely feel, and cannot communicate, that things are not exactly right; Benjamin thinks that it is in the nature of the world that things go wrong. The potential hope of the book is finally expressed only in terms of ignorance (Boxer), wistful inarticulateness (Clover), or the tired, cynical belief that things never change (Benjamin). The inhabitants of this world seem to deserve their fate.

One must finally ask, however, with all this despair and bleakness what are the actual bases for the tyranny of *Animal Farm*. Is the terrorism of the dogs the most crucial aspect? Is it this that rules the animals? Boxer's power is seen as superior to this violence and force. Is the basis of the tonal despair the pessimistic belief in the helplessness of the mass of the animals? Orwell elsewhere states again and again his faith in the common people. It seems to me that the basis of this society's evil is the inability of its inhabitants to ascertain truth and that this is demonstrated through the theme of the corruption of language. So long as the animals cannot remember the past, because it is continually altered, they have no control over the present and hence over the future. A society which cannot control its language is, says Orwell, doomed to be oppressed in terms which deny it the very most elemental aspects of humanity: To live in a world which allows the revised form of the seventh commandment of *Animal Farm* is not merely to renounce the belief in the possibility of human equality, but in the blatant perversion of language, the very concept of objective reality is lost.

The mode by which the recognition of reality is denied is the corruption of language. When a society no longer maintains its language as a common basis by which value, idea, and fact are to be exchanged, those who control the means of communication have the most awful of powers – they literally can create the truth they choose. *Animal Farm*, then, seems to be in one respect only an extension of *Burmese Days* – the common problem is the failure of communication and its corollary, community. But if in *Burmese Days* their failure was contingent, in *Animal Farm* it is brought about by willful manipulation. The next logical step is seen in *1984*, where the consequences press to the premonition of apocalypse.[7] □

Robert Lee's argument is that Orwell sees the revolution as being betrayed not purely through the selfish machinations of the pigs, but, on a more basic level, through the disputed territory of language. The corruption of language, including the rewriting of history and the amendments made to the commandments of Animalism, generates an instability in both the perception of the world and the subsequent expression of any desire to change that world. Here Lee points towards the crude hijacking of language by ideological forces that was ultimately to become such a central feature of *Nineteen Eighty-Four*. The corruption of the guiding principle of Animalism – All Animals are Equal – into the equivocal – All Animals are Equal but Some are more Equal than Others (p. 90) – is a perfect example of an embryonic doublethink and shows Orwell to be aware of the potential for social control offered by the domination of language. In *The Language of George Orwell*, Roger Fowler has gone one step further than Lee to explore the specific disproportions of speech acts among the animals:

■ One feature of this disastrous animal utopia is a marked disproportion in the allocation of language to the various classes of animal. Success in language relates directly to the amount of power enjoyed by the different species: power to understand the processes of farming and of government, power to control the fates of other species. The pigs learn to read and write fluently, the others learn less well, their success diminishing according to the conventional stereotype of their intelligence: Orwell analyses their relative attainments in detail, constructing the descending hierarchy pigs-donkey-goat-dogs-horse-sheep-hens-ducks. Their different commands of language correspond roughly to their degrees of control over their lives in this new regime.

There is a marked difference in the amounts of *speech* assigned to the different animals. Except for one small oration by Pilkington at the end, humans do not speak, though their rumours and plots are to some small extent reported. All the rest of the animals are imagined to have speech, though as far as the lower orders go, this seems to be limited to confessing crimes, and these confessions are reported, not direct. In the early days the animals participate in debates, but their contributions (other than those of the pigs) are reported rather than direct speech. Only the horses, the goat and the donkey hold conversations, and then in a very limited way, and – scanning the text as a whole – surprisingly rarely, at least in direct speech . . . . . .

It can be seen that language is of fundamental significance in *Animal Farm*, and in a number of respects. It is first of all the medium for narration, the telling of the tale, and in that role it has a specific stylistic character, which both models the mind-style of the animals (in its underlying mundane, pastoral simplicity) and slightly distances them (by the somewhat elevated narrator's register). When we look at the language of the pigs, comparing it both in quantity and in style with that associated with the other animals, we realise that language is also part of the *action* of the book, and that the relationship of language and power symbolised by linguistic actions is a theme examined by this fable. This theme becomes more specifically focused as the pigs' regime gets indefensibly brutal and selfish: language can be used in a perverted way in order to support a distorted, untruthful, version of reality. There is a hint of this in the first presentation of Squealer . . . as a brilliant talker who 'could turn black into white' (p. 9). This is precisely Squealer's role throughout the narrative, a role which he takes over from the banished Snowball. The Seven Commandments, initial moral code of Animalism, are by Snowball reduced for ease of memorisation by the animals (also to blur its details) to the maxim 'Four legs good, two legs bad' (p. 22) which even the dim-witted sheep can bleat enthusiastically. The text continues:

> The birds at first objected, since it seemed to them that they also had two legs, but Snowball proved to them that this was not so.
>
> 'A bird's wing, comrades,' he said, 'is an organ of propulsion and not of manipulation. It should therefore be regarded as a leg. The distinguishing mark of Man is the *hand*, the instrument with which he does all his mischief.'
>
> The birds did not understand Snowball's long words, but they accepted his explanation, and all the humbler animals set to work to learn the new maxim by heart (pp. 21–2).

The long words stand out against the simple language of the narrative, and are a patent grotesquerie of language by which Orwell mocks the lying logic of Snowball as Snowball squares the world with the maxim by redefining wings as legs. The animals, though handled sympathetically rather than patronisingly, are naive, and take in Snowball's explanation. It is Squealer who performs this function of redefining black as white for the animals for most of the story.[8] □

Again the focus of Fowler's attention is the malicious manipulation of language and distances us further from interpretations of the text as a simple and uncomplicated fable. What Fowler and Lee both highlight is the degree to which Orwell investigates the dynamics of power in the most basic units of communication. Orwell is thus seen to explore not just the phenomenon of betrayed revolution, but, much more forcefully, the necessary pre-conditions of totalitarianism. In order for totalitarian government to be effective, a fundamental subjection of will in the populace has to be enacted; anti-democratic measures require, on one level, the acquiescence of the majority. In a libertarian society such acquiescence is unlikely to be forthcoming if the methods for social control are overtly and arbitrarily enforced. The subtle implementation of those methods is necessary to ensure their passive acceptance. Forms of ideological conditioning enable, and indeed encourage, the subjection of the individual self to the collective and, as Orwell shows, one of the most effective means by which that conditioning can be guaranteed is through centralised control of linguistic systems.

Animal Farm and the Totalitarian Temper

That Orwell is contemplating the nature of totalitarianism in *Animal Farm* is something that many critics, perhaps beguiled by its simplicity, have failed to note. As we know, plans for the novel that was to become *Nineteen Eighty-Four* had been laid prior to the writing of *Animal Farm* and so it is not illogical to see a much greater correspondence between the final texts than some critics would suggest. In fact much critical space has been devoted to exploring the relationship between the two novels and whilst we should heed the warning against reading Orwell backwards, it is important to establish how these texts interlink and how *Animal Farm* can be seen as a novel of transition.

One area that has naturally excited much critical attention is the presentation of the animal revolution not as an historically specific metaphor of the Russian Revolution, but as a broader commentary on the nature of rebellion and the progress of dictatorships. That we should read *Animal Farm* as a disquisition on the evils of totalitarianism is something stressed by Alex Zwerdling in the following passage:

■ In Orwell's speculations about revolution as a method for achieving socialist goals, he became far less confident than Trotsky that real progress was achieved through revolution, and his own view at times approaches Lord Acton's gloomy conviction that every revolution 'makes a wise and just reform impossible.' As early as 1938, the central idea of *Animal Farm* was running through Orwell's mind: 'It would seem that what you get over and over again is a movement of the proletariat which is promptly canalised and betrayed by astute people at the top, and then the growth of a new governing class. The one thing that never arrives is equality. The mass of the people never get the chance to bring their innate decency into the control of affairs, so that one is almost driven to the cynical thought that men are only decent when they are powerless.' Clearly Orwell still hesitates to accept this idea: he says he is 'almost driven' to it. It remained an unresolved issue in his mind for years, and one can see why. His socialist faith made him need to deny it; his temperamental pessimism must have found it congenial. He could neither resolve the question nor forget it – perhaps the ideal condition for the creation of a vital literary work.

Orwell's uncertainty about revolution eventually produced *Animal Farm* and was responsible for the considerable ambiguity of the book. An ironic allegory is bound to mystify many of its readers, no matter how easy it is to identify the historical parallels on which it is based. We know that Orwell had a great deal of difficulty getting *Animal Farm* into print, and it is generally assumed that publishers rejected it because they did not want to publish an anti-Soviet satire in the middle of the war. Yet T. S. Eliot's letter of rejection from Faber makes it clear this was not the only problem the book raised. Eliot complains that 'the effect is simply one of negation. It ought to excite some sympathy with what the author wants, as well as sympathy with his objections to something: and the positive point of view which I take to be generally Trotskyite, is not convincing.' He goes on to suggest that Orwell 'splits his vote' by refusing to confirm any of the standard Western attitudes toward the Soviet Union.

Eliot's argument suggests a thoroughly confused sense of Orwell's purpose. If *Animal Farm* can be said to have a 'positive point of view' at all, it is certainly not Trotskyite: Snowball is hardly its tragic hero. The difficulties of understanding *Animal Farm* largely stem from its interpretation as an exclusive attack on the Soviet Union. Orwell's purpose, however, is more general: he is interested in tracing the inevitable stages of any revolution, and he shapes his fable accordingly. This is not to deny that the literal level of the story is almost exclusively based on Soviet history. But although Russia is his immediate target, Orwell says the book 'is intended as a satire on dictatorship in general.' He was faithful to the details of Soviet history, yet he did not hesitate to transform some of its most important elements.

The most striking of these is the omission of Lenin from the drama. Major (the idealist visionary who dies before the revolution takes place) is clearly meant to represent Marx, while Napoleon and Snowball act out the conflict in the postrevolutionary state between Stalin and Trotsky. Lenin is left out, it seems to me, because Orwell wants to emphasize the enormous disparity between the ideals of the revolution and the reality of the society it actually achieves. Lenin was the missing link in this process, both visionary and architect of the new state, but from Orwell's longer historical perspective, his brief period of power must have seemed like an irrelevant interlude in the stark drama that was unfolding. The heirs of Lenin had in fact begun to transform him into a myth even before he was dead; they legitimized their power by worshipping at his shrine. In order to demythify the Russian Revolution and present the Bolshevik leaders as they really were, Orwell must have felt compelled to eliminate the mythical hero altogether.

Such radical departures from history are of course Orwell's prerogative in constructing a story intended to have more general significance. He says in a preface to *Animal Farm* that 'although the various episodes are taken from the actual history of the Russian Revolution, they are dealt with schematically and their chronological order is changed; this was necessary for the symmetry of the story.' (p. 113) One might add that it was also necessary in order to achieve Orwell's purpose in writing it. This raises the question of how the topical and generic levels of satire in the book are related, and one might clarify the issue by citing the case of Jonathan Swift, who was in some sense Orwell's model.

When *Gulliver's Travels* was first published, many read the book as an essentially partisan political document, a propaganda piece for the opposition party. Yet Swift himself wrote to his French translator that, if *Gulliver's Travels* could only be understood in England, it was a failure, for 'the same vices and the same follies reign everywhere and the author who writes only for a city, a province, a kingdom, or even an age, deserves so little to be translated, that he does not even deserve to be read.' In the same way, *Animal Farm* is concerned both with the Russian Revolution and, by extension, with the general pattern of revolution itself. As the Stalinist period recedes into the distant past, Orwell's book (if it survives as a literary work) will more and more be appreciated as generic rather than topical satire, just as *Gulliver's Travels* has come to be.

Orwell chose to write his book in the form of a fable partly to give the pattern of historical events permanent mythic life, to emphasize that he was dealing with typical, not fortuitous, events. He is interested in constructing a paradigmatic social revolution, and the pattern that emerges is meant to apply to the Spanish Civil War and to the French Revolution (the main character, after all, is named Napoleon) as well as to the Russian one. Orwell's story suggests that revolutions inevitably go through several predictable stages. They begin with great idealistic fervor and popular support, energized by millennial expectations of justice and equality. The period immediately following a successful revolution is the Eden stage. There is a sense of triumphant achievement; idealistic vision is translated into immediate reality; the spirit of community and equality are everywhere apparent. Old laws and institutions are broken and replaced by an inner, yet reliable, concern for the common good. The state has, for the moment, withered away.

Slowly the feeling of freedom gives way to the sense of necessity and bondage, 'we' becomes 'I–they,' spirit turns into law, improvised organization is replaced by rigid institutions, equality modulates to privilege. The next stage is the creation of a new elite which, because of its superior skill and its lust for power, assumes command and recreates the class structure. Its power is first universally granted but gradually must be upheld against opposition by terror and threat. As time goes on, the past is forgotten or expunged; the new elite takes on all the characteristics of the old, prerevolutionary leadership, while the rest of the society returns to the condition of servitude. The transition is too gradual to be dramatic, although it has its dramatic moments, and it is constantly presented in the guise of historical inevitability or as a necessary response to conspiracy or external danger. A scapegoat is found to explain the disparity between ideal and actual. The exploited class remains exploited basically because of its doggedness and stupidity but also because, having no taste for power, it is inevitably victimized by the power-hungry. In every new society – even if it consists exclusively of those without previous experience of power – some will rise above their fellows and assume the available positions of authority. When their power and privileges are consolidated, they will fight to keep them. The only surviving vestiges of revolution will be its rhetoric and its (conveniently altered) history. The reality of 'equality' and 'justice' will have withered away, to be replaced by the state.

'The effect,' Eliot had said, 'is simply one of negation.' His objection raises the question of whether *Animal Farm* should be considered in moral terms at all. At this point in his career Orwell's mind had begun to work in an increasingly analytic way. He was interested in understanding the structure of revolution rather than in proposing a better way to achieve social goals. Eliot complains that the book fails to 'excite some sympathy with what the author wants.' Yet great satire has often been written out of the despairing sense that 'what the author wants' may be unattainable. Orwell's socialism is not an act of faith. If he has a 'positive point of view' at all in writing *Animal Farm*, it is the hope that socialists will be able to face the hard truths he presents rather than continue to accept the various consoling illusions their movement has generated to account for its disappointments.

And yet realism is not his only goal; he is also finally a moralist. In the essay on Dickens, Orwell makes an important distinction between the moralist and the revolutionary, which I take to be crucial for an understanding of his purpose in *Animal Farm*. Dickens, he says, is a moralist: 'It is hopeless to try and pin him down to any definite remedy, still more to any political doctrine. . . . Useless to change institutions without a 'change of heart' – that, essentially, is what he is always saying.' Orwell realized that the need for a 'change of heart' has been used as 'the alibi of people who do not wish to endanger the *status quo*,' but he insists that this does not make Dickens a reactionary apologist. The paradox can only be explained by understanding the writer's relation to the moment in which he writes:

> I said earlier that Dickens is not *in the accepted sense* a revolutionary writer. But it is not at all certain that a merely moral criticism of society may not be just as 'revolutionary' – and revolution, after all, means turning things upside down – as the politico-economic criticism which is fashionable at this moment. Blake was not a politician, but there is more understanding of the nature of capitalist society in a poem like 'I wander through each charter'd street' than in three-quarters of Socialist literature. Progress is not an illusion, it happens, but it is slow and invariably disappointing. There is always a new tyrant waiting to take over from the old – generally not quite so bad, but still a tyrant. Consequently two viewpoints are always tenable. The one, how can you improve human nature until you have changed the system? The other, what is the use of changing the system before you have improved human nature? They appeal to different individuals, and they probably show a tendency to alternate in point of time.

The passage is remarkable for the sense it gives of Orwell's long historical perspective and his ability to see a particular artistic choice (Dickens's and, at this point, his own) as being in perpetual conflict with its equally legitimate opposite. The attitude could be described as dialectical, except that Orwell does not stress the synthesis which grows out of each clash. Rather, he sees the conflict as eternal: the point of view is far from the ultimate optimism of Hegel and Marx. At a particular moment in time, then, the moralist who voices his outrage at what is accepted, even though he has no idea how things might be changed, is more of a revolutionary than the 'revolutionary' writer who endorses the most advanced form of social engineering. Most revolutionaries, as Orwell also points out in the Dickens essay, 'are potential Tories, because they imagine that everything can be put right by altering the *shape* of society; once that change is effected, as it sometimes is, they see no need for any other.' It is at this moment – when a given revolution has more to preserve than to transform – that it is ripe for the moralist's exposé. Orwell felt that Soviet society had reached this stage, although most of the socialist camp still saw in it only its earlier, triumphant achievement. In performing this task, he hoped he might also make his audience aware that the illusion they cherished was only a particular example of a temptation they would meet again – the habit of substituting wish for reality.[9] □

Zwerdling argues against purely historicised readings of *Animal Farm*, whilst acknowledging that the novel clearly owes much to the *dramatis personae* of the Socialist movement. Orwell's text offers us insights into the social dynamics of class revolution but, for Zwerdling, the Russian Revolution was merely an example of a broader political paradigm rather than a model in itself. In this way, *Animal Farm* can be seen as a stepping stone on the path to *Nineteen Eighty-Four*, even though both texts are born from a similar moment of disillusion with the direction of Socialism. It is important to recognise, though, that *Animal Farm* is not a dry run for *Nineteen Eighty-Four*, nor is it a simplified version of the later text. Instead, it is an individual work of art, making distinct points about the nature of power, which nevertheless proves a vital bridge between Orwell's earlier realism and the complex fantasy of the last work.

Nineteen Eighty-Four

To synthesise the body of critical writing on *Nineteen Eighty-Four* into a few short indicative passages is a very difficult task and to attempt to organise those passages into a coherent narrative of critical response is even more problematic. As we have seen, *Nineteen Eighty-Four* has been subjected to numerous appropriative readings and employed as an exemplum for widely divergent and often contradictory causes. Its critical history is, therefore, a confused babble of voices each striving for prominence. Unlike *Animal Farm*, *Nineteen Eighty-Four* has not suffered from claims of over-simplicity and whilst some critics have queried Orwell's writing abilities, few have failed to appreciate the broad cultural and political implications of the novel. So far this Guide has striven to establish the broad terms by which readers can engage with the novel. This section provides more specific readings based around debates that have consistently been at the forefront of study of the text. Broadly these can be broken down into three principal arenas of criticism: the nature of totalitarian power; the compromise of selfhood and the corruption of language.

Nineteen Eighty-Four and the Politics of Power

Orwell's representation of the totalitarian state is persuasive and unsettling to such a degree that it has become lodged within the cultural memory of the Western world and is consistently resurrected as a metaphor for repressive state governance. Yet Orwell's vision of a dystopian future is rooted in both the temporal and the timeless; its parameters are defined by the historical realities of the Communist Soviet Union and Nazi Germany, but also by an ahistorical inquiry into the nature and workings of power. The ostensible simplicity of *Animal Farm*'s moral – that power corrupts – is given new weight and texture by *Nineteen Eighty-Four* which seeks to discover the manner in which power corrupts and the ways in which that corruption extends to the individual's sense of autonomous selfhood. Considering whether Orwell's political vision was an enduring one, Richard Rorty writes as follows:

■ Orwell's best novels will be widely read only as long as we describe the politics of the twentieth century as Orwell did. How long that will be will depend on the contingencies of our political future: on what sort of people will be looking back on us, on how events in the next century will reflect back on ours, on how people will decide to describe the Bolshevik Revolution, the Cold War, the brief American hegemony, and the role of countries like Brazil and China. Orwell thought of our century as the period in which 'human equality became technically possible' and in which, simultaneously,

> practices which had long been abandoned, in some cases for hundreds of years – imprisonment without trial, the use of war prisoners as slaves, public executions, torture to extract confessions, the use of hostages, and the deportation of whole populations – not only became common again, but were tolerated and even defended by people who considered themselves enlightened and progressive.[10]

Someday this description of our century may come to seem blinkered or shortsighted. If it does, Orwell will be seen as having inveighed against an evil he did not entirely understand. Our descendants will read him as we read Swift – with admiration for a man who served human liberty, but with little inclination to adopt his classification of political tendencies or his vocabulary of moral and political deliberation. Some present-day leftist critics of Orwell (e.g., Christopher Norris) think that we *already* have a way of seeing Orwell as blinkered and shortsighted. They think that the facts to which he called attention can already be put in a context within which they look quite different. Unlike Norris, I do not think that we have a better alternative context. In the forty years since Orwell wrote, as far as I can see, nobody has come up with a better way of setting out the political alternatives which confront us. Taking his earlier warnings against the greedy and stupid conservatives together with his warnings against the Communist oligarchs, his description of our political situation – of the dangers and options at hand – remains as useful as any we possess.[11] □

Rorty warns against reading Orwell as a prophet or savant, suggesting instead that his relevance is to a world with the same conception of politics as those outlined in *Animal Farm* and *Nineteen Eighty-Four*. Orwell is curiously of his time, Rorty feels, but his enduring reputation stems from the continuing threat of dictatorial and ideologically driven government. Only when we move into a new political paradigm will Orwell's legacy begin to appear antiquated. This is an interesting and sensitive caveat to the cult of authorial reputation and positions Orwell in the centre of twentieth-century political discourse, but in a role which is evolutionary rather than ahistorical. Such a precise distinction leads us into our first extract on the portrayal of power in *Nineteen Eighty-Four*. Alan Kennedy challenges the received wisdom that *Nineteen Eighty-Four* presents the lust for power as an absolute, incorrigible desire for the experience of power itself:

■ Our analysis has been hovering around the subject of power and we might hope a close consideration of power will clear up all the confusions we have been encountering. In fact we can construct a satisfying hypothesis that goes something like this. The novel wants to demonstrate that the lust for power is an absolute, an ultimate and therefore ultimately inexplicable desire. It is all-mastering, and irreducible to reason. Power is desired not for any reason, not for any end, not as a means. Power is desired for its own sake. In that sense it is like God, beyond reason. Since power lust is inexplicable, then it doesn't make sense to try to make sense of the ways in which the power-hungry seek to maintain their power. Such a commentary seems totally inadequate on the surface, and there are other, more satisfactory theoretical accounts of power.

If we could discover that the account of power in *1984* is itself inadequate, then we might be able to conclude that the novel does indeed fail to achieve its conscious intention. We can reach such a conviction, in fact, simply by denying that power can be treated as an absolute in human society. It turns out that selfishness is not the driving power of human society as we know it. Anthropologically speaking, human beings are successful for the same reasons as animals such as coyotes are successful: the sex drive is powerful, in the general sense. That is, people like to reproduce themselves. Which is to say that their deepest drives are directed towards the continuation of the species; or that in fact individual needs are overcome by the needs of the group. Our success now is a result of the selflessness of evolutionary forces. And, of course, we have to recognise that we live in paradox, and that our success in building societies is what gives us the technological mastery to destroy ourselves.

The conundrum of power as conceived by O'Brien can perhaps best be grasped by the image he gives of the future: 'a boot stamping on a human face – for ever' (p. 280). Now, it is very difficult for O'Brien to avoid the master/slave paradox: that the master is bound to his slave; or that, for the boot to feel power, it is dependent on the existence of the face. This fact I want to interpret to mean that even power is not self-sufficient: in order to exist, power needs to be perceived. O'Brien himself makes this point indirectly: 'We control matter because we control the mind. Reality is inside the skull' (p. 277). In his period of acceptance, Winston begins to echo this 'truth': 'What knowledge have we of anything, save through our own minds? All happenings are in the mind. Whatever happens in all minds, truly happens.' (p. 291) O'Brien's final word on the matter is, 'Nothing exists except through human consciousness' (p. 213). Which of course means that power exists only through human consciousness. If power is a kind of God, then it requires the consciousness, as Winston indicates, of all human minds for it to 'truly happen'. 'We are the priests of power', says O'Brien. 'God is power' (p. 276). So it seems that, for God to exist, for God as power to exist (especially since he is an idea), he and it must be perceived.

If God is power, then we can comprehend that he had to create the world so as to be perceived. Which leads us to consider the logic of the Party's repressive methods. The Party is superior to Stalinist Russia, to Hitler, we are told, because it refuses to make martyrs. It requires rebellious individuals to become conscious of its power, and O'Brien is at the height of his voluptuous enjoyment when he can see Winston squirming in the agony of consciousness of O'Brien's power. The boot is never happier than when it is recognised as a boot by the face. Then, of course, when the individual freely submits to the Party, he is killed. The brain is to be made perfect before it is blown out. Which means that, with the elimination of the rebellious individual, the Party needs another one; it needs to create another dissident consciousness, in order to be able to put the boot in again and reaffirm the reality of its power by creating consciousness of power. So the Party itself is caught in a dangerous double game of having to survive by creating opposition to itself. No wonder it does not see the only logical way to perpetuate itself (by means of radicalising the Oedipal rebellion).

Which makes one wonder why the Party stops short of making martyrs. O'Brien notes that previous totalitarian regimes failed by making martyrs and so creating crystalline centres of opposition, and, since the Party cannot stand opposition, it will not make martyrs (pp. 265–6). Which contradicts the need of the Party to have opposition, or at least to have general consciousness of its power for it to exist. If the Party is never openly perceived as exercising its power, then it will not be perceived as having power. As Canetti[12] so tellingly shows, those in genuine human societies have power only because they are perceived as having the power of death over members of a society. In societies in which power is clearly recognised, there is a regular public demonstration of the power of the ruler by means of death . . . Hence the importance of capturing enemies and bringing them back to the home village before slaughtering them. So, it turns out that perhaps O'Brien, while he is a better metaphysician than Winston, is not in fact the best metaphysician, or at least not the most astute analyst of the real nature of power. Which of course makes us think again that perhaps Orwell's novel is not at all a prophecy or a warning, but a challenge: a challenge to our reading ability; a challenge to become a better metaphysician than O'Brien; a challenge to question O'Brien's claim that all reality is in the mind, or that all reality is available in the form of knowledge.[13] □

Kennedy's polemical analysis applies a deconstructive reading to the novel and searches for the gaps, silences and inconsistencies within the text. Turning his attention to the dynamics of power, he argues that the machinery of repression that Orwell creates for Airstrip One, and which is embodied by O'Brien, is effectively self-defeating. Power is not power without its visual display, he contends, and the Party in Oceania seeks only to extend the threat of forceful subjection in order to maintain public control. Kennedy's position is legitimate, if debatable, and does open Orwell's novel to readings via Foucauldian notions of discipline and punishment. Foucault argues that the threat of physical retribution upon the recalcitrant social subject can ultimately lead to a systematic internalisation of the codes of 'acceptable' public and private behaviour, after which the need for the visual articulation of power is dramatically reduced. One striking example of this in *Nineteen Eighty-Four* is the threat of Room 101, which symbolises the ultimate sanction that the state can bring to bear upon the individual. The existence of the threat of a personalised and specific horror (in Winston Smith's case, the terror of rats), without the necessity of employing that measure, is fundamental to the acknowledgement of the discriminating control of the state on the individual. With the actualisation and overt display of the repressive power of the governing body, some of that threat is diminished, as its parameters are delineated. At root, Kennedy sees this paradoxical enactment of power as a spur to the reader to construct readings of these power relations which are resistant to the absolute bondage which O'Brien implies is the inherent nature of power. As readers, Kennedy suggests, we have a duty to challenge the hegemony not only of O'Brien but also of Orwell and to read against the grain of the text.

Winston's torture and 'rehabilitation' have fascinated critics inquiring into the dynamics of repression in the novel. The figure of O'Brien, with whom Winston develops an ambivalent relationship of fear/dependence, has featured as central to many of these critiques. In the following extract, Erika Gottlieb examines the interplay between the sadistic and masochistic impulses that constitute the torturer/tortured interdependence of Winston and O'Brien. She begins, however, by considering the origins of Orwell's painful vision of a society driven to insanity by power hunger. Gottlieb's essay is an attempt to reconcile political readings of the novel with those based on psychological interpretation. In the first part of the extract, she dismisses as irrelevant the psychobiographical identification that many have seen in the construction of Winston's character. To find parallels between the lives of author and main character is not difficult, she intimates, but it is ultimately unsatisfactory. To pursue this limited line of investigation is seen as a wilful ignorance of the broader implications of Orwell's attack on totalitarianism:

■ The critic insisting on Orwell's sado-masochistic tendencies or on Winston's paranoia inevitably overlooks an important factor: Freud's definition of the neurotic personality has been so influential that it is often accepted as axiomatic that the source of neurosis resides in the individual's failure to adjust to a societal standard, a commonly accepted 'norm' of sanity. Orwell's *Nineteen Eighty-Four* is one of the first works which genuinely and systematically challenges this assumption.

One cannot come to grips with the novel without understanding that Orwell here introduces a paradox of numbers. By juxtaposing the single individual's sanity and humanity with the insanity and inhumanity of an entire state, he proposes that in certain societies the exclusive norm of sanity may indeed reside in the 'minority of one' (p. 261). The dictator of a totalitarian society can hold on to power only by convincing the masses that the unnatural, hate-filled and topsy-turvy world he created out of his insane obsession with power is normal. Orwell's political allegory contains the psychological warning: in a totalitarian state, paranoia becomes the norm. Consequently, in a society which is based on suspicion, spying, fear and hatred, Winston is not a paranoid [*sic*] when he feels persecuted.

Therefore, it is really quite beside the point here whether or not *Nineteen Eighty-Four* reflects the writer's paranoia or sado-masochistic tendencies related to an unhappy childhood; what is essential is that we realise that the novel is based on the uncannily accurate analysis of the paranoid and sado-masochistic tendencies of dictatorship as exemplified by Stalin's Russia and Hitler's Germany.

Readers of *Nineteen Eighty-Four* who have lived under totalitarian rule have often been amazed at the novel's exceptional insight into the workings of the Police State, an insight more likely to come from

Orwell's wide reading in contemporary history, including first-hand accounts of political prisoners in Germany and Russia, than from the subconscious projections of his own psycho-pathological problems.

Also, whether or not Orwell's political insights were accurate, his definition of totalitarianism in *Nineteen Eighty-Four* matches those of his political commentaries, and no intelligent reader has yet come forward to claim that these commentaries are distorted by the essayist's paranoia.

Indeed, Orwell has explored the psycho-dynamics of the contemporary dictators' power over their subjects in many of his essays:

> The interconnection between sadism, masochism, success worship, power worship, nationalism and totalitarianism is a huge subject whose edges have barely been scratched. . . . Fascism is often loosely equated with sadism, but nearly always by people who see nothing wrong in the most slavish worship of Stalin.[14]

Confronted with ample historical evidence about mass insanity, Orwell is understandably concerned about the prospects of dictatorship on an even larger scale, should the Western world not recognise the falsehood of *both* Hitler's and Stalin's propaganda.

> The truth is, of course, that the countless English intellectuals who kiss the arse of Stalin are not different from the minority who give their allegiance to Hitler or Mussolini. . . . All of them are worshipping power and successful cruelty. It is important to notice that the cult of power tends to be mixed up with a love of cruelty and wickedness for *their own sakes*.[15]

Whether or not Orwell was on his deathbed when he conceived Winston's torture scenes (as a matter of fact, there is evidence he had a detailed outline for the book under the title *The Last Man in Europe* as early as 1943, well before his last illness),[16] *Nineteen Eighty-Four* emerges as a dramatic warning against the dehumanising power, the successful cruelty, of the totalitarian state. Reading *Nineteen Eighty-Four* as a case study of Winston's or Orwell's private neurosis clouds the issue that *Nineteen Eighty-Four* is a harrowing indictment of totalitarian governments because it happens to be a strikingly accurate anatomy of the way such governments have been functioning in the past and are still functioning in the present.

When in search of latent references to the author's childhood tendencies for paranoia, the 'psychological' critic may completely miss Orwell's explicit and by now widely accepted political diagnosis of the paranoia inherent in a totalitarian regime. The Two Minutes Hate which at its climax turns into the ecstatic worship of the daily ritual of the dictatorship turned state religion. Only by whipping up hatred against the arch-enemy, Goldstein, the satanic Betrayer, can the Inner Party prepare the atmosphere for the worshipful prayer to Big Brother the 'Saviour' (p. 18). What Orwell is pointing out in this scene is the theological underpinning of both Stalin's and Hitler's cult of leader worship. Both relied on justifying the persecution of a scapegoat accused of the treachery of Satan (whether we look at Hitler's use of the Jew linked to a Jewish world conspiracy, or Stalin's use of Trotsky linked to imperialist hirelings and counter-revolutionaries). In both cases the whipping up of hatred against this Satanic enemy allowed the dictator to justify his persecution of any individual or group he chose to associate with the scapegoat – an effective ploy leading to the subjugation of his own people to slavery.

Of course, what concerned Orwell in the novel was not merely the analysis of atrocities actually committed by Hitler's or Stalin's regimes, but what he felt was the Western intellectual's susceptibility to the psychosis of nationalistic leader worship. He was also concerned that prolonged periods of war may call forth or increase this susceptibility.

> . . . we are in danger of . . . the centralised slave state, ruled over by a small clique who are in effect a new ruling class, though they might be adoptive rather than hereditary. [The] dynamic [of such a state] would come from some kind of rabid nationalism and leader worship kept going by literally continuous war.[17]

Concerned with the impact of totalitarianism on the Western mind, in *Nineteen Eighty-Four* Orwell presents us with a haunting demonstration of the psychodynamics of this particular political system; the political and psychological aspects of the novel are inextricably intertwined. To recognise the organic unity of political and psychological dimensions is also essential to the recognition of *Nineteen Eighty-Four* as a well-integrated work of art – something neither the political nor the psychological critic has been ready to acknowledge without reservations, in spite of the novel's undeniable power and success.[18] □

Gottlieb proceeds to analyse this 'demonstration of the psychodynamics' of power in relation to the scenes of Winston's torture and in particular those involving the threat of Room 101:

■ Critical assessment of the climactic scene in Room 101 springs from the same two basically irreconcilable schools of opinion that inform attitudes to the book as a whole. Critics concentrating on the political parable tend to skim over this scene either by dismissing its importance or by admitting distaste for what they call the melodramatic or the theatricality of Grand Guignol, which to some verges on the ridiculous.

On the other hand, critics who examine the scene in terms of its psychological dimension usually follow the assumptions of Freudian depth psychology. They may find the scene crucial, but only as far as it reveals the particular nature of Winston's neurosis – paranoia, latent homosexuality, sado-masochistic tendencies[19] – all attributed to the Oedipal situation. What these psychological interpretations imply, and often explicitly state, is that Winston deliberately provokes his own punishment; that is, what happens to him in the Ministry of Love is just what he has been subconsciously craving for all along.

There is no doubt that psychological scrutiny of this scene is essential to an understanding of the dramatic climax in the novel. But Freudian interpretations tend to have trouble reconciling their emphasis on Winston's (and ultimately on Orwell's) neurotic tendencies with the humanistic message of the political allegory. They fail to see that although Winston's ordeal in Room 101 unmistakably follows from his inner life, it is also the ordeal of Everyman, indeed of our common humanity in confrontation with the dehumanising forces of totalitarianism. ... ...

What is at stake in Room 101 is not Winston's potency or manhood. It is his loss of face. The rats' cage is mask-like. They will devour his face from within. And it is not the Oedipal sexual offence that he is guilty of. He is guilty of denying the fundamental values of the private self. In his selfish and uncontrollable hunger he denied his mother and tore himself away from the primary bond of belonging, loyalty, and love. Now, in his uncontrollable fear of the rats, he re-enacts this first act of betrayal: he offers up the body of the only person he loves, as a surrogate for his own. When he screams, 'Do it to Julia', he offers her as a human sacrifice to the hungry rats (p. 300). Once again, symbolically, he devours the one he loves.

In Room 101 he can no longer stay 'in front of' the wall of darkness: he is forced to get over to 'the other side' (p. 297). And as the walls of the private self are being destroyed, he feels that he is falling 'through the floor, through the walls of the building, through the earth, through the oceans, through the atmosphere, into outer space, into the gulfs between the stars – always away, away, away from the rats' (p. 300). The irony is, of course, that having broken through the walls of darkness, he can no longer get away. Exposed to the cage of 'starving brutes' (p. 299) in Room 101, Winston hears *himself* become 'insane, a screaming animal' (p. 299). By allowing himself to be degraded to the level of the starved rats, he has become what he had been most afraid of. O'Brien did successfully conclude his experiment:

the 'inner heart' of loyalty and self-sacrifice is only sentimental illusion. Ultimately man is nothing but a beast, and like a beast, he can be degraded until he is deprived of his will, until he becomes an instrument in the hands of the Party.

At this point we should realise that Orwell's strategies lead to conclusions fundamentally different from those of the Freudian critic. The starved rats, just like the child Winston, were themselves the victims of the Party's brutality. Ultimately the real face behind the mask-like cage of the rats is the face of Big Brother himself. It is Big Brother who turns his subjects into ferocious, hate-filled beings like himself, forcing them to act out the ritual of his own prime betrayal as human sacrifice. Winston's own final and crucial act of betrayal is some kind of horrible *imitatio dei*: in the moment he betrays his loved one, he becomes one with the godhead, acting out the inevitable yet horrible mystery, the loving union between victim and victimiser (p. 300).

In effect, all the citizens of Oceania are kept in their cage, systematically starved, deprived of food, love, sexual and emotional satisfaction, so that the Party may channel all their pent-up energy into the hysterical quest for new victims, leading to the equally hysterical worship of their leader. All the people of Oceania become instruments in the hands of the Party, ready to denounce one another in order to assure their own survival. Yet there is a tragic irony in this process: as the victim's last bond of personal loyalty is broken, he has become the agent of his own enslavement, and ultimately that of his own extinction.

Room 101 is the dramatic centre of the novel because it both repeats and reverses two previous crises. It is the reversal of the break-through scene in which Winston liberates himself from the long repressed guilt by pledging loyalty to Julia: 'only feelings matter. If they could make me stop loving you – that would be the real betrayal' (p. 173). It is also the re-enactment of his childhood crisis (pp. 167–71). Forced to revisit the crucial trial of his childhood, in Room 101 Winston fails again. The failure destroys his hard-won liberation, the maturity of his selfhood, and pushes him into another, far more terrifying infancy. The private self is enslaved, wiped out by the collective self. He becomes the image of his Maker, the prodigal son returning to the 'loving breast' (p. 311) of his parent.

Politically, Winston's capitulation was pre-ordained by the dynamic of totalitarianism. Thus, a sense of personal responsibility, guilt, or shame would be quite out of order. Yet the moral paradox here puts Orwell in a category quite distinct from both the Freudian critic and the critic studying the novel only in terms of the political spectrum. For thirty years Winston's sense of guilt has been a burden, but it also served as a reminder that he still had a sense of personal loyalty and could feel shame. In fact, it was this mysterious sense of guilt or shame that made him start his search for the Truth in the past, the search which led ultimately to moral regeneration.

Significantly, once he repeats his act of betrayal, he no longer carries the burden of guilt. Of course, he is also free of his sense of humanity, of the basic moral attitudes defining the private self. Once reborn, united with the collective self of Oceania, he is no longer capable of regret or guilt because he has no further claim to a private conscience.

Room 101 is a climactic scene in the novel, bringing together all the betrayals in a series of symbolic reversals. Visually, '101' suggests two parts of the self, face-to-face through zero: reduced to nothingness through fear and shame, Winston faces the rats in himself. The number '101' also suggests repetition after a reversal: repeating the childhood trial, Winston reverts to another state of childhood.

In yet another visual allusion, '101' suggests links of a chain, that is, not only one, but a whole series of continuous, repeated reversals. Room 101 is at the heart of the novel because it is the centre of the mythical, the political, and the psychological drama of betrayal. It is here that any victim is turned victimiser, by giving up, betraying, his bond of private loyalty. Paradoxically, it is precisely at this point that he will be finally trapped, 'chained' to become a true victim, willing to stay in the cage forever.

Ironically, it is by adjusting to the norm of the majority that Winston has now become, finally, insane. Having joined in the collective insanity imposed upon the population by Big Brother, Winston now willingly joins the other rats in their cage.[20] □

Selfhood and Freedom

Moving on to a discussion of the terror induced by the prospect of Room 101, Gottlieb suggests that these climactic scenes reveal the deracination of the self. Faced with the possibility of being subjected to our worst fears, and in particular of those fears being known and exploited by others, the individual can no longer maintain a discrete and autonomous selfhood. The subsequent self-betrayal – Winston's emotional and psychological breakdown at the prospect of being devoured by rats – is crucial to the exercise of power and to the disintegration of individual will. Gottlieb thus sees in the Room 101 scenes the purest form of totalitarian control, which is self-control (or ironically the loss of self-control). The efficiently repressive state induces in its subjects a perpetual state of guilt formed from the knowledge of betrayal – betrayal of the self, of others and ultimately of Big Brother. Before Winston can be dispatched, his dangerous tendency for independent thought must be eradicated and replaced by a sense of guilt at the betrayal of the ideals of Ingsoc.

The status of the self within a total state has also been explored by the next two critics in this chapter. Mason Harris develops similar ideas to Gottlieb about the sadomasochistic relationship between O'Brien and Winston and argues that the nature of their dialogue reveals their inter-dependence:

■ In the Ministry of Love, O'Brien treats Winston as a case for reli-gious conversion. If Winston turned to O'Brien to bolster a faltering attempt at independence, O'Brien states that the very coherence of the Party's world depends on Winston's voluntary submission, his enthu-siastic acceptance of the faith: 'When finally you surrender to us, it must be of your own free will. We do not destroy the heretic because he resists us: so long as he resists us we never destroy him. We convert him . . . we bring him over to our side, not in appearance, but genuinely, heart and soul' (p. 267).

O'Brien tortures Winston not so much to intimidate him as to break down his sense of self and cause him to develop a love-relationship with his torturer. In Winston's vision, O'Brien 'was the tormentor, he was the protector, he was the inquisitor, he was the friend' (p. 256). As the treatment proceeds, he experiences a 'peculiar reverence for O'Brien, which nothing seemed able to destroy' (p. 286). He comes to feel that O'Brien's mind entirely contains his own, and that he is a helpless infant cared for by O'Brien (pp. 262–3). The more helpless and ashamed Winston feels, the more he experiences himself through O'Brien's consciousness, as part of O'Brien's strength (p. 268).

O'Brien reveals to Winston a utopia of sado-masochism where the highest joy is the loss of self to absolute authority, accompanied by regression to infancy and escape from time into the immortality of the Party: 'The individual only has power in so far as he ceases to be an individual . . . if he can make complete, utter submission, if he can escape from his identity, if he can merge himself in the Party so that he *is* the Party, then he is all-powerful and immortal' (pp. 276–7). O'Brien describes this ideal world in terms which alternate between submis-sion and domination. It will be 'a world of trampling and being trampled upon' in which 'there will be no emotions except fear, rage, triumph and self-abasement' (p. 279). Here the fear is essential to the rage, and the self-abasement to the triumph. Utterly penitent, Winston will crawl into a 'world of victory after victory, triumph after triumph' (p. 281). O'Brien promises, 'Always, at every moment, there will be the thrill of victory, the sensation of trampling on an enemy who is helpless. If you want a picture of the future, imagine a boot trampling on a human face for ever' (p. 281).

The key word in this famous statement is 'imagine'. The citizens of Oceania are not allowed to do much face-trampling on their own; that is reserved for specialists in the Ministry of Love. Rather, the 'sensation' of triumph is experienced vicariously through victories reported on the telescreen, news films such as the one recorded in Winston's diary, public executions of traitors and prisoners of war, and the various 'hate' periods. The new Winston produced by O'Brien's therapy is a gin-sodden, sentimental masochist, but still capable of experiencing 'triumph' when a blast of trumpets from the telescreen announces a great military victory. In this final scene, Winston's fear of a 'smashing defeat in Africa' is actually ambivalent – it might bring about 'the destruction of the Party!' (p. 303) – but he does not know this because he no longer attempts to understand his feelings. When victory with great slaughter is announced, he sits drunkenly while experiencing vicarious action: 'Under the table Winston's feet made convulsive movements. He had not stirred from his seat, but in his mind he was running, swiftly running, he was with the crowds out-side, cheering himself deaf' (p. 310). Thus the sense of triumph can be enjoyed in complete passivity. Only at this moment does Winston achieve the 'healing change' (p. 311) by projecting his ambivalence into love for Big Brother and hatred for the enemy.

In addition to representing submission to external authority, the relation between O'Brien and Winston could represent the super-ego sadistically tormenting the ego. The Party with its all-seeing tele-screens could be an extreme manifestation of a guilty conscience. Freud says that the cruellest aspect of the super-ego lies in its refusal to distinguish between thoughts and actions: 'nothing is hidden from the super-ego, not even thoughts . . . the intention is counted as equiv-alent to the deed.'[21] . . . O'Brien confirms that 'The Party is not interested in the overt act: the thought is all we care about' (p. 265). In 'The Prevention of Literature', an essay of the mid-forties, Orwell describes, in terms close to Freud's concept of repression, the 'self-censorship' which a writer may be led to impose on himself by dogmatic political loyalties: 'Even a single taboo can have an all-round crippling effect upon the mind, because there is always a danger that any thought which is freely followed up may lead to the forbidden thought'.[22] As he recovers from torture, Winston becomes adept in a technique of mental hygiene called 'Crimestop': 'The mind should develop a blind spot whenever a dangerous thought presented itself. The process should be automatic, instinctive' (p. 291). Winston's ego sinks in self-esteem until he becomes dependent for his moral being on O'Brien and Big Brother. Social authority can gain complete control over the individual only by crushing the ego and appropriating the super-ego, thus setting up a sado-masochistic relationship within the self as well as between the self and others.[23] □

Harris concurs with Gottlieb that the way to absolute domination in

Oceania is not through pressure of external forces, but through the willing submission of the self to the macrocosm of the state. Only by the compliant identification of Winston with O'Brien can a successful 'conversion' be effected. The perverse father/son relationship that is engendered conceals the immersion of the individual self in the body of the state, as represented by the paternal O'Brien, and at a greater remove by the fraternal influence of Big Brother. This process of subsuming autonomy within collectivity is transformed, in Harris's view, into the submission of the ego to the super-ego. The warring parts of the psyche act as a potent metaphor for the internalisation of the state/subject dichotomy. Freedom as it exists in *Nineteen Eighty-Four* comes from the acceptance of the renegotiated boundaries of the self and not from the expression of autonomous will. This is a point addressed by Richard Rorty:

■ I take Orwell's claim that there is no such thing as *inner* freedom, no such thing as an 'autonomous individual', to be the one made by historicist, including Marxist, critics of 'liberal individualism'. This is that there is nothing deep inside each of us, no common human nature, no built-in human solidarity, to use as a moral reference point.[24] There is nothing to people except what has been socialised into them – their ability to use language, and thereby to exchange beliefs and desires with other people. Orwell reiterated this point when he said, 'To abolish class distinctions means abolishing a part of yourself', and when he added that if he himself were to 'get outside the class racket' he would 'hardly be recognisable as the same person'. To be a person is to speak a particular language, one which enables us to discuss particular beliefs and desires with *particular* sorts of people. It is a historical contingency whether we are socialised by Neanderthals, ancient Chinese, Eton, Summerhill, or the Ministery [*sic*] of Truth. Simply by being human we do not have a common bond. For all we share with all other humans is the same thing we share with all other animals – the ability to feel pain.

One way to react to this last point is to say that our moral vocabulary should be extended to cover animals as well as people. A better way is to try to isolate something that distinguishes human from animal pain. Here is where O'Brien comes in. O'Brien reminds us that human beings who have been socialised – socialised in any language, any culture – do share a capacity which other animals lack. They can all be given a special kind of pain: They can all be humiliated by the forcible tearing down of the particular structures of language and belief in which they were socialised (or which they pride themselves on having formed for themselves). More specifically, they can be used, and animals cannot, to gratify O'Brien's wish to 'tear human minds to pieces and put them together again in new shapes of your own choosing' (p. 269).

The point that sadism aims at humiliation rather than merely at pain in general has been developed in detail by Elaine Scarry in *The Body in Pain: The Making and Unmaking of the World*. It is a consequence of Scarry's argument that the worst thing you can do to somebody is not to make her scream in agony but to use that agony in such a way that even when the agony is over, she cannot reconstitute herself. The idea is to get her to do or say things – and, if possible, believe and desire things, think thoughts – which later she will be unable to cope with having done or thought. You can thereby, as Scarry puts it, 'unmake her world' by making it impossible for her to use language to describe what she has been.

Let me now apply this point to O'Brien's making Winston believe, briefly, that two and two equals five. Notice first that, unlike 'Rutherford conspired with the Eurasian General Staff', it is not something O'Brien himself believes. Nor does Winston himself believe it once he is broken and released. It is not, and could not be, Party doctrine. (The book O'Brien co-authored, *The Theory and Practice of Oligarchical Collectivism*, notes that when one is 'designing a gun or an airplane' two and two *have* to make four.) The *only* point in making Winston believe that two and two equals five is to break him. Getting somebody to deny a belief for no reason is a first step toward making her incapable of having a self because she becomes incapable of weaving a coherent web of belief and desire. It makes her irrational, in a quite precise sense: She is unable to give a reason for her belief that fits together with her other beliefs. She becomes irrational not in the sense that she has lost contact with reality but in the sense that she can no longer rationalise – no longer justify herself to herself.

Making Winston briefly believe that two plus two equals five serves the same 'breaking' function as making him briefly desire that the rats chew through Julia's face rather than his own (p. 300). But the latter episode differs from the former in being a final, irreversible unmaking. Winston might be able to include the belief that he had once, under odd conditions, believed that two and two equals five within a coherent story about his character and his life. Temporary irrationality is something around which one can weave a story. But the belief that he once wanted them to *do it to Julia* is not one he can weave a story around. That was why O'Brien saved the rats for the best part, the part in which Winston had to watch himself go to pieces and simultaneously know that he could never pick up those pieces again.

To return to my main point: the fact that two and two does not make five is not the essence of the matter. What matters is that Winston has picked it as symbolic, and that O'Brien knows that. If there were a *truth*, belief in which would break Winston, making him believe that *truth* would be just as good for O'Brien's purposes.

Suppose it were the case that Julia had been (like the purported antique dealer, Mr Charrington) a longtime member of the Thought Police. Suppose she had been instructed by O'Brien to seduce Winston. Suppose that O'Brien told Winston this, giving him no evidence save his own obviously unreliable word. Suppose further that Winston's love for Julia was such that only the same torture which made him able to believe that two and two equals five could make him believe that Julia had been O'Brien's agent. The effect would be the same, and the effect is all that matters to O'Brien. Truth and falsity drop out.

O'Brien wants to cause Winston as much pain as possible, and for this purpose what matters is that Winston be forced to realise that he has become incoherent, realise that he is no longer able to use a language or be a self. Although we can say, 'I believed something false', nobody can say to himself, 'I am, right now, believing something false'. So nobody can be humiliated at the moment of believing a falsehood, or by the mere fact of having done so. But people can, their torturers hope, experience the ultimate humiliation of saying to themselves, in retrospect, 'Now that I have believed or desired *this*, I can never be what I hoped to be, what I thought I was. The story I have been telling myself about myself – my picture of myself as honest, or loyal, or devout – no longer makes sense. I no longer have a self to make sense of. There is no world in which I can picture myself as living, because there is no vocabulary in which I can tell a coherent story about myself.' For Winston the sentence he could not utter sincerely and still be able to put himself back together was 'Do it to Julia!' (p.300) and the worst thing in the world happened to be rats. But presumably each of us stands in the same relations to some sentence, and to some thing.

If one can discover that key sentence and that key thing, then, as O'Brien says, one can tear a mind apart and put it together in new shapes of one's own choosing. But it is the sound of the tearing, not the result of the putting together, that is the object of the exercise. It is the breaking that matters. The putting together is just an extra fillip. When Winston comes to love Big Brother, for example, it is irrelevant that Big Brother is in fact unlovable. What matters is that there is no way of going back and forth between a Winston who loves Big Brother and the Winston who loved Julia, cherished the glass paperweight, and could remember the clipping which showed that Rutherford was innocent. The point of breaking Winston is not to bring Winston into line with the Party's ideas. The Inner Party is not torturing Winston because it is afraid of a revolution, or because it is offended by the thought that someone might not love Big Brother. It is torturing Winston for the sake of causing Winston pain, and thereby increasing the pleasure of its members, particularly O'Brien. The only object of O'Brien's intensive seven-year-long study of Winston was to make possible the rich, complicated, delicate, absorbing spectacle of mental pain which Winston would eventually provide (p. 256). The only point in leaving the thing sitting in the Chestnut Tree Café alive for a while is that it can still feel pain when the telescreen plays 'Under the spreading chestnut tree/I sold you and you sold me.' (p. 307) Torture is not for the sake of getting people to obey, nor for the sake of getting them to believe falsehoods. As O'Brien says, 'The object of torture is torture' (p. 276).[25] □

For Rorty, the exercise of absolute power involves the unmaking of the self and this takes us a step further than Harris, for the breaking and unmaking of the self necessitates the reduction of the individual to incoherence. It can be inferred from these interpretations that totalitarianism depends upon the inability of the individual subject to formulate, or even conceive a self other than that applied from without. Effectively, this means that language itself becomes untenable in the state of incoherence, for it cannot be constructed in a condition of non-selfhood. It is only after the resistance to state ideology has been eliminated that a new language (literally 'newspeak') can be introduced. The torture of Winston and the threat of Room 101 is designed to inflict such a significant trauma on his consciousness that he cannot possibly conceive of his prior life, or subsequently of any seditious act. For Orwell, the power of totalitarianism is its ability to reconstitute the self so that resistance is unthinkable.

'Newspeak' and the Compromising of Language

As suggested above, the mechanisms of social control in Oceania are oiled by the official discourses of the Party. Language becomes a crucial tool in the suppression of rebellion and more importantly in the normalisation of the diktats of Big Brother. Orwell had long been fascinated by the potential for popular control offered by propaganda and rhetoric. His time working for the BBC during the years of the Second World War had convinced him of the corruptibility of language and the endless flexibility of meanings. As we saw with *Animal Farm*, he was exploring the nature of propaganda and censorship in the early 1940s and with *Nineteen Eighty-Four* he produced a definitive treatise on the manipulation of language in the interests of ideological conditioning. The extracts in this section explore Orwell's decreasing faith in language's capacity clearly to express truth. Robert Lee cites the voiding of meaning from words as fundamental to the control which the Party exerts over heterodoxy:

■ The end of human reason may be the ultimate indignity that man can suffer. But the fabric of the novel suggests that Orwell's concern is with means and not ends. If power is an end in itself, the essential means to the attainment of that power is the same concept that Orwell has articulated, in varying contexts and with differing implications, since his first book and which had dominated his thoughts since his experiences in the Spanish Civil War – the corruption of language.

Too many details of the novel are unexplained if the theme of language corrupted and corrupting is slighted. For even O'Brien's view of the 'perfected' world is couched in terms of the future: The world the Party is creating is a world that 'will' happen:

> No one dares trust a wife or a child or a friend any longer. But in the future there will be no wives and no friends. Children will be taken from their mothers at birth, as one takes eggs from a hen. The sex instinct will be eradicated. Procreation will be an annual formality like the renewal of a ration card. We shall abolish the orgasm. Our neurologists are at work upon it now. There will be no loyalty, except loyalty toward the Party. There will be no love, except the love of Big Brother. There will be no laughter, except the laugh of triumph over a defeated enemy. There will be no art, no literature, no science. When we are omnipotent we shall have no more need of science (p. 280).

O'Brien admits, in passing, that the Party is not yet omnipotent. In terms of control over the deviant, it is, for all practical purposes, all-powerful; but the power is not yet absolute, and the tense and terms which describe the absolutism are radically utopian. However, the control of language is seen in more definite, empirical realizations; it is even possible to date it. Winston is talking to Syme, whose work in the 'Research Department' is the continuous rewriting of the Newspeak dictionary.

> 'The Eleventh Edition is the definitive edition,' he said. 'We're getting the language into its final shape – the shape it's going to have when nobody speaks anything else. When we've finished with it, people like you will have to learn it all over again. You think, I dare say, that our chief job is inventing new words. But not a bit of it! We're destroying words – scores of them, hundreds of them, every day. We're cutting the language down to the bone. The Eleventh Edition won't contain a single word that will become obsolete before the year 2050.' (pp. 53–4)

Like so many other norms which are reversed in the world of *1984*, the dictionary becomes a means to narrow language, a way to diminish the range of vocabulary. The dictionary predicts and thus determines the choices of speech – and thus thought – and thus action – available to the inhabitants of Oceania. For language is the means by which men move out of their isolation; it is the means by which they particularize their concept of self, distinguishing it from another self – in the world of *1984*, the state's self. . . . The loss of choice in language leads to the loss of particularization, and this leads to unconsciousness. Syme again speaks to Winston.

'Don't you see that the whole aim of Newspeak is to narrow the range of thought? In the end we shall make thought-crime literally impossible, because there will be no words in which to express it. Every concept that can ever be needed will be expressed by exactly one word with its meaning rigidly defined and all its subsidiary meanings rubbed out and forgotten. Already, in the Eleventh Edition, we're not far from that point. But the process will still be continuing long after you and I are dead. Every year fewer and fewer words, and the range of consciousness always a little smaller. Even now, of course, there's no reason or excuse for committing thought-crime. It's merely a question of self-discipline, reality control. But in the end there won't be any need even for that. The Revolution will be complete when the language is perfect. . . . By the year 2050, at the very latest, not a single human being will be alive who could understand such a conversation as we are having now. . . . The whole climate of thought will be different. In fact there will be no thought, as we understand it now. Orthodoxy means not thinking – not needing to think. Orthodoxy is unconsciousness.' (pp. 53–4)

The world which O'Brien is able only to predict can be casually assumed and fixed by a minor clerk, one whose fate is to himself vanish: 'Syme had ceased to exist; he had never existed' (p. 154). In a world where the past is always mutable in the constant alteration of language, existence is indeed indeterminable.

. . . though the past is alterable, it never has been altered in any specific instance. For when it has been recreated in whatever shape is needed at the moment, then this new version is the past, and no different past can ever have existed (pp. 214–15).[26] □

Language as an expression of selfhood and as an instrument for bridging the gulf between self and other is made increasingly redundant by the totalitarian state and instead is replaced by a form of words designed purely for functional purposes. Lee points out that without the ability to verbalise their alienation, the inhabitants of Airstrip One have no means to escape their isolation. Rather than being the means by which the individual can articulate the difference of her/his ideas, language moves towards a monologic status which reflects only the uniqueness of the state. 'Newspeak' strives to distance further the individual from any sense of coherent selfhood because it demands repeated verbal acknowledgement of the integrated nature of the individual within the state. When language itself cannot encompass semantic rebellion or variance, the consciousness of the individual struggles to conceive of any viable alternative to express dissatisfaction.

In the following passage, Alok Rai explores the concept of 'Newspeak' in relation to Orwell's views on language generally:

■ The matter of language – 'Newspeak' – is central to Orwell's conception of the suffocating tyranny of *Nineteen Eighty-Four*. Language is one of the key instruments of political domination, the necessary and insidious means of the 'totalitarian' control of reality. As Syme explains to Winston:

> The Revolution will be complete when the language is perfect. Newspeak is Ingsoc and Ingsoc is Newspeak (p. 55).

Winston's struggle in the novel is, to a large extent, a struggle to find an adequate language or, what is nearly the same thing, an adequate critical location from which he can regard the world whose language holds him in bondage. The struggle is, we know, a failure – Goldstein's language, which Winston needs as much as Orwell himself does to describe the tyranny of Big Brother, is revealed to be another manifestation of that same, enveloping tyranny. Thus, Winston's rebellion is quenched in an involuntary, unconscious complicity. The suffocation is total. The idea of Newspeak, thus, is crucial to Orwell's conception of *Nineteen Eighty-Four*. ... ...

Orwell's most powerful insight is into the political/ideological sensitivity of language, and into the areas of use and misuse which that opens up – into how language can be a subtle and insidious instrument for the enforcement of particular, desired perceptions of 'reality'. This insight is, obviously, relativistic in tendency, suggesting as it does the necessary mediation of 'reality' through different linguistic 'systems', and the implicit impossibility of bringing supra-lingual criteria to bear upon inter-lingual comparisons. Clearly, there is a limit beyond which such relativism slips into absurdity – that is, we cannot function as human beings except in terms of a historically variable 'positivist' consensus. Thus, Orwell's relativism has, perhaps inevitably, a positive core, which derives its substance from his everyday world, and from the commonsensical consensus on which it rests.

This world is the world of ordinary, 'decent' human beings, who instinctively *know* what is right and what is wrong, what is true and what is not. It seems to me, however, that on the rebound from excessive relativism, Orwell is led into adopting an excessively uncritical attitude to the ambient world of common sense, to its language and to the forms of its understanding. I would suggest that the conservative tendency in Orwell's temperament is evident not so much directly in his language itself as in the limits which it sets to Orwell's thinking about language. Typically, again, his radicalism is subverted by his own conservatism.

Few people, I believe, would fail to accept Orwell's criticisms of the samples of prevalent political styles which he selected for castigation in 'Politics and the English Language', or disagree with his view that 'in our time, political speech and writing are largely the defence of the indefensible'; and that therefore 'political language has to consist largely of euphemism, question-begging, and sheer cloudy vagueness'.[27] This observation, it should be noticed, cuts right across political systems. . . . Orwell's strictures apply equally to the 'totalitarian' rhetoric which he inveighs against and the 'anti-totalitarian' rhetoric to which he is himself prone. However, the point of immediate interest to me is the interaction between the relativism of Orwell's conception of language and the residual (or emergent, or threatened) positivism of his temperament.

In a famous sentence in 'Politics and the English Language', after listing all the things one ought not to do, Orwell synthesised, as it were, the wisdom he had gleaned:

> What is above all needed is to let the meaning choose the word, and not the other way about.

This sounds unobjectionable enough until one reflects that that is, more or less, the manner in which that ultimate horror is to be constructed – by shedding the words that do not correspond to pre-determined meanings. My contention is that Orwell is here evading or bypassing his insight into the inevitable interdependence between words and meanings. He is tempted, compelled, or merely permitted by the positivism of his temperament into thinking that the meaning, or more precisely *his* meaning, is pre-verbal and pre-conceptual, and thus unsullied by the particularity of perception which, unacknowledged, manifests itself as dishonesty in political language, as awkwardness and a lack of facility in 'choosing words'. It is immaterial at this point whether or not the conceptions and meanings which Orwell wished to put across are preferable to those urged by the persons whose language he holds up for ridicule in 'Politics and the

English Language'. What is crucial is the fact that Orwell fails to extend his insight into the interweaving of political conceptions and language to the dialects favoured by ordinary 'decent' people like himself. Orwell, it is important to note, resists the obvious inference that, to use his own terms, Newspeak is only a refinement, especially malign but also especially unsubtle, of Oldspeak. After all, even 'ordinary' language restricts the range of expressible meanings, as every bilingual person knows – in other words, there is no open, unconstraining Oldspeak, there are only variations, at different levels of complexity, of Newspeak. Still, one should also note that Orwell is, at this stage, secure enough in his affirmation of the ordinary 'decent' world, its language and its durability, to be *able* to resist the implications of his own linguistic insight. . . . . . . If we return now to 'Politics and the English Language' we find that whereas the demolition work is done with gusto, Orwell is curiously weak and negative about what needs to be done to promote the right kind of political language. . . . In the same essay Orwell also writes: 'The great enemy of clear language is insincerity'[28] the implication being that sincerity will of itself produce clarity and that lack of clarity reflects back on the credibility of the belief that is sought to be articulated. The thrust of all this – clarity, fluency, the banishment of all that is rough and 'barbarous' – is obvious enough, and implies a kind of cultural centrality which the 1930s Orwell did not feel.

In the context of wartime democracy, in the flush of that 'patriotic' sentiment which the Government had skilfully manufactured out of the disaster of Dunkirk, Orwell had written:

> to *preserve* is always to *extend*. The choice before us is not so much between victory and defeat as between revolution and apathy.[29]

If we apply this to Orwell's activity in the area of language we find that while he is admirable in the protective aspect, he is rather less certain about the radical extensions of which his critique of language is capable. There is, of course, an absolute sense in which an overriding concern with language represents a narrowing of the generous political (and literary) conceptions which Orwell had entertained earlier. However even apart from that, I believe that the specific form of that concern with language is marked by the conservative tendency which becomes dominant during this phase, whether the theme be language or, in a beautiful essay, the common toad.

The positivism in Orwell's linguistic conceptions – the sense which he conveys that while other people's language distorts reality, his own offers unmediated access to it – is not, I believe, accidental. This positivism is, I suggest, the form in which the process of reconciliation or accommodation manifests itself in language. In defending language against the 'barbarous' critics of the social order at a time when his own faith in his alternative conceptions was under stress, Orwell is led into accepting uncritically the ordinary language, the self-conceptions, of his ambient society, and so, following his insight, the implicit attitudes as well. It is perhaps some renewed awareness of his radical critique of that society which accounts for the fact that in *Nineteen Eighty-Four*, as I have pointed out above, the crucial positivist assertion with which Winston attempts to resist the 'insanity' of Newspeak takes an arithmetical rather than a verbal form.

For the linguistic insight into relativism, which is merely adumbrated in 'Politics and the English Language', to grow into the nightmare of Newspeak in *Nineteen Eighty-Four*, certain changes must take place: changes not only in the external, public circumstances of the time – the sense of purpose generated by the war being dissipated and distorted by the deepening tensions of the Cold War – but also, and relatedly, in Orwell's own thinking. 'Politics and the English Language' is written on the explicit assumption that the decay of language is corrigible, that if language can be corrupted through malign intent or through sheer inattention, it can also be cleansed. There is also the related assumption, implicit in the interpenetration of language and politics, that such a process of linguistic cleansing can react back on politics, that hope is not lost. One half of the insight Orwell came upon in 'Politics and the English Language' – into the ideological sensitivity of language and the consequent possibilities of ideological bondage – is, as we have seen, preserved in *Nineteen Eighty-Four*, in the conception of Newspeak. But 'Politics and the English Language', as we have seen, not only confronts the threat, and emergent reality, of the political degeneration of language, it also carries the promise of its regeneration in conjunction with a higher politics. Of this aspect of 'Politics and the English Language' little survives in the bleak world of *Nineteen Eighty-Four*. Again, the attenuation of Orwell's faith in ordinary 'decency' and common sense (that which had, so to speak, provided a limit to the depredation of *his own relativism*), this too is essential for the possibility of Newspeak, implicit in 'Politics and the English Language', to be realised. Orwell's despairing, unconvinced and unconvincing affirmation of decency in *Nineteen Eighty-Four* illustrates the general argument . . . that in the wartime phase of reconciliation or accommodation with his ambient society, Orwell is lulled into making a 'conservative' commitment which he can later neither live with nor reject. That is to say, the roots of Orwell's terminal despair are to be found in the hope of his wartime writings. He is his own prisoner, imprisoned in conceptions and forms of understanding which he can neither relinquish nor use without guilt. Consider, for instance, Winston's dilemma in *Nineteen Eighty-Four*: Orwell invents the language of Goldstein – different alike from Newspeak and from the language of the novel – as a means of characterising the State of which Newspeak is the impenetrable armour; as a means whereby Winston (and we) can gain a critical perspective on the oppressive society. However, as we know, Orwell's imagination subverts itself: Goldstein's language also turns out to be an invention of the rulers of Oceania, and offers no escape from the nightmare. Winston Smith, therefore, is imprisoned not only in Newspeak but also in the language in which he seeks to criticise the world of Newspeak.[30] □

Rai interprets these experiments with language in the context of Orwell's deepening personal despair at the political conditions of the 1930s and 1940s. The vulnerability of language to political or ideological inflection troubled Orwell and, in particular, his belief in the necessary clarity of words to reflect the stability of reality. Rai argues that the infiltrations of language by ideological influences is one of Orwell's lasting insights but, at the same time, he declares that this insidious appropriation of language was, for Orwell, a reversible evil. At the heart of his vision of the world, Rai suggests, was a conviction that there exists a stable and commonsensical core of decency and consensus against which the vagaries of politics tend to pale. Orwell is thus a strangely ambivalent analyst of language for Rai. On the one hand, he is acutely aware of the susceptibility of language to political manipulation and is conscious of the increasingly indeterminate relationship of word and world. On the other hand, he retains a sense of the logical and 'natural' interdependence between a coherent reality and a representational discourse. It is this fundamental paradox that enables the construction of 'Newspeak', and simultaneously undermines it as a viable linguistic system. Orwell's 'terminal despair' derives from the residue of positivity that had characterised his earlier contemplations of language and it is manifested in *Nineteen Eighty-Four* through the elimination of private and apolitical modes of expression. The language which Winston Smith attempts to adopt as a resistant act of intellectual rebellion turns out to be the invention of the state itself and thus encoded within the ideological dictates of that repressive system. Rai sees Orwell's despair as engendered by a deeply felt suspicion that the distance between a real, concrete world and the means by which that world is articulated is becoming ever wider and increasingly mediating that gap is a self-conscious and politically inscribed reinvention of that reality.

Many critics would disagree with Rai and dismiss 'Newspeak' as a practical impossibility, and it should be remembered that even in the novel the institution of the language as the official speech of Oceania is projected to take place by 2050. Nevertheless, Rai makes a number of significant points about Orwell's fears for the integrity of expression under total-itarianism, and his argument that Orwell is essentially a conservative thinker interestingly echoes some of the early criticism that has already been discussed in this Guide. Rai's book was published in 1988 and understandably reflects many of the theoretical and intellectual concerns of its time. Criticism of both *Nineteen Eighty-Four* and *Animal Farm* during the 1980s embraced new paradigms of interpretation and succeeded in re-energising critical assessment of the novels. Unsurprisingly, much of this new wave of attention was focused on, or developed out of, the defining Orwellian moment – the year 1984.

CHAPTER FIVE

1984 – The Orwellian Moment

'THE BEST thing that could happen to George Orwell is unquestionably 1985.'[1] So writes Alan Sandison in *George Orwell: After 1984*, an attempt to reassess the impact of Orwell's novel on the cultural map of the late twentieth century. His comment attests to the intensity of attention that was paid to Orwell, and in particular to *Nineteen Eighty-Four*, in the years leading up to the Orwellian moment of 1984. Sandison also implies that much of that attention had distracted and detracted from the critical debates surrounding Orwell's work as a whole. How seriously Orwell's final work was to be taken in the run-up to 1984 provided a topic for vigorous discussion in both academic and non-academic contexts. The apparent lack of totalitarian regimes in the West to match that of Oceania did not prevent enthusiastic arguments about whether Orwell had been wrong, partially wrong or prophetically accurate. Earlier debates about whether the novel should be read as a warning or a prediction resurfaced as critics, the media and the general public renegotiated the legacy of Orwell's text. Sandison's assertion that the Orwellian moment could not be over soon enough points towards the frenzy of interest in the novel – a frenzy which was inevitable, but which was ironically to play itself out relatively swiftly. This chapter provides extracts written during and around 1984, or which comment on the Orwell phenomenon of that time. What these passages show is both a deep-seated fear that much of what had been projected had come to pass and a sceptical cynicism about comparisons between the book and the year. What they all exhibit is a slice of cultural and critical history, revealing a contemplative and introspective society assessing how much political ground had been covered since the end of the Second World War.

John Rodden has provided a very useful summation of the build-up to 1984:

■ The extraordinary degree to which 'Orwell' was employed in such promotional campaigns, sometimes even before the 1980s, is yet another indication of his enormous public reputation – and a comment upon Orwell's own writing practices. For Orwell himself liberally used the popular and mass art of his day as background and motif for his fiction; reciprocally, his work itself has in turn become part of popular and mass culture. . . . Orwell wrote about postcards and comic strips; the 1984 countdown witnessed Orwell postcards, comic strips, T-shirts, pop songs (Laurie Anderson's 'Good Morning, Mr. Orwell,' Van Halen's '1984'). Campaign buttons ('Orwell in '84!!') came from a Pennsylvania advertising company, which launched the Orwell for President campaign in 1983–84, nominating their favorite-son candidate on April Fool's Day, 1983.

Some spinoffs pegged to '1984' laced their humor with political invective. The left-slanted *Big Brother Book of Lists*, with a sinister Thought Police agent in a black trench coat on the cover, used '1984' as a handy hook for its numerous compilations . . . *The 1984 Calendar: An American History* similarly noted about 250 dates in history which the creators considered anniversaries of government intrusion into the lives of individuals.[2] In addition, the national campaign committees of both the Democratic and Republican parties sent out cover letters referring to the 'Orwellian spectre' in soliciting funds from party supporters, on issues ranging from defense spending to abortion.

So in 1984 the socialist author was exploited not only as an ideological patron but also as a capitalist money-maker. 'Orwell' was a hot item; the date's approach ignited a conflagration which lasted for several months. Orwell's popular reputation blazed like a shooting star, radiating into numerous spheres outside the literary-academic scene. An in-depth analysis of his treatment in hundreds of popular periodicals in 1983–84 – quite possibly unprecedented for a literary figure – would probably offer insight into the relation between commercial fanaticism and celebrity. Just a partial list of the specialized magazines and trade journals which ran stories on Orwell and '1984' in late 1983 and early 1984, some of them with utterly outlandish angles of interest, gives a hint of the phenomenal range of Orwell's reception among non-intellectual audiences during this time.

Roofing Spectator	*Four Wheeler*
Art Material Trade News	*Cruising World*
The National Clothesline Monthly	*Ohio Farmer*
Racing Wheel Times	*Tennis Monthly*
Construction Equipment Distribution News	*Cablevision*
Computer Decisions Monthly	*Hospitals*

Electronic Packaging and Production Monthly   *Metal News*
Insulation Outlook Monthly   *American Medical News*

The presentation of Orwell and *Nineteen Eighty-Four* in these organs indicates how a writer's image can alter – sometimes beyond recognition – as his name and work radiate beyond the sphere of the serious literary community into the wider public. Take, for example, the following banal use of *Nineteen Eighty-Four* by *The Welding Journal*. Addressed to industry employees, the February 1984 article ('1984 Is Here!') began by confusing *Nineteen Eighty-Four* with *Animal Farm*:

> *Are you more equal than others?* This is your chance to become one who is more equal than others, more expert in the welding field. . . .
> Is Big Brother watching you? If to you Big Brother is your boss, a board of directors, a steering committee, or a review board, they too will be watching – and they will be wondering if you are keeping aware of today's fast-moving welding technology.[3]

Such hilarious examples of commercial defacement suggest the difference between the popularization and vulgarization of a work of art, a line hard to draw conceptually yet often quite identifiable in practice. Because its title was a date, *Nineteen Eighty-Four* is probably unique in the way it was used by commercial and ideological interest groups. But the general process of its incorporation into commercial culture nevertheless broadly illustrates how the reputation of a relatively popular writer inevitably alters in response to changes in the time and place of his reception. Two trade journal editorials in 1983–84 underline this last point even more clearly. They also show how Orwell's public image as a 'dark prophet' readily served as a pretext for industry spokesmen to counterpose themselves as 'true,' optimistic prophets. Their treating *Nineteen Eighty-Four* as a historical forecast, rather than as a warning against totalitarian thinking, allowed them to 'trump Orwell' with sunny counter-forecasts about their own industry. The first editorial is from *The Casual Living Monthly*; the second is from *The Shooting Industry*:

> If I were to play George Orwell for one brief fleeting moment, I would predict a bright future for the casual furniture industry in 1984. My prediction is based strictly on fact and empirical observation, leaving fantasy and hypothesis to Orwell and his like.
> Unless George Orwell's predictions come true and 1984 sees Big Brother remove the accessibility of handguns from the majority of citizens the handgun business should recover at least as fast as the general economy.[4]

As one might expect, however, the commercialization of Orwell and *Nineteen Eighty-Four* was carried out chiefly by the major Anglo–American mass media. By late 1983, the American press was shrieking that 'Orwellmania!' has seized the U.S. and Britain. One headline in January 1984 summed up the ubiquity of Orwell's name: 'Where Will the Orwellian Fascination End?'[5] In the opening months of the year, gratefully christened 'The Year of the Book' by Penguin Books, *Nineteen Eighty-Four* made publishing history, topping the *New York Times* and *Publisher's Weekly* lists of best-selling mass market fiction for five weeks, the first time any book several years old (let alone thirty-five) had ever risen to occupy the number one position.

The promotional campaigns associated with *Nineteen Eighty-Four* and the book's sales explosion in 1983–84 were actually the culmination of a decade-long trend. By 1979, popular magazines like *Time* and *Playboy* were warning readers that '1984' was 'only' five years away. The first signs that the countdown was turning *Nineteen Eighty-Four* into a mass culture object came in 1980–81. The 1980 Yale University's freshman 'facebook' for the class of 1984 featured dozens of photographs of George Orwell, included to replace those 'faceless' student 'unpersons' who had failed to include a snapshot with their college applications. In the next year 'Orwell' and '1984' appeared in several advertisements. 'We're betting $2.3 million that Orwell was wrong' ran an ad headline in early 1981 in *Time* for the Boise Cascade paper company. The full-page ad pictured a scene reminiscent of the Golden Country in *Nineteen Eighty-Four*. A husband, wife, and little boy stroll arm-in-arm through a quiet glen, and then step lightly through the pages of a titanic calendar labeled '1984': 'We see a sunnier future than George Orwell did in 1948,' the ad copy begins, 'which is one reason why we've launched our most ambitious capital investment program ever.'[6] In succeeding months other firms and stores spun ambitious ad campaigns off '1984.' . . . On New Year's Day, 1984, Apple Computers kicked off its Macintosh computer promotion using *Nineteen Eighty-Four*. The firm's controversial $500,000 one-week TV spot, probably seen by 60 million football fans on New Year's Day alone, stopped just short of labeling arch-rival IBM 'Big Brother.' A television image of rows of marching, chanting, zombie-citizens ('We are one people with one will, one resolve, one cause!') – presumably IBM patrons tutored in Room 101 – was shattered when a beautiful woman in Olympic uniform hurled a sledgehammer through the screen. . . . . . .

Yet nothing recedes like success. 'Orwellmania' proved to be short-lived. With the exception of . . . a few promotions associated with *Nineteen Eighty-Four*, the gimmickry was over by March 1984. By the date on which Winston Smith makes his first fateful diary entry, 4 April 1984, the 'Orwellian fascination' had finally ended. The mutability of the present had rendered '1984' obsolescent as a mass-cult object.[7] □

As Rodden's contextualisation shows, the response to the Orwellian year was diverse and largely tangential to the text which had inspired it. Certainly, many inconsistent readings of the text were perpetrated in the interests of product-marketing and consumerism and, as Rodden indicates, little reference to the content of the novel is evident in these appropriations. 1984, as a mythical date and as a symbolic expression of state repression, overrides the actualities of the text and of Orwell's warning about all ideological systems. The response that Rodden charts reveals a largely superficial and irrelevant selection of images and concepts from the novel which are, more often than not, employed comparatively to assert the liberality of the present and the potential for capitalism and consumerism to increase a liberal version of individual freedom. Rodden's account is, admittedly, centred on the American reaction to, and commodification, of the Orwell moment, but the response in Britain, whilst more understated, was not markedly different in content. Such responses are very valuable, however, for the degree to which they reveal the ideological posturing of the Cold War period. The explicit presentation of life in America as wholly distanced from the world predicted by *Nineteen Eighty-Four* excites comparisons with a Soviet Union dominated by political intolerance and constraint of personal freedom. Such simplifications were a hallmark of the popularisation of Orwell in the early 1980s and intrinsically countermand his warnings against notions of ideological inviolability.

As Rodden suggests, the regenerated interest in Orwell was not long lasting and the novelty of correspondence between year and book soon dwindled. However, whilst public attention faded, much critical material was stimulated and serious reconsideration was given to the ongoing value and significance of Orwell's work. This is observable in the next group of extracts which seek soberly to test Orwell's theories of totalitarian power structures against contemporary models of governance. In the first passage, Raymond Williams, writing in the 1984 reissue of his 1971 monograph on Orwell, interrogates the novel's assumptions about the articulation of power over the intervening decades:

■ It would be possible, for example, to run a silly kind of checklist on the projections. Is there an Anti-Sex League? Is there a two-way telescreen for spying on people in their homes? Is there a statutory Two Minutes Hate? No? Well then it just shows, as some said at the time, that the book is a wild kind of horror-comic, or at best stupidly exaggerated. But these are elements of the parodic superstructure. The structure then? Yet in the predominant political resonance which has surrounded the novel we do not even have to look at these arguments, because their proof is already given in the real world. 'This is where socialism gets you.' 'This is where it has already got, in Russia and Eastern Europe.' But Orwell was quick to separate himself from this interpretation, which accounted for much of the early success of the book and which is still offered as if it were beyond question.

My recent novel is NOT intended as an attack on Socialism or on the British Labour Party (of which I am a supporter) but as a show-up of the perversions to which a centralised economy is liable and which have already been partly realised in Communism and Fascism.[8]

'*Partly* realised', in the social orders directed by Stalin and Hitler. The full perversions are shown as going further. Moreover the easy response, to put down the book and look East, where 'it is all already happening', should be checked by Orwell's emphasis:

The scene of the book is laid in Britain in order to emphasise that the English-speaking races are not innately better than anyone else and that totalitarianism, *if not fought against*, could triumph anywhere.[9]

The point is more than one of local correction, against the use and abuse of the novel during the cold war. It is central to Orwell's arguments that what is being described, in its main tendencies, is not only a universal danger but a universal process. That is the true source of his horror. If the novel is absorbed into the propaganda of this or that state, as a basis for hating and fearing an enemy state, against which there must preparation for war, there is the really savage irony that a citizen of Oceania, in 1984, is thinking as he has been programmed to think, but with the reassurance of the book to tell him that he is free and that only those others are propagandised and brain-washed. Orwell was offering no such reassurance. He saw the super-states, the spy states, and the majority populations controlled by induced ideas as the way *the world* was going; to the point where there would still be arbitrary enemies, and names and figures to hate, but where there would be no surviving faculty of discovering or telling the truth about *our own* situation: the situation of any of us, in any of the states and alliances. This is a much harder position than any simple anti-socialism or anti-communism. It is indeed so hard that we must begin by examining what he took to be its overpowering conditions, leading first to the super-states and to limited perpetual war. ... ... *Nineteen Eighty-Four* is so often quoted as a vision of the worst possible future world that it may seem odd to say that in at least one respect Orwell notably under-estimated a general danger. It is not often remembered that in the novel a war with atomic bombs has been fought in the 1950s. There are not many details, though it is mentioned that an atomic bomb fell on Colchester. This is one of several instances in which, read from the actual 1984, the novel can be clearly seen as belonging to the 1940s. Orwell was quick to comment on the importance of the new weapon. He wrote in *Tribune* in October 1945 that it was dangerous mainly because it made the strong much stronger; its difficult manufacture meant that it would be reserved to a few powerful societies that were already heavily industrialised. 'The great age of democracy and of national self-determination' had been 'the age of the musket and the rifle'. Now, with this invention,

> we have before us the prospect of two or three monstrous super-states, each possessed of a weapon by which millions of people can be wiped out in a few seconds, dividing the world between them.[10]

This is not only the outline of the world of *Nineteen Eighty-Four*. It is also an intelligent recognition of the actual power of the new weapons. Yet still, after this, he included in his story a war with atomic weapons after which, though with its own kinds of horror, a relatively recognisable land and society survived. This is no discredit to Orwell. Again and again it has been almost impossible to imagine the true consequences of an atomic war, as distinct from the one-sided use of the bomb which has been the only actual event. Indeed there has been a familiar kind of *doublethink* about nuclear weapons, in which it is simultaneously if contradictorily known that they would lead to massive and in many cases absolute destruction and yet that, with suf-ficient political determination of whatever kind, they could be absorbed and survived. ... ...

The next stage in Orwell's development of the idea, while he was in the middle of writing his novel, follows from his definition of three political possibilities: a preventive war by the United States, which *would* be a crime and would in any case solve nothing; a cold war until several nations have atomic bombs, then almost at once a war which would wipe out industrial civilisation and leave only a small popula-tion living by subsistence agriculture; or

> that the fear inspired by the atomic bomb and other weapons yet to come will be so great that everyone will refrain from using them. This seems to me the worst possibility of all. It would mean the division of the world among two or three vast super-states, unable to conquer one another and unable to be overthrown by any internal

rebellion. In all probability their structure would be hierarchic, with a semi-divine caste at the top and outright slavery at the bottom, and the crushing out of liberty would exceed anything that the world has yet seen. Within each state the necessary psychological atmosphere would be kept up by complete severance from the outer world, and by a continuous phony war against rival states. Civilisations of this type might remain static for thousands of years.[11]

This is, in effect, the option taken by the novel, though an intervening and less damaging atomic war has been retained from earlier positions. In his directly political writing, at this time, Orwell saw an alternative to all three dangers: the building of 'democratic Socialism . . . throughout some large area . . . A Socialist United States of Europe seems to me the only worthwhile political objective today'.[12] But in the perspective of the fiction this is entirely absent.

Obviously we must ask, in 1984, why none of Orwell's three (or four) possibilities has occurred. Yet we must do this soberly, since we shall not be released from any of the dangers he and others foresaw by the mere passage of a fictional date. It is not, in some jeering way, to prove Orwell wrong, but to go on learning the nature of the historical developments which at his most serious he was trying desperately to understand, that we have to ask what he left out, or what he wrongly included, in his assessment of the world-political future.

First we have to notice that what came through, in this period, were not unitary super-states or empires but the more complex forms of military superpowers and primarily military alliances. There are times, especially as we listen to war propaganda, when we can suppose that the . . . vision has been realised, in the monolithically presented entities of 'East' and 'West', and with China as the shifting partner of either. But the full political realities have turned out to be very different. There is, for example, a coexistent and different hierarchy of *economic* power, with Japan and West Germany as major forces. In significantly different degrees in 'East' and 'West', but everywhere to some extent, old national forms have persisted and continue to command the loyalty of majorities, though also in every such nation, including those of 'the West', there is a significant minority who are conscious agents of the interests of the dominant power in the military alliance.

At the same time, in ways that Orwell could not have foreseen, these elements of political autonomy and diversity – within very narrow margins in the Warsaw Pact, within broader margins in NATO which contains most kinds of political state from liberal democracies to military dictatorships – are radically qualified by the nature of modern nuclear-weapons systems. The atomic war of *Nineteen Eighty-Four* is damaging but not disastrous; in fact it is made to precipitate the 'perpetual limited war' which is a central condition of the novel, in which the super-states are unconquerable because their rulers cannot risk atomic war. The war actually being fought, with its distant battles and its occasional rockets, belongs technologically to the 1940s. But then it is not only that the effects of atomic war have been under-estimated; it is that the military and political consequences of a relative monopoly of nuclear weapons have turned out to be quite dif-ferent from anything that Orwell and most others supposed.

> Suppose – and really this is the likeliest development – that the surviving great nations make a tacit agreement never to use the atomic bomb against one another? Suppose they only use it, or the threat of it, against people who are unable to retaliate? In that case we are back where we were before, the only difference being that power is concentrated in still fewer hands and that the outlook for subject peoples and oppressed classes is still more hopeless.[13]

Between the powers that have acquired atomic weapons there has been neither formal nor tacit agreement never to use the weapons against one another. On the contrary, the predominant policy has been one of mutual threat. Within this policy there has not, as Orwell thought, been technical stagnation, but a continual enlargement and escalation – of weapons systems, each typically developed under an alleged threat of the superiority of the other side. And these have now reached the point at which national autonomies, within the alliances, contradict in one central respect the technical requirements of the most modern systems, which require instant response or even, some argue, preventive first use, if the other power is not to gain an early and over-whelming advantage.

It would be easy to argue from this, yet again, that the . . . super-state, with the necessary unitary command, is inevitable, as a product of the new weapons. But to move to that kind of super-state, for all its strategic advantages, would be to provoke major political problems – especially, for example, in Western Europe – which would endanger and probably break the now fragile compromise between surviving political autonomies and loyalties and the military strategic alliance which has been superimposed on them. Thus Britain, in 1984, both is and is not, in Orwell's phrase, Airstrip One. It is dense with its own and foreign air and missile bases but it is also – and crucially, by a majority, is valued as – an independent political nation. To force the question to the point where it would have to be one thing *or* the other would bring into play all the forces which Orwell recognised in his essays but excluded from the novel. For the agents of paranational military economic planning Britain has become, in a true example of Newspeak, the UK or Yookay. But for the peoples who live on the actual island there are more real and more valued names and relationships and considerations.

It is in the exclusion of even these traditional elements of resistance to what might seem a logical new order that Orwell, in the novel though usually not in the essays, went most obviously wrong. But there is an even larger error in the exclusion of new forces of resistance: most notably the national-liberation and revolutionary movements of what he knew as the colonial world. The monopoly of nuclear weapons, in the major industrialised states, has not prevented major advances towards autonomy among the 'subject peoples' whose condition he predicted as more hopeless. This is the peculiar unreality of the projection, that the old world powers, newly grouped into super-states, are seen as wholly dominant, and that the rest of the world is merely a passive quarry of minerals and cheap labour. Again, however, what has actually happened is complex. There have been political liberations in this vast area that Orwell reduced to passivity, but there is a limited sense in which what he foresaw has happened: not in super-state wars for its control, but in a complex of economic interventions, by paranational corporations which have some of the technical attributes of super-states; of political interventions, manoeuvres and 'destabilisations'; of exceptionally heavy arms exports to what in the worst cases become client states; and of military interventions, in some cases, where heavy and bloody fighting still excludes the use or threat of use of the nuclear weapons which in the perspective of the 1940s had seemed decisive for either conquest or blackmail.

Thus there has been, in one sense, the 'perpetual war' that Orwell thought likely, but it has been neither of a total nor of a phoney kind. The complex political and economic forces actually engaged have prevented the realisation of the apparently simple extrapolations from technical necessity or political ambition. It is sometimes hard to say, at this world-political level, whether the real 1984 is better or worse than the projected Nineteen Eighty-Four. It is more complex, more dynamic, more uncertain than the singular nightmare. Many more people are free or relatively free than the projection allowed, but also many more people have died or are dying in continuing 'small' wars, and vastly more live in danger of annihilation by nuclear war. The rationed and manipulated shortages of the projection have been succeeded by an extraordinary affluence in the privileged nations, and by actual and potential starvation in extending areas of the poor world. It is then not for showing danger and horror that anyone can reproach Orwell. If there is to be reproach, it is for looking so intently in one direction, with its simplified and easily dramatised dangers, that there is an excuse for not looking at other forces and developments which may, in the end, prove to be even more disastrous.[14] □

Williams here explores the parallels between the geopolitical conditions of 1984 and those in Orwell's novel. Superficial correspondences are brushed aside, as are the numerous differences – those who look to make simplistic comparisons fail to appreciate the macrocosmic level on which Orwell constructs his projected world. Interestingly, Williams asserts that the absorption of the novel into the ideological armoury of any state is in direct contravention to Orwell's desires and brings about a perverse trivialisation of the novel's import. To use *Nineteen Eighty-Four* as direct evidence of one state's democracy and another's diabolism is to ignore completely the message contained in the novel's warning. Ironically, in that circumstance, the text becomes an instrument of the propaganda and cultural indoctrination against which Orwell inveighs. The typical popular response noted by Rodden reflects just such an appropriation and would doubtless have troubled Orwell as, indeed, it troubles Williams. For Williams, Orwell's imaginative projections for the future are astute and logical prognoses whose impact Orwell has, if anything, underestimated. The atomic war that takes place as a background to the novel is a curious misjudgement for Williams, but it does give way to a condition of small-scale, perpetual war which is indicative of the Cold War political arena. Williams sees Orwell's greatest projection as the emergence of super-power blocs, which retain the threat of nuclear attack but seek to avoid the consequences of such actions by promoting military, political and economic intervention in surrogate states. Ultimately, Williams is equivocal as to the accuracy of Orwell's predictions; they do not go far enough and, whilst they reveal a strikingly sensitive political consciousness, they also display the limitations of that consciousness.

George Woodcock, Orwell's friend and eulogist, is more certain about the interrelationship of text and actuality:

■ The geopolitics of *Nineteen Eighty-Four* developed out of Orwell's perceptions of that now-distant world of Teheran and Hiroshima in which he lived and died. Oscar Wilde would have probably considered it an extraordinary instance of his principle of nature imitating art that history in 1984 should offer us a world so similar to that of the novel. We do in fact live in a world of three super-powers, the United States, the USSR, and the People's Republic of China, which respectively dominate roughly the same areas that Oceania, Eurasia, and Eastasia dominate in the novel, except that Europe west of the Elbe is in the American rather than the Russian camp. They are not, indeed, formally at war with each other, but if Clausewitz's maxim that 'war is the continuation of politics by other means' is true, it is equally true that, in the modern world, geopolitics is the continuation of war by other means, and that, without actually declaring war or assaulting each others' territories directly, the three great powers have been carrying on, by massive political manoeuvres and by peripheral and large indirect wars, strategies aimed at winning a position of ascendancy in the modern world.

Sometimes, like the great powers in Orwell's novel, the superpowers do venture with their own armies into the great disputed rectangle (which in real life, as in the novel, consists mainly of Africa and South Asia) as the USA did in Vietnam and the USSR has done in Afghanistan, but usually they are more comfortable using the peoples of the disputed areas to fight their battles for them, as the USA has used Israel in the Middle East and right-wing military leaders in Latin America, and as the USSR has used Syria in the Middle East and Cuba (whose armed forces have become a veritable foreign legion of the Red Army) in Africa and Central America. This pattern of cruel little wars on the verges of the great power blocs has become the accepted strategic style of the late twentieth century. The atom bombs are, as in the novel, being stored up, but, though agreements restricting their use are habitually aborted, the bombs are not dropped; they have, in fact, become the guarantees for the perpetuation of the balance of power between the three blocs.

The general effect of this situation on large parts of the world has been disastrous. Anyone who has travelled widely since the end of World War II is appalled by what has happened, during relatively recent years, to many of those countries that were previously free of access, and peaceful if not always prosperous. The misfortunes of countries like Afghanistan, Vietnam, Cambodia, and Lebanon began when their strategic situations tempted the direct or indirect intervention of one or other of the three super-powers, ever watchful for the opportunity to gain an advantage over the others. Such countries have been brought not merely war and physical destruction; they have been subjected in a variety of ways to ruthless totalitarian or quasi-totalitarian regimes, sometimes alien and sometimes native and collaborating.

The list of casualties among the nations other than super-powers is appalling. A few areas were annexed in the old-fashioned imperialist way; ironically, this has been done only by the two Communist powers, so that the Baltic republics of Latvia, Lithuania, and Estonia, the Finnish province of Karelia, and the Roumanian [sic] province of Bessarabia were absorbed directly into the USSR and subjected to immediate and ruthless purges by the NKVD, while Tibet was taken over by the Chinese and its traditional religious life was equally ruthlessly eliminated. In the next circle of the totalitarian hell are those countries which are nominally independent Communist states; some of them, like Poland and the other Warsaw Pact countries, are mere satellites with Russian armies of occupation, though there are others, like Jugoslavia [*sic*] and Albania in Europe, and Vietnam and North Korea in Asia, that remain ideologically and politically subordinated to strong oppressive 'native' Communist regimes, yet are not under the direct control of Russia or China. All these countries are totalitarian in political structure and in what remains of fading ideologies; they range in degree from the comparatively relaxed regime of Jugoslavia, to the fanatically destructive regime of Pol Pot in Cambodia which set about the establishment of the new order by annihilating, with more than Stalinist fervour, whole classes of Cambodian society. This regime succeeded in largely depopulating the country and even depriving it of technicians and professionals of every kind, so that when Pol Pot and his assassins were driven out of the country by another totalitarian gang, sponsored by the Vietnamese, hardly a medical practitioner was found to have survived. Here and there in such settings, ideology may still be a strong motivating factor, as it was in Cambodia and possibly still is in Albania; more often, as in Russia itself, it is power rather than ideological purity that is the aim of the all-powerful parties and secret police forces which have been established in all these countries in imitation of the structural patterns of the Stalinist USSR.

In a less obvious but no less real way, the power bloc dominated by the United States and principally sited in the Americas and in Europe is formed of like-minded regimes. Sometimes, as in the Communist blocs, coercion plays or has played its part. There are plenty of cases here as well where adherence was imposed by some kind of external intervention in the politics of a country. This took place directly in Greece after World War I, and as recently as 1983 in the Caribbean island of Grenada, but more often it has been achieved indirectly through the subsidization and arming of local right-wing takeovers, as in Chile in 1973 and Guatemala in 1954. But in most cases, the United States and its allies or satellites are united by the bonds of common fear of Russia and shared opposition to the Communist type of society. This is a situation perfectly fitted by the Orwellian maxim: 'All animals are equal, but some are more equal than others.' Whatever roles the other countries may play in the councils of NATO and NORAD, the United States is unassailably the dominant power, and its partners tend always to act as Washington decides, as when, despite enormous popular opposition in their own cities, the countries of western Europe accepted the deployment of Cruise and Pershing missiles on their territories.[15] □

But for Woodcock the implications of this political brinkmanship extend deep into the social psychologies of 1948 and 1984:

■ In turning away from the geopolitical view, and regarding again what the year 1984 has brought to the circumstances in which we live from day to day among our neighbours, I proceed from the fact that *Nineteen Eighty-Four* was set not in Russia, but in Oceania, which includes the countries we have up to now regarded as bulwarks of the democratic world – the United States and Britain. For people living in that democratic world, the novel's relevance to Russia, unlike that of *Animal Farm*, is secondary, and its prime role is that of a warning, or a cluster of warnings, directed at the societies we inhabit. Considered for its polemical rather than its literary qualities, as warning it must stand or fall.

The society portrayed in *Nineteen Eighty-Four* formed the sum of the probable consequences of tendencies that Orwell saw at work in the western societies of his day. Looking into the future, he envisaged the possibility of a society that, except perhaps among the despised proles who had 'stayed human,' was entirely malign; even Winston and Julia, in the extremities of their rebellion, take on the malign qualities of the forces they oppose. But the original social impulses and initiatives that started the world on its way to Orwell's nightmare future were by no means entirely malign. One of the saddest lessons of history is that generous impulses, once they become institutionalized, can lead to negative consequences, as the long records of world religions like Christianity, and of world movements for social amelioration like socialism, have shown. Whatever may be true of the path to Hell, the paths that led to the cellars of the Spanish Inquisition and of the NKVD's Lubianka Prison in Moscow were, sadly, paved with good intentions.

And when we look at the signs that suggest how far since 1948 we have gone towards the world of Orwell's imagination, we can do no better than begin with that characteristically benevolent phenomenon of the post-World War II democratic world, the welfare state.

Robert Nisbet has remarked, in an essay . . . that:

Totalitarianism involves the demolishment of authentic social ties in a population, but involves, no less, their replacement by new ones, each deriving its meaning and sanction from the central structure of the State.

In fact, we do not have to wait for the totalitarian millennium to see 'the demolition of authentic social ties in a population.' For many generations, the tendency of the state has been to replace by bureaucratic initiatives those generous impulses and processes which, in most relatively free societies, led in the past to the voluntary performance of a good many social functions by the practice of mutual aid; the coming of the welfare state was accelerated by the process of bureaucratizing and institutionalizing social benevolence.

The negative consequences of this development have been twofold. First, whenever the state persists in carrying out, or at least controlling, activities aimed at the welfare of individuals, the 'authentic social ties' inevitably atrophy. The result of the transfer of responsibilities – as experience shows particularly in urban centres where the manifestations of mutual aid first die away – is a growing dependence on the state to do things people should be doing for themselves or their neighbours. Dependence, of course, narrows the freedom of the individual and his opportunities to act with independence and originality, and it automatically increases the power and influence of the welfare bureaucracy, which becomes all the more dangerous because its members justify their interference in other people's lives by the excuse that they are doing good; the social worker who uses his power and his sense of personal virtue to tyrannize the poor has become a familiar manifestation of Pecksniffery in all welfare states. Such a situation leads to a growing atomization and hence subordination of the population, whose members, becoming less involved with their neighbours in community activities, suffer that crippling sense of alienation which makes individuals who are lost in the mass society ready victims for the kinds of propaganda that are based on the fears of the lonely, for whom Big Brother finally appears as a friend in need.

Secondly, and in the long run perhaps even more harmful in its consequences, there is the part played by the welfare state in regimenting the population through its systems of registration. In a society where everyone is a potential recipient of a pension, or of medical service provided out of public funds, or of doles during unemployment, everyone is inevitably docketed, with enough personal particulars to authenticate his or her claims to benefits. As only highly organized and centralized states can provide welfare aid efficiently and with enough sufficiency, this means that personal information regarding every citizen who receives a social security number is stored in centralized data banks. At first it was assumed that such information would be used only for benevolent purposes, i.e., to ensure that everyone received the benefits due to him. In practice, as the years have gone on, social security numbers – and presumably therefore the other stored data – have been made available to other government agencies, some of which, like the taxation and security services, harbour intents that are often not very friendly to the individual. The welfare state, in other words, has made notable inroads into the privacy of individuals, and a society where privacy rapidly diminishes is on its way to the totalitarian state. For once data banks have been established, there is no curb on the use that might be made of them by unimaginatively zealous bureaucrats or by some future dictator. In fact, the boasted confidentiality of government files has long been vulnerable. For many decades the United States government has used tax files as a means to attack and imprison supposed enemies it could not get at in any other way. And recently in Canada, when Helmut Rauca was being sought, the Minister for Foreign Affairs authorized the opening of the hitherto sacred passport files to the RCMP; whatever the merits of the Rauca case in itself, the precedent was alarming.

Thus, by weakening the natural impulses within society towards mutual aid and voluntary co-operation, and by centralizing information about private individuals, the welfare state, for all its originally benevolent intent, has weakened our ability to resist the more malevolent assaults of governments that may come in harsher times. We are all there, meticulously registered, awaiting their attention.[16] □

The welfare state as an oppressive intervention of the institution in the life of the individual is a curious and intriguing notion. Woodcock contends that the prospect of welfare and care induces people willingly to forego their liberty in the interests of materialistic gain. This insidious infiltration of the state into the private and individualistic needs of the subject effects an efficient and covert form of totalitarian control. It is a short step from this conclusion to the idea of Big Brother as inherent in all state practices – a construction that some critics have made, as we shall see. The next group of extracts explores the parallels between the methods of social control employed in Oceania and those pertaining to the late twentieth century. The first passage, from Mark Crispin Miller's essay 'Big Brother is You, Watching', attempts to draw parallels between the ubiquity of the television in contemporary American society and the pernicious influence which the telescreens have on the integrity of the self in *Nineteen Eighty-Four*. Moreover, he construes the omnipresence of the media in 1984 as indicative of a counter-Enlightenment which he regards as active in present-day America. Fundamental to this notion of counter-Enlightenment is the paralysing effect television is seen to have on free will whilst simultaneously espousing such liberation as its guiding *raison d'être*:

■ As we leave the world of Orwell's novel dissolving into its own flux, we must turn back to our more tangible society, wherein the novel now receives so much perfunctory attention, and ask how Orwell's vision reflects on American life in 1984. We can best begin to answer this unpleasant question by pointing out that most of those who have raised it have done so only to dismiss it, proclaiming in a flood of essays, editorials, and advertisements that *Nineteen Eighty-Four* cannot relate to our free society, whereas the novel does, of course, apply directly – and exclusively – to the Soviet Union. This conception of the novel is nearly as old as the novel itself, which, once published, was immediately hailed by some American conservatives as a vivid anti-Communist manifesto. Although Orwell himself publicly deplored this propagandistic reduction of his work, in the work itself he had already satirized just such warlike interpretation. In Oceania there can be no lasting animus against the status quo, since every individual reaction to the Party's rule is deflected by the Party into collective hatred of the Party's latest enemy. Thus the reader who appropriates the novel as a weapon succeeds only in resembling its most benighted characters, who also bolster their own system through the very discontent in which it keeps them. (As we might expect, the chauvinistic misreading of *Nineteen Eighty-Four* suits the purposes of those Soviet ideologues who jeer America, just as it has helped express the American condemnation of the Soviet Union.)

Such jingoistic interpretation exemplifies the paralysis of Enlightenment, wherein the means of liberation becomes an object that prolongs captivity: the warlike reader keeps himself forever moving forward in aggressive readiness, justifying his repressive posture with the very text that calls it into question. However, it is not only such reactionary misreadings that inadvertently demonstrate the truth of *Nineteen Eighty-Four*. Because the novel's power derives primarily from Orwell's apprehension that the most progressive attitudes demand their own eventual reversal, the ruthless left-liberal reader vindicates that apprehension even more directly than his right-wing counterpart. That enlightened reader who, in the name of justice or equality, treats the novel as a guide to some vast campaign of mechanistic social engineering therefore only advocates the same process that motivates the Inner Party. What we may call the vulgar feminist position, for instance, which argues that we must get rid of 'traditional sexual love' in order to preempt Big Brother,[17] repeats O'Brien's way of thinking and even anticipates one feature of his program: 'We shall abolish the orgasm. Our neurologists are at work upon it now.' (p.280)

In short, those who, whether on the left or the right, use the novel as a social or political instrument thereby betray their inability to step outside of it, much less read it, illuminating nothing but their own inclusion in the iron process which the novel criticizes. But *Nineteen Eighty-Four* enables us to read with clarity not just itself but the whole current moment in which it is so widely celebrated and distorted. Orwell was, of course, not thinking of this moment in America when he conceived and wrote his novel; nor would it make sense to demonstrate a crude equation of America with Oceania. Orwell wrote not as a prophet but as an artist. Rather than simply itemize the world of *Nineteen Eighty-Four* into those details that have 'come true' and those that haven't, then, we must discover within this satire of Enlightenment its oblique reflections on our own enlightened culture, whose continuities with Orwell's time and place demand our critical consideration. We can best begin this project of discovery by analyzing one explicit similarity between the novel's world and ours. In Oceania, as in America, the telescreens are always on, and everyone is always watching them.

The Oceanic telescreens are not actually televisual. Writing in the late forties, Orwell could not come to know TV's peculiar quality but conceived the telescreen, understandably, as a simple combination of radio and cinema. Its sounds and images therefore suggest these parent media, which, beginning at mid-century, turned out to be alike in their capacity to drum up violent feeling. The telescreens' voices are abrasive and hysterical, like the mob whose regulated violence they catalyze; and the telescreens' images are also explicitly suasive, arousing primitive reactions, paradoxically, through sophisticated cinematic techniques. Ingenious tricks of Eisensteinian montage enable the telescreens to inspire extreme reactions, whether foaming hatred of this year's foe or cringing reverence for Big Brother (reactions that are fundamentally the same).

Television, on the other hand, inspires no such wildness, but is as cool and dry as the Oceanic telescreens are hot and bothered. Its flat, neutralizing vision automatically strains out those ineffable qualities wherein we recognize each other's power; nor can it, like film, reinvest its figures with such density, but must reduce all of its objects to the same mundane level.[18] In order to overcome the muting effect of TV's essential grayness, the managers of all televisual spectacle try automatically to intensify each broadcast moment through the few sensational techniques available: extreme close-ups, marvellously heightened colors, dizzying graphics, high-pitched voices trilling choral harmonies, insistent bursts of domesticated rock'n'roll, and the incessant, meaningless montage that includes all things, events, and persons. And yet these compensations for the medium's basic coolness merely reinforce its distancing effect. Repeatedly subjected to TV's small jolts, we become incapable of outright shock or intense arousal, lapsing into a constant dull anxiety wherein we can hardly sense the difference between a famine and a case of body odor. And the televisual montage bolsters our inability to differentiate, its spectacle of endless metamorphosis merely making all those images seem as insignificant as any single image seen for hours.

Because of these formal properties, TV is casually inimical to all charisma and therefore seems an inappropriate device for any program like the Inner Party's. Televised, the 'enormous face' of Big Brother would immediately lose its aura of 'mysterious calm,' . . . On TV, furthermore, the maniacal intensities of actual Party members would also lose their sinister allure, not by being cancelled out but by coming off as overheated, alien, and silly. At those moments when his face takes on a 'mad gleam of enthusiasm,' even O'Brien would seem to have been bypassed, and therefore exterminated, by TV.

Thus TV would seem to be an essentially iconoclastic medium; and yet it is this inherent subversiveness toward any visible authority that has enabled TV to establish its own total rule – for it is *all* individuality that TV annihilates, either by not conveying it, or by making it look ludicrous. TV would therefore suit the Party's ultimate objective perfectly, if Orwell had lived to watch and understand it. As TV would neutralize Big Brother's face and O'Brien's transports, so would it undercut the earnest idealism of Winston Smith, dismissing his indignant arguments about 'the spirit of Man' by concentrating coolly on his 'jailbird's face,' just as O'Brien does. With its clinical or inquisitorial vision, TV appears to penetrate all masks, to expose all alibis, thereby seeming to turn the whole world into a comic spectacle of unsuccessful lying, pompous posturing, and neurotic defensiveness, behaviors that appear to be seen through the moment they are represented. It is from this apparent penetration that TV's documentary programs derive the ostensible incisiveness that makes them so engrossing: 'Sixty Minutes,' 'The People's Court,' 'Real People,' and so on. And it is the need to withstand TV's derisive penetration that has dictated the peculiar self-protective mien of all seasoned televisual performers, whether they play love scenes, read the news, or seem to run the country. The muted affability and thoroughgoing smoothness that make these entertainers seem acceptable on TV also serve as a defense against its searching eye; and yet by thus attempting to avoid subversion, these figures – finally interchangeable as well as evanescent – merely subvert themselves, giving up that individuality which TV would otherwise discredit.

Thus, within the borders of its spectacle, TV continues automatically that process of Enlightenment which the Party hastens consciously – the erasure of all lingering subjectivity. Whereas the Oceanic telescreens are the mere means used by the ironists in power, our telescreens are themselves ironic, and therefore make those powerful few unnecessary. For it is not only *on* TV that TV thus proceeds to cancel selves; it also wields its nullifying influence out in the wide world of its impressionable viewers. Television's formal erasure of distinctness complements – or perhaps has actually fostered – a derisive personal style that inhibits all personality, a knowingness that now pervades all TV genres, and the culture which those genres have homogenized. That corrosive irony which emanates from the Oceanic elite has been universalized by television, whose characters – both real and fictional – relentlessly inflict it on each other and themselves, defining a negative ideal of hip inertia which no living human being is able to approach too closely. ... ...

Guided by its images even while he thinks that he sees through them, the TV viewer learns only to consume. That inert, ironic watchfulness which TV reinforces in its audience is itself conducive to consumption. As we watch, struggling inwardly to avoid resembling anyone who might stand out as pre- or non- or antitelevisual, we are already trying to live up, or down, to the same standard of acceptability that TV's ads and shows define collectively, the standard that requires the desperate use of all those goods and services that TV proffers, including breath mints, mouthwash, dandruff shampoos, hair conditioners, blow-driers, hair removers, eye drops, deodorant soaps and sticks and sprays, hair dyes, skin creams, lip balms, diet colas, diet plans, lo-cal frozen dinners, bathroom bowl cleaners, floor wax, car wax, furniture polish, fabric softeners, room deodorizers, and more, and more. Out of this flood of commodities, it is promised, we will each arise as sleek, quick, compact, and efficient as a brand-new Toyota; and in our effort at such self-renewal, moreover, we are enjoined not just to sweeten every orifice and burnish every surface, but to evacuate our psyches. While selling its explicit products, TV also advertises incidentally an ideal of emotional self-management, which dictates that we purge ourselves of all 'bad feelings' through continual confession, and by affecting the same stilted geniality evinced by most of TV's characters, the butts excluded. The unconscious must never be allowed to interfere with productivity, and so the viewer is warned repeatedly to atone for his every psychic eruption, like Parsons after his arrest for talking treason in his sleep: "'Thoughtcrime is a dreadful thing, old man,' he said sententiously. "It's insidious. . . . There I was, working away, trying to do my bit – never knew I had any bad stuff in my mind at all.'" (p. 245)

Thus, even as its programs push the jargon of 'honesty' and 'tolerance,' forever counselling you to 'be yourself,' TV shames you ruthlessly for every symptom of residual mortality, urging you to turn yourself into a standard object wholly inoffensive, useful, and adulterated, a product of and for all other products. However, this transformation is impossible. There is no such purity available to human beings, whose bodies will sweat, whose instincts will rage, however expertly we work to shut them off. Even Winston Smith, as broken as he is at the conclusion, is still impelled by his desires, which the Party could not extinguish after all, since it depends on their distorted energy. For all its chilling finality, in other words, the novel's closing sentence is merely another of the Party's lies (p. 311). And what O'Brien cannot achieve through torture, we cannot attain through our campaigns of self-maintenance, no matter how many miles we jog or how devotedly, if skeptically, we watch TV. . . . . . .

TV, however, is not the cause of our habitual self-scrutiny, but has only set the standard for it, a relationship with a complicated history. It is through our efforts to maintain ourselves as the objects of our anxious self-spectatorship that we consummate the process of American Enlightenment, whose project throughout this century has been the complete and permanent reduction of our populace into the collective instrument of absolute production. This project has arisen not through corporate conspiracy but as the logical fulfillment, openly and even optimistically pursued, of the imperative of unlimited economic growth. Thus compelled, the enlightened captains of production have employed the principles, and often the exponents, of modern social science, in order to create a perfect work force whose members, whether laboring on products or consuming them, would function inexhaustibly and on command, like well-tuned robots. As the material for this ideal, Americans have been closely watched for decades: in the factory, then in the office, by efficiency experts and industrial psychologists; in the supermarkets, then throughout the shopping malls by motivational researchers no less cunningly than by the store detectives; and in the schools, and then at home, and then in bed, by an immense, diverse, yet ultimately unified bureaucracy of social workers, education specialists, and 'mental health professionals' of every kind. The psychic and social mutations necessarily induced by this multiform intrusion have accomplished what its first engineers had hoped for, but in a form, and at a cost, which they could never have foreseen: Americans – restless, disconnected, and insatiable – are mere consumers, having by now internalized the diffuse apparatus of surveillance built all around them, while still depending heavily on its external forms – TV, psychologistic 'counseling,' 'self-help' manuals, the 'human potential' regimens, and other self-perpetuating therapies administered to keep us on the job.

And so the project of industrial Enlightenment has only forced us back toward that same helpless natural state that Enlightenment had once meant to abolish. Both in America and in Oceania, the telescreens infantilize their captive audience. In *Nineteen Eighty-Four* and in 1984, the world has been made too bright and cold by the same system that forever promises the protective warmth of mother love, and so each viewer yearns to have his growing needs fulfilled by the very force that aggravates them. So it is, first of all, with Orwell's famished hero. The figure who had slipped quickly into Victory Mansions, 'his chin nuzzled into his breast,' (p. 3), had tried unknowingly to transcend the Oceanic violence by mothering himself, but then ends up so broken by that violence that he adopts its symbol as his mother: 'O cruel, needless misunderstanding!' he exults inwardly before the image of Big Brother's face. 'O stubborn, self-willed exile from the loving breast!' (p. 311) And, as it is with Winston Smith in his perverted ardor, so it is with every vaguely hungry TV viewer, who longs to be included by the medium that has excluded everyone, and who expects its products to fulfill him in a way that they have made impossible.[19] □

Mark Miller's article postulates a counter-Enlightenment at work in post-1945 Western culture, brought about, largely, by a dependence on television which, he suggests, divorces the individual from her/his own selfhood by providing televisual simulacra of 'real' lives which in turn become objectified and consumed by the watchers and integrated into a relationship of dependence between watcher and watched. The endless cycle of dependence that is engendered creates, so Miller contends, the perfect capitalist workforce – unimaginative but aspirational automatons. In this way, contemporary American society is seen to reflect the conditions of the totalitarian machine and the ultimate irony is that the individual subject-workers have internalised their materialistic torpor as the very indicative mark of their freedom from totalitarian constraint. 'Big Brother' no longer needs to control his citizens because they have become their own most effective monitors.

Anthony Burgess is also interested in the potential for self-regulatory impulses in the modern state. In his treatise-cum-novel, *1985*, he cogitates on the separation of sex and love in *Nineteen Eighty-Four* and the way in which that reflects a social phenomenon:

■ Traditionally, we have always hated a thing because it is intrinsically hatable. Christianity, though it enjoins love of people, commands hatred of certain qualities that may inhere in them – cruelty, intolerance, greed and so on. There was a time when we knew what the hatable qualities were; now we are no longer sure. Traditional vices are presented in the popular press as virtues. A man, film star or tycoon, who has been proud, covetous, lustful, envious and gluttonous and achieved a name in the world through the exercise of such vices, is a hero, not a monster. Tolerance is weakness, cowardice is prudence. The notion of intrinsic loathability no longer exists.

It seems to follow that lovability does not exist either. Love comes into *Nineteen Eighty-Four*, but it is neither the disinterested, generalized love of the Gospels nor the romantic love of nineteenth-century novelists. It is certainly not a love appropriate to marriage vows. Winston receives a note from a girl whose name he does not even know. It says simply, 'I love you.' He at once palpitates with fear and excitement (pp. 113–15). The love that the girl, whose name turns out to be Julia, claims to feel for him is, we learn, based on a recognition that his political orthodoxy is imperfect, and that his disaffection is ready to be expressed in the only form she knows – a willingness to fornicate. Fornication is forbidden by the State, since it offers a pleasure the State cannot control. To make love physically is an act of rebellion. This imposes on the sexual act a bundle of virtues which it is not, in itself, well able to sustain. But the statement 'I love you' is here as much a mockery of the values traditionally attached to the phrase as is the State's own institution of a Ministry of Love.

The main fictional weakness of *Nineteen Eighty-Four* lies here. There is an insufficiency of conflict between the individual's view of love and the State's. Winston and Julia do not oppose to Big Brother the strength of a true marital union and, by extension, the values of the family. They have fornicated clandestinely and been caught naked in the act. There is a sad moment when Julia, whose sole notion of freedom is the right to be sexually promiscuous, gives Winston a potted history of her love affairs (pp. 131–2). Winston rejoices in her corruption, and Orwell seems to abet the false antithesis – oppose to the moral evils of the State the moral evils of the individual. And yet, as we know, the history of Orwell's own love life is one of trust and devotion: he was not extrapolating a frustration in his fiction. He was perhaps merely being prophetic. In 1984, whether Big Brother is there or not, the traditional view of love will have disappeared, and through no fault of the repressive State.

One of the achievements of American civilization is the devaluation of the institution of marriage. This has had much to do with the Puritan condemnation of adultery as a deadly sin; the scarlet letter is burnt into the American soul. Divorce is preferable to adultery, divorce sometimes being a euphemism for serial polygamy. But divorce is rarely presented, in American fiction or American life, as the wholly regrettable, unavoidable, last-resort surgical operation of a less permissive tradition. Love is a sort of car that has to be replaced by a newer model. It is an electric light bulb whose hours of illumination are numbered. It is equated, as in the mind of Orwell's Julia, with sexual desire. Sexual desire does not die, but it requires a change of object. Like hatred, it is a gun.

Love, however, could be defined as a discipline. It is big enough to encompass transient phases of indifference, dislike, even hatred. Its best physical expression is sexual, but the expression should not be confounded with the essence, the word confused with the thing. Both Winston and Julia love in the sense that they form a self-contained community whose main activity is the sexual act, the act and its concomitants begetting fondness, companionship, and other benign essences. They know, however, that there is no permanency in the relationship; their only discipline is directed to not being found out. It is a brief phase of superficial tenderness to be ended by punishment. 'We are the dead,' says Winston, and Julia dutifully echoes him. 'You are the dead,' says the voice from the wall (p.230). The relationship had death in it from the start. So do many relationships in our permissive age, and the death is not imposed from without; it is self-induced.

Separate the sexual act from love, and the language of love is devalued. An aspect of our freedom is our right to debase the language totally, so that its syntagms [sic] become mere noise. Big Brother, though regretting the promiscuity enjoined by our society and abetted by our films and magazines, will be delighted to see the weakening of marital values. Communism has tried to kill the family – with great difficulty in China – since the family is the original of which the State tries to make a grotesque blown-up copy; it is far better for the family to kill itself.

The reduction of love to the sexual act, and then to the promiscuous sequence of sexual acts, has the effect of reducing sexual partners to mere objects. It becomes easy then to regard all human beings, in whatever social connection, as objects, on to whom we can spray whatever emotion is expedient. An object has no individual essence; it is a common noun. Generalization follows – women, not this woman and that; workers, the working class. The shocking demotion of millions of individual souls to a generalized class called the proles is perhaps, after the devaluation of love, the most terrible thing in *Nineteen Eighty-Four*.[20] □

Burgess's very personal identification of the loss of love with the advent of the sexual revolution may reveal more about the society that is consuming *Nineteen Eighty-Four* in the early 1980s than it does about the novel itself. Critics like Burgess and Miller reflect their own anxieties about the direction in which society is seen to be heading onto the text. In so doing, they replicate the interpretations of the early political critics who claimed the novel as an explicit affirmation of their partisan views. *Nineteen Eighty-Four* has always been a canvas onto which readers have projected their concerns with society and in the self-conscious *fin de siècle* this has been no different. The observations of many of these critics are temperate, logical and reasoned, and strive, at least in part, to refer back to Orwell. Some criticism produced in the build-up to 1984 sought more emotionally to respond to what its authors saw as the degeneration of the social order into an Orwellian nightmare. The following extracts represent extreme reactions to the dangers predicted by *Nineteen Eighty-Four* and, although at such a remove they may appear dated and hysterical, they do provide a flavour of the fear and anger that was engendered by the novel. Tom Winnifrith and William Whitehead, in *1984 And All's Well?*, write in this first passage on the insidious infiltration of an Orwellian 'Newspeak' into public discourse:

■ But Newspeak is something more than a bad joke. Aspects of Newspeak have already entered our vocabulary and our lives. Let us start with the way we write down our thoughts. In *Nineteen Eighty-Four* the pen is an archaic device, long since replaced by the inkpencil and the speakwrite. The invention of the biro or ballpoint pen fascinated Orwell, and he was anxious to get hold of what in 1947 was an expensive toy. Now in banks, post offices, examination rooms, and almost everywhere, ballpoints or their even more modern successors rule supreme, with pen and ink being relegated to the dusty classrooms of a few old-fashioned schools. Likewise busy and important men are thought extremely eccentric if they write their letters in longhand, an activity deemed suitable only for maiden aunts. Instead they dictate them to their secretaries, and the resulting product is usually less satisfactory. University professors can blame their typists for errors of which any fifteen-year-old would be ashamed. Similarly the ballpoint pen has increased the fluency and speed of writing, but decreased the accuracy and pleasure.

In *Nineteen Eighty-Four* we have a device for the destruction of information, known with a savage irony as the memory hole. In 1984 we will have a variety of devices like xerox machines, microfilms and now all the resources of the silicon chip designed to act as memory banks. It is sad, but perhaps hardly surprising, that these technological innovations do not seem to have improved our memory of the past, although it would clearly take some major catastrophe to destroy all the information thus stored. But with so much information at our disposal we find it hard to discover what information is important. Because it is easy to copy information we do not bother to remember it. . . . . . .

We are told in a fairly meaningless cliché, worthy of *Nineteen Eighty-Four*, that the medium is the message. A multiplicity of devices for improving the publication of books and newspapers has not produced any startling results. Photocopiers, electric typewriters and word processors do not seem to have meant that printing has become quicker, cheaper, more accurate or more beautiful since the time compositors laboriously typeset manuscripts written in copperplate with quill pens. It might be argued that an increase in quantity has meant a decrease in quality.

That standards of literacy have deteriorated cannot be doubted. It is true that we do not yet say *mans* for *men*, or *thinked* for *thought*, but *whom* is now regarded as an anachronism even by university students who are equally patronising towards the apostrophe and the hyphen. . . . It was clever of Orwell to see that *shall* and *should* will yield to *will* and *would*, although among our new illiterate elite both tend to give way in speech and even sometimes in writing to *I'll, you'll, he'll, I'de, you'de, he'de*. What is required for our new vocabulary are short clipped words of unmistakable meaning which can be uttered rapidly and rouse the minimum of echoes in the speaker's mind. In Newspeak *Nineteen Eighty-Four* euphony outweighs every consideration other than exactitude of meaning. In Newspeak 1984 exactitude of meaning is the last consideration of many public speakers, but euphony has certainly prevailed over grammar.

It may seem old-fashioned to deplore these changes or to regard them as sinister, or to see them as part of the world of Orwell's novel. Certainly progressive educational methods, encouraging free expression at the expense of correctness, seem very different from the jackboot philosophy of *Nineteen Eighty-Four*, and the bewildering variety of spelling perpetuated and permitted in our schools appears a total contrast to the narrow uniformity enforced in Newspeak. But illiteracy breeds confusion, and that is worrying for our confused world in which the wicked and unscrupulous can promote confusion to further their own ends. It is bad to be depraved and sad to be deprived, but we are in sad bad way if we confuse the two, and the confusion is in fact as reductive as the diminution of vocabulary foreseen in Newspeak. A failure to observe the correct grammar and the etymological meaning of a word is of course also part of the blurring of the past which leads to the destruction of the truth. At the moment we can afford to laugh at feminist writers who say that history is a sexist word and should be replaced by herstory, but the time may come when ignorance of the Greek derivation of history may be as disturbing as the abuse of the word democracy. . . . . . .

As well as precision reduction, the useful Newspeak word *crimethink* covers both peaceful protest and violent revolution, rational argument and mindless chanting of slogans. In 1983, though we have modish and meaningless terms like freedom fighters and guerrillas to cover a vast range of activity and to show on which side we are, on the whole it is a feature of our present vocabulary, at any rate the vocabulary of the supposed intelligensia, that we have added to the number of words in use, not reduced them. It is when we consider some of these words that Orwell seems to be uncannily prophetic. Consider *feedback, flowchart, input, matrix, interface, parameter* and *database*. These words have a number of features in common with the vocabulary of Newspeak.

First of all they are ugly. This may seem a subjective judgement, but most people would agree that words like *halcyon* and *hyacinth* sound beautiful quite apart from their connotations, whereas *input* and *feedback*, like *Newspeak* itself, sound ugly, although they have very few connotations. Perhaps *feedback* with its uncomfortable anatomical associations is the nearest equivalent we have to *bellyfeel*. Apart from *Newspeak* and *doublethink* none of the words mentioned in *Nineteen Eighty-Four* has entered the vocabulary of modern English, but perhaps this is because Orwell has warned as well as prophesied. As a lover of the English language, Orwell would have been displeased by both *input* and *feedback*, but he would have been pleased by the fact that the words he put into *Nineteen Eighty-Four* had been fed back in this disgusting way.[21] □

On the dissociation of love and sex, Winnifrith and Whitehead comment:

■ In some ways we are of course in a better position than Orwell's generation. The hypocrisy and secrecy surrounding many a pre-marital and extra-marital affair have given way to a new frankness, of which Orwell would have approved. He would perhaps have seen that hypocrisy and secrecy spring from a sense of shame, and that this shame might have nipped in the bud many a rash affair leading to nothing but disaster. It is however difficult to believe that anyone, especially Orwell, could approve of a return to Victorian morality, or sanction any progress towards *Nineteen Eighty-Four* morality. In both Victorian society and in *Nineteen Eighty-Four* there is much hypocrisy and furtive adultery; in Victorian novels those who are found out are sent to Australia, and in *Nineteen Eighty-Four* they are sent to room 101, and in neither case do we approve of the penalty.

All however has not been sheer gain. The new sexual permissiveness does not seem to have brought about greater happiness in marriage, if the divorce figures are any indication. In 1982 in Great Britain it was concluded that one in every three marriages would end in divorce, and in the United States the proportion is even higher. The family is a deeply hallowed institution, but these figures seem to threaten its long reign. In *Nineteen Eighty-Four* the only marriage mentioned is that between Winston and the frigid Katherine, and the only family we see is the horrible Parsons family. There are of course haunting glimpses of Winston's own family with rare moments of happiness playing snakes and ladders, but this belongs to the past.

Lots of families are still playing snakes and ladders, and more advanced video games, but the threat to family life remains as serious in sexually permissive 1984 as it is in sexually tyrannical *Nineteen Eighty-Four*. It is true that the cripplingly harsh difficulty of obtaining a divorce, and the stigma attached to even the innocent party in a divorce, which lasted in England until well beyond 1948, produced many unhappy families who would not otherwise have kept together. But the comparative ease of divorce at the present time has produced many families who have not kept together, and this makes them even unhappier. Probably, given the ease of divorce, marriages are undertaken more lightly. One sometimes wonders why people bother to get married at all, since every encouragement is given to young men, and now even to young women, to satisfy their sexual instincts outside marriage, and little encouragement is given to people to satisfy their paternal or maternal instincts. Democratic and non-democratic governments alike both pay lip service to the family as something which should be preserved, but in spite of such cosy institutions as family allowances, successive governments have done little to save the family.[22] □

There is little doubt that such complaints against the modern world are heart-felt and passionately argued. There is a degree, however, to which Winnifrith and Whitehead appear excessively conservative about social change, almost to the point of paranoia. A social paradigm shift seems to be occurring against which these respected academics inveigh in overtly nostalgic and mournful terms. The loss of that world rather than the iniquities of Orwell's dystopia seems to be the principal, if largely unspoken focus. Another equally fascinating document of its time is Donald McCormick's *Approaching 1984*, which takes features of Orwell's vision and extrapolates them onto the conditions of society in the early 1980s. On censorship McCormick comments:

■ One of the paradoxes of life as we approach 1984 is that in many respects ultra-liberalism and oppressive censorship go together: in fact, the former leads to the latter. This is perhaps the one grave danger that is not generally visualised. Yet history should show that inevitably the sudden exposure of a nation to uninhibited freedom produces a counterreaction and repressive measures. Immediately after the French Revolution the cries of *'Liberté, Egalité, Fraternité'* were silenced in the zeal for tyranny and executions; after the Russian Revolution the insistence on free love and the end to bourgeois marriage produced so much anarchy that there was a swift return to the principles of family life. But today ultra-liberalism may eventually produce more censorship, not less, and of a far more drastic kind. The right to total freedom of expression whether in terms of pornography or violence may swiftly be replaced by a distorted censorship aimed at curbing any form of self-expression. You give people the right to strike and they demand pickets to support strike action. You allow them six pickets and they immediately introduce 600. You allow them 600 and you have riots and violence. You fail to take prompt action against that violence and you have widespread injuries and deaths. You have injuries and deaths and what happens? Why, not prosecution of the pickets or the criminal activists masquerading as pickets, but the charging of an employer for provocative actions which cause breaches of the peace.

Similarly, if there is a song-hit called 'Cannabis Turns Me On' or 'LSD Sets Me Free', and it reaches the top of the record charts, hundreds of youngsters may be impelled to experiment with drugs. But who find themselves in court, charged with breaking the law? Not the songwriters and commercial pluggers of these musical incitements, but the young people urged on by a permissive society to try out the very things which that society still legally condemns.

This is censorship turned inside out. You create the climate for a permissive and over-indulgent society and then punish those who take one step too many. Yet the effects of an ultra-permissive and liberal society such as one sees all too frequently in the West often mask the cause of some of the sicknesses of that society which is, quite simply, an actual easing of the censorship over books, plays, songs and other art forms. As Orwell detected at that PEN conference, there was even in the late 1940s a trend towards this, while little was being done to combat the evils of increased political censorship in other areas of the world. The result has been the continued existence of harsh regimes in the totalitarian world and the production of rubbish (impertinently described as the highest form of self-expression), pornography and civilisation-destroying propaganda in the guise of art in the West.[23] □

On the prevalence and protean shapes of Big Brother, McCormick also has much to say:

■ That 'Big Brother' is ubiquitous, watchful and operating over large areas of the world is surely evident from the fact that the phrase is now in everyday use in the languages of all countries except where he holds sway – and even in Poland he is sometimes slyly referred to as 'Our Big Cousin'.

What is rather more disturbing is that this title is now so generally used that it is applied not merely to all-powerful dictators, but to trade union leaders, minor bureaucrats and even parish councillors and traffic wardens. Power has corrupted people who would never have dreamed of overstepping their authority in the past. . . . . . .

The supreme Big Brother, Josef Stalin, has gone, and for one thing we can be grateful – none of his successors in any part of the world has been quite as blatantly ruthless and cruel as this despot who sent hundreds of thousands of his countrymen to their death. This is not to say that another Stalin never could emerge, but the death-blow which has been dealt to the personality cult since the removal of Stalin and Hitler from the human scene ensures that nobody can remain in power for long and be quite as evil as these two men. As George Orwell once said, a theocracy which imposes a single creed on all its people cannot operate a modern science-based economy, where progress depends on innovation, inquiry and willingness to think dangerous thoughts.

There are a number of Big Brethren still in control of their countries' destinies, but on the whole they have been (or are) less frightening and far less harsh than Hitler or Stalin. It is perhaps easier today for the so-called 'free world' to laugh at the antics of our ruler Big Brothers than it was in Orwell's time. There is the bemedalled, strutting, self-styled Field Marshal Idi Amin Dada of Uganda, whose behaviour at times has caused us to rock with mirth. There is his boast that he 'knows Queen Elizabeth II even more intimately than her husband does'. Perhaps we laugh too easily: the ridiculous conduct of this buffoon to some extent masked the fact that for several years in Uganda thousands of people disappeared without trace overnight. Only after he was actually deposed did we learn that on his orders the ears of all whites executed over the years in the State Research Bureau in Kampala were delivered to him on a platter. . . . . . .

It is true that the twentieth century's own mad Dervish in the person of Colonel Gaddafi of Libya sometimes fills us with fear as to where his influence may lead the Arab world, but so far his extremism has been firmly rejected by his neighbour, Egypt, and some other Moslem states. On the whole the Big Brothers of recent years have been much less awe-inspiring than those of thirty or forty years ago. In the Soviet Union, for example, nobody has tried to recreate a Stalin or a Beria. For Big Brother read Big Brothers in Moscow today and somehow the Politburo gives one a feeling that there is some kind of safety in numbers. One feels that the rather staid, conservative-minded members of that body cannot all be compulsive criminals. Disarmament talks such as SALT would have been impossible under Stalin's régime and, even if they have not made any spectacular progress, the fact that such talks have now lasted for some years is in itself a form of safety-catch.

As for Mr Yuri Andropov, the chief of the KGB, this quiet, scholarly bureaucrat is in complete contrast to the sinister Lavrenti Beria, his predecessor, who drove around Moscow at nights in his bullet-proof ZIS, abducting and seducing tiny girls off the streets. As for those posters of Big Brother, of which Winston Smith wrote in his diary; when the life-size portraits of Chairman Mao appeared all over China they depicted a benevolent uncle, or father-figure, rather than some all-seeing robot dictator from outer space. Mao Tse-tung created an entirely new image for Big Brother, possibly because he was very much a rural figure and one of the very few dictators who have concerned themselves with the lot of the peasant rather than of the industrial workers. He saw that his people were better fed: for that he will be remembered on balance as a relatively respectable dictator.

But the fact that the image of Big Brother may seem to have changed in some countries is no reason for complacency. The threat lying behind the image is there all the same, and today Big Brother in some form or other is to be found everywhere. The fact that he lends himself more to farce and satire in some instances is apt to blind us to realities. ... ...

O'Brien, chief counter-espionage agent in *Nineteen Eighty-Four*, says: 'The Party seeks power entirely for its own sake. We are not interested in the good of others; we are interested solely in power.' (p.275) This is, of course, something that no Big Brother or Big Sister, whether of the political, trade union, Women's Lib or gangster sphere, will ever admit. If they all did admit this, then it would be much easier to identify all the Big Brethren and we might be surprised to find how they have multiplied. ... ...

... the USA's most awful example of a Big Brother over several decades was undoubtedly J. Edgar Hoover, the dictatorial, power-loving boss of the FBI. Just because he wanted to cling on to power at all costs, Hoover hushed up the evidence that President Kennedy's killer, Lee Harvey Oswald, had been associated with the KGB, and used his influence with some senior executives of the CIA to stifle any further investigation of this. Why? Because further inquiries would have showed that Hoover's FBI had slipped up badly in not keeping tabs on Oswald after he came back to the USA from the USSR.

Big Brothers could easily come about even in the so-called 'free world', in the form of a state-run computer network. Dr M.V. Wilkes, writing in the *New Scientist*, asked: 'How would you feel if you had exceeded the speed limit on a deserted road in the dead of night, and a few days later received a demand for a fine that had been automatically printed by a computer coupled to a radar system and vehicle-identification device? It might not be a demand at all, but simply a statement that your bank account had been debited automatically.' ... ...

In Orwell's nightmare, Big Brother was always visible – on the television screens, peering into every home like the house detective in a huge departmental store watching for shoplifters. The nightmare was controlling the masses by fear alone. For why else should the wretched prisoner, Parsons, locked up with Winston Smith, call out 'Down with Big Brother' in his sleep? (p.245)

'Thought-crime is a dreadful thing, old man,' said Parsons to his fellow prisoner. 'It's insidious ... do you know how it got hold of me? In my sleep! ... My little daughter ... listened at the keyhole. Heard what I was saying and nipped off to the patrols the very next day.

Pretty smart of a nipper of seven, eh? I don't bear any grudge against her. It shows I brought her up in the right spirit, anyway.' (p.245)

The awful lesson of this is not at first obvious. Slowly, the horror of Parsons' comments are borne in on one. He was imprisoned for thought-crime at the behest of his nasty-minded little daughter. Yet he doesn't blame her – rather admires her, in fact – for, after all, this is what a decently educated child should do. Then one sees that from this state of mind to one in which nobody fears Big Brother, but actually loves and accepts him, is not such a long step. Today the minds of millions have been so completely captured and controlled by Big Brother in some form or other that his presence is unnoticed. This is especially so in the democracies where Big Brother, if he does not wear kid gloves, at least has calloused hands to make us all feel he is just an ordinary fellow, suffering like the rest. We have been conditioned to accept instinctively and without question what he decrees.[24] □

It would be easy to dismiss many of these observations as paranoid anachronisms, but to do so would be a grave disservice. The genuine fears that are expressed in these texts suggest an articulate expression of a widely felt, but largely unarticulated concern, about the political, ethical and ideological paths down which principally Western societies appeared to be heading. These anxiously self-reflective diatribes reveal a great deal, not just about how Orwell was interpreted in the mid-1980s, but also about how Britons and Americans saw themselves and their uneasy relationship with authority. The fact that many of the more panicky prognostications seem to us to be wildly over-exaggerated does not mean that they have been disproved by time. An alternative interpretation, and one which would no doubt be advocated by these critics, is that the examples of state intervention that they cite have not only become accommodated within a sense of the normal but have also been assimilated into an understanding of the contemporary condition.

The frenzy of interest in Orwell which was inspired by the approach of the year of the book passed very quickly and was replaced by a curious apathy towards Orwell. Whilst most readers had been rationally aware that the likelihood of a Big Brother-like state coming to pass by 1984 was slim, an irrational fear of the future fuelled an ongoing interest in the accuracy of the projected model. With the passing of the date, the novelty value of the book also disappeared and Orwell's profile diminished considerably – although, as the final chapter of this Guide will show, Orwellian notions such as Room 101 and Big Brother have persisted, in mutated forms, in popular culture. Critical appraisal throughout the rest of the 1980s and 1990s, however, has continued at a steady but declining pace and this decline prompts the question: has Orwell's moment passed for good? Perhaps 1985 was not the best thing to happen to Orwell after all.

CHAPTER SIX

Watching Big Brother Watching: Orwell on the Screen

IT IS difficult to overemphasise the impact that *Animal Farm* and *Nineteen Eighty-Four* have had on late twentieth-century culture, particularly in Britain and America where the terms 'Orwell' and 'Orwellian' have become potent bywords for state control of the individual and for the strangulation of freedom by bureaucracy and managerial autocracy. This Guide has examined some of the ways in which Orwell and his most notorious texts have been co-opted to support various, often divergent, causes, but in recent times that co-option has taken a new turn. With the proliferation of the mass media throughout the second half of the century and, in particular, with the ubiquity of television within the home, the notion of the ever-vigilant Big Brother, remorselessly examining the lives of private individuals, has taken on a new significance. The telescreens which continuously monitor the lives of the inhabitants of Airstrip One seem to have their natural correlative in the television sets that have become indispensable parts of domestic life. Whether or not the world of 1984 mirrored that of the novel, certain elements of Orwell's vision have been prophetically accurate and whilst the two-way observation of the telescreen is not a current reality, changes in television's entertainment content point increasingly towards the position of viewer not only as observer, but also as active participant in the context of the programme being broadcast.

The contemporary prevalence of what is called 'reality television', that purports to provide real-life drama as entertainment, has brought about a situation in which the viewer, traditionally removed and distanced from a pre-recorded visual experience, is thrown into a live and unpredictable context where their distance from the drama is (notionally at least) reduced. What is invoked in this form of entertainment is not the viewer's passivity, but conversely their active participation in the events portrayed. Such participation is of course illusory – viewers have little or no effect on what they witness, but such television seeks to question the solidity of the barriers between the watcher and watched. The viewer, comfortably ensconced in their domestic security, becomes a surrogate for Big Brother, convinced of their own impenetrability, whilst willingly destabilising that of those they watch. The phenomenon of the *Big Brother* gameshow, which captivated British audiences in the summer of 2000, but which has had similar impact in its various incarnations around the world, is a ready example of the re-negotiation of the watcher/watched dynamic. Yet whilst the programme maintained the Orwellian symbol of Big Brother in the public eye, there were distinct semantic and conceptual differences between the figure implied as Big Brother and that contained within Orwell's original text. This discrepancy suggests an intriguing divorcing of the author from his creation, which in many ways reflects the current attitude towards Orwell. Though concepts such as 'Big Brother', 'doublethink', the 'Thought Police' and 'Newspeak' still have some common currency, their original context and creator is often forgotten. This is indicative of the degree to which Orwell's work has outgrown its author and has mutated to reflect upon changes in society that Orwell could not have predicted. This process of mutation is the focus of this final chapter. By looking at the screen history of *Animal Farm* and *Nineteen Eighty-Four* and at the ways that those texts have been variously altered, it is possible to see how the cultural phenomenon of Orwell has, in fact, all but eclipsed Orwell as writer.

Animal Farm and *Nineteen Eighty-Four*: A Screen History

Orwell's last two novels undoubtedly have a strong visual impact that lends itself to film adaptation. The stark, futuristic austerity of Airstrip One, with its overtones of wartime London melded to a Stalinist Soviet Union, has instant shock appeal, as does O'Brien's torture of Smith. The possibilities for striking cinema offered by *Animal Farm* are obvious – the combination of endearing animal imagery with a strong, clear moral is immediately commercial. Film-makers have striven to fulfil this potential but have, on the whole, failed to make both money and convincingly robust adaptations. Nevertheless, the influence of Orwell's texts is evident in a plethora of films, as we shall see.

John Rodden has claimed that, more than any other factor, the film and television adaptations of Orwell's work have lodged him within the popular imagination.[1] Orwell is a cultural icon largely because of the fear that he induced with his vision of 1984, and the filmic treatments of the novel brought him to the attention of audiences that would never have considered reading his fiction. The critical date in this transformation of Orwell to a household name is Sunday 12 December 1954. It is possible to date this so specifically because, on the evening of that day, a television adaptation of *Nineteen Eighty-Four* by Nigel Kneale was broadcast by the BBC as their Sunday Play. Up until this point Orwell's reputation was chiefly maintained by a quorum of critics, friends and admirers, and had it not been for the TV broadcast of the play, his popular fame may well have dwindled to relative obscurity. Instead, he and his work were catapulted into the public eye and into a controversial debate about moral decency, family life and the uses of television.

The play was shown at prime viewing time on the sole channel that was available in that era. It was preceded by the popular gameshow *What's My Line* and prefaced with a warning that it was unsuitable for children or the nervously infirm. The play itself starred Peter Cushing as Winston Smith and Yvonne Mitchell as Julia; two of the small screen's most popular performers. The setting was a bleak, post-nuclear war London and the adaptation was relatively faithful to both the mood and political tenor of Orwell's text. The controversial aspects of the drama revolved around the representations of violence during O'Brien's torture of Smith, notably his use of electric shocks, and of the horrors of Room 101. Rodden points out that such portrayals of violence were not intrinsically excessive or offensive (and he contrasts them with the much more graphic violence depicted on American television at the time), but the British viewing public was unprepared for the brutality of Orwell's vision.[2] From the critics the play received much praise as a thought-provoking adaptation which the BBC was courageous to present. Such approbation, however, was swamped by a tide of public disgust and disapproval. The BBC and newspaper offices were inundated by angry callers who described the play as 'sadistic' and 'horrific',[3] a reaction that was taken up by the popular press the following morning. The extracts below detail some of the responses to the drama and reflect the intensity of emotion generated. The first is from the *Daily Express*:

■ *'1984*: Wife Dies As She Watches'
A forty-year-old mother of two children collapsed and died while watching the TV horror play *1984*, it was disclosed last night. She was Mrs Beryl Kathleen Mirfin, a local beauty queen of 1936, who was watching the play on Sunday night at her home in Carlton Hill, Herne Bay. With her was her husband, who is a real estate agent, and two friends. In the early part of George Orwell's nightmarish fantasy of a Police State Future, Mrs Mirfin collapsed. A doctor who was called asked at once: 'Was she watching the TV play?'[4] □

The second response is from *The News Chronicle*:

■ *'1984* Shocks Viewers'
Hundreds of angry television viewers telephoned the BBC and news-

paper offices last night after the TV presentation of George Orwell's *1984* – the story of a nightmare era. All complained that it was too ghastly for television. Not one caller praised the play.

Mrs Edna Burgess of Holborn rang *The News Chronicle* to say: 'I trembled with fear as I watched; it was not fit for ordinary decent-minded human beings. It was nothing but unoriginal bits of horror put together.'

Miss Vivienne van Kampen of Muswell Hill, demanded an immediate campaign to prevent the BBC from repeating the play . . . 'Some of the scenes are the most ghastly things I have ever seen' she said.

It was not only women viewers who were upset. Mr Frederick Poate of Woking was looking in with Canadian friends. 'None of us is particularly squeamish, but we found the torture scene where a man was being given electric shocks in a coffin more than we could stand.' he said. Callers told the BBC that the play was worse than horror comics and not fit for public viewing.[5] □

The controversy that ensued dominated the newspapers for the week that followed and was still rumbling a month later. A hastily convened discussion programme was aired on the Monday evening which pitted irate viewers against BBC officials, and the Corporation was placed under extreme pressure not to broadcast a repeat showing on the Thursday of that week, as had been planned. In the event the repeat was shown, generating an even larger audience than the first screening and causing a fresh tumult of complaints. The effects of the fracas were wide-ranging. Firstly, it brought Orwell firmly back into the public's gaze and boosted sales of his book from 150 per month to 19,000 in the week after the play.[6] A novel which seemed to have had its moment was suddenly thrust into the public's consciousness, where it has remained ever since. The fear that was generated by the drama, a crushing sense of the inevitability of Orwell's prophecy, recuperated a reputation that was beginning to fade and brought him to the attention of new readers, particularly amongst the working classes, that he had previously failed to attract.

More broadly the controversy around the play excited debate about the purpose of television and about the moral landscaping of popular entertainment. The two extracts which follow, both taken from popular journals, were written in the week after the screening and point towards the key areas of discussion which sustained the debate. Writing in *The Listener*, Philip Hope Wallace commented:

■ Art is always suspect in Britain and we do well to remember that she has her enemies. Artists, except at general elections, are not asked to air their opinions of politicians, but how swift is the politician to denounce the artist. . . . And at this point may I say that a line taken by many others, i.e. 'We are still free. This is not 1984. You could have switched off if you didn't like it' is just as absurd? [*sic*] People don't have television to switch it off. No, the inescapable fact is that democratic or majority-monopoly television means in the long run that all one can serve up is the pap which may rot the mental teeth in the long run but turns not even the queasiest stomach at the time.

Meanwhile a Mr and Mrs George Orwell of Woolwich have been . . . telephonically assailed from all quarters. How the real 'Orwell' would have loved it all.[7] □

Meanwhile, in the *New Statesman and Nation*, William Salter argued that the controversy brought the BBC's required inclusiveness into disrepute:

■ The real storm over the TV version of *Nineteen Eighty-Four* is that it exposes as glaringly as possible the cultural situation in terms of which the Television Service has to work. There is nothing new in the situation itself. We have known all about it for years: highbrow, middlebrow, lowbrow, categories given formal recognition in sound broadcasting by the example of the Third Programme, Home and Light. Yet though we know all about it, when a storm does blow up, as over the Orwell adaptation, it always comes as a shock, the cultural rifts between us are revealed as greater than we had supposed. ... ...

The counterpart of this predigested reading matter forms a large proportion of the programmes the BBC puts out in the Television Service. It is now apparent that any violent departure from this is regarded by many viewers as a malign attack on their sense not only of what is right and proper but of their security: it seems that even before the interval of *Nineteen Eighty-Four*, that is, well before the visual horrors had been reached, the BBC was already being assaulted by indignant telephone calls. What was being defended, it seems was the sanctity of the Sabbath which, so far as TV is concerned, should be sacred to pap, and the innocence of children; for viewing, it must be remembered, is largely a family concern. This means in effect that any given programme is judged by its suitability for the youngest member of the family present. ... ...

Obviously the only cure for the situation lies in the schools, in better education. But that is a long-term cure. What is the BBC to do in the meantime? It was surely wholly right to withstand the pressure to abandon the repeat broadcast of *Nineteen Eighty-Four* . . . If the BBC can put nothing on its Television Service that will be unsuitable for a ten-year-old child, then it had better close the shop altogether, for we shall have no TV worth looking at.[8] □

Both these commentators are aware of the power of television in the cultural life of the nation and equally aware of its dual potential to unite and divide the populace along lines of morality, class and education. Hope Wallace represents the body of critics who praised the play on aesthetic grounds and who expressed deep suspicion at the convenient intrusion of political indignation into an artistic matter. Yet he also makes the pertinent comment that the autonomy of the individual viewer is seriously threatened by the authority and ubiquity of television. Here we begin to see the emergence of concerns with the addictive qualities of television programming and the potentially harmful effects that may accrue. Salter also points to the diverse impacts of television and the dangers of trying to please all sections of the population. For Salter, the hysterical reaction to the screening of *Nineteen Eighty-Four* proves the existence of an entrenched cultural divide which cannot be bridged by single-channel broadcasting. The drama provoked such an outcry, he argues, because many viewers simply did not understand its import. Such cultural collisions, as are evidenced in the response to the play, reveal the impossibility of a consensual broadcasting policy. Having schedules dictated by the most junior member of the viewing family renders the medium, in Salter's opinion, a limited and essentially conservative force which must always pander to a moral majority for fear of opprobrium. Such strident attitudes were freely expressed in the weeks after the play's airing and they show how seriously the role of television within the entertainment culture of the nation was being considered. Ultimately, the issue of intellectual compromise, to which Salter points, was addressed by the institution of a second BBC channel, devoted in the main to a diet of serious programming, and by the arrival of the independent, entertainment-oriented channel ITV.

What could not be denied was the influence that television was increasingly having on moral and aesthetic debates. One side-issue to emerge from the fiasco, and one which has not been extensively considered, is that the experience of watching the play of *Nineteen Eighty-Four* in one's home is markedly different from the experience of going to the cinema to see a film production. Suddenly, the viewer is aware of their passivity and their lack of choice about what they see. Apologists for the programme did argue that those horrified by the content could easily have switched off but, as Hope Wallace stated, one does not have a television to turn it off. The 'invasion' of privacy that is perpetrated by the violence of *Nineteen Eighty-Four* is therefore all the more intense because it seems to the viewer that they are powerless before it. Much of the outrage against the BBC and Orwell could be ascribed to the sudden realisation of the intrusive power of television. As John Sutherland argues in the next extract, the controversy, whilst relatively short-lived, created an impact on the culture of television which was to be long-lasting:

■ The *Nineteen Eighty-Four* controversy articulated the case for diversity, heterogeneity and audience choice. . . . It was, at the very least, evident that the BBC, with its one channel, could no longer please all the British television viewing people. Nor could television any longer remain ignored, or relegated to the status of visual radio. It was now proven to be a medium capable of unprecedented impact. . . . . . .

The programmers got the message: *Nineteen Eighty-Four* may have attracted 'hundreds' of hostile phone calls. But it also drew the highest viewing figures of any television event to date. Henceforth, no television play could argue itself successful unless it jammed the switchboard. Audience provocation . . . was established as television theatre's main ingredient.[9] □

Hot on the heels of the *Nineteen Eighty-Four* scandal came the first screen adaptation of *Animal Farm*, an event which further cemented Orwell in the consciousness of the public. Radio versions of the play had been produced in 1947 and 1952, but the film of 1955 brought Orwell's work to an ever wider audience and, with the hardening of the Cold War, the novel's clear political overtones chimed well with an increasingly anti-Soviet mood in the West. The film is notable for being the first, full-length, non-American animated cartoon, a feat achieved by the British husband-and-wife team John Halas and Joy Bacheler. It is equally notable for its bowdlerisation of Orwell's original work – with the appending of a happy ending being perhaps the most significant of alterations. Again, the context of the film is important. Rodden suggests that the film's ambivalent reception in America has largely to be read in the context of the 1954 McCarthy trials which had sought to uncover Communist sympathisers in many areas of American public life. By 1955, Senator Joseph McCarthy had fallen dramatically from grace and an American viewing public greeted the political commentary of *Animal Farm* with a bemused sense of *déjà vu*. Part of the problem with the animated feature was the decision to decontextualise the story from the events surrounding the Russian Revolution. Instead, the film portrays the struggle for control of *Animal Farm* as a generalised tale about the evils of power, without the intricate system of character correspondences and parody of historical events. There are parallels between the animals and political figures, but they are largely based around contemporary historical personages – Old Major is given the voice and mannerisms of Winston Churchill, one pig resembles the Labour leader Ernest Bevin, whilst another calls Hermann Goering to mind. Such obvious interference with the text's original set of correspondences served only to confuse viewers and to trivialise the portentous message that Orwell was trying to convey. In an article written shortly after the film's release, David Sylvester condemned the production on all levels:

■ This film is a failure aesthetically, imaginatively, and intellectually. The style of the drawing is a feeble parody of Disney: even Boxer the cart-horse, symbol of the working class, might be a reject from the Olympian pastures in *Fantasia*. The humour as well as the idealisations are largely Disney-esque: thus much of the would-be comic relief comes from a well-meaning goofy gosling which is a pure Disney type. The main thing about the film that is not Disney-esque is its poverty of comic invention, and it is not as if the blame for this could be placed upon the book. On the credit side, there are a few moments of tragic invention which have been added to the story and add to its impact. When the 'traitors' are slaughtered, a carrion-bird averts its eyes. After the slaughter, when the words 'without cause' are added to the slogan 'No animal shall kill any other animal,' they are painted in in blood. And the sound-track is quite harrowing when Benjamin the donkey runs braying shrilly down the road in pursuit of the knacker's van with Boxer in it.

The essential weakness of the film lies, not in the realisation of detail, not even in that the drawing is as second-rate as it is second-hand, but in its wilful misinterpretation of Orwell's central intention. The point of *Animal Farm* is that it is not an allegory of ideas, not a speculative fantasy. It is a precise satire on the most terrible phenomenon of recent history, the tragedy of Bolshevism, and nobody who has read the book can fail to be aware of this. When the film critic of *The Spectator* describes the film as 'this bitter satire on the Welfare State,' it has to be inferred that the lady is ignorant of the book-of-the-film rather than that she has missed the point of the film itself. For the film does everything it can to obscure the book's meaning, to treat it as a vague, general sermon instead of an indictment of events that actually happened.

The thing that obsessed Orwell most of all about Soviet totalitarianism was its ruthless dishonesty, its practice of 'doublethink.' Orwell's loathing for this is manifest in three themes in *Animal Farm*. One is the gradual transformation of the revolutionary slogans ('All animals are equal but some animals are more equal than others' and the rest). The second is the opportunism with which the porcine government suddenly make allies of their enemies and enemies of their allies. The third is the establishment of a legendary traitor-figure whose machinations can be held responsible for all mistakes of government and even circumstantial misfortunes. The importance for Orwell of these latter two themes is shown by their recurrence in *Nineteen Eighty-Four*, where the roles of the neighbouring farmers, Mr. Pilkington of Foxwood and Mr. Frederick of Pinchfield, are taken over by the states of Eurasia and Eastasia, and that of Snowball, the Trotsky of the piece, by Emmanuel Goldstein. . . . But both these themes all but disappear from the *Animal Farm* film. It suppresses the destruction of the half-completed windmill by a storm, which, in one of the book's supreme ironies, gives Comrade Napoleon the opportunity to put the blame on Snowball. And it excludes Mr. Pilkington and Mr. Frederick altogether. This, incidentally, entails handing over the leadership of the invasion of Animal Farm from Mr. Frederick to Mr. Jones, the exiled proprietor. So distortion by omission leads to positive distortion which makes nonsense of history – or would if the film, like the book, bore any relation to history.

These expurgations have been made, no doubt, in the interests of simplification. But there are other distortions for which no such justification is conceivable. The most cheap and inept is that of giving old Major, the prophet of the Revolution, the voice and appearance of Sir Winston Churchill. This again is absurd only if *Animal Farm* is supposed to bear some relation to the facts. But the closing scenes introduce an absurdity which is internally nonsensical. The guests of the pigs at the banquet are not men but other pigs. Does this mean that there are other farms where the animals have revolted and the pigs taken over? We have not hitherto been told that this has happened. Furthermore, surely the point of the banquet should be that the pigs have sold out to the human leaders of other states, that is, to creatures of the same species as those they once deposed? And surely this remains a point that has to be made even if the film is trying to be general and not particular in application? Not to have made it destroys all the poignancy of the ending.

> 'No question, now, what had happened to the faces of the pigs. The creatures outside looked from pig to man, and from man to pig, and from pig to man again; but already it was impossible to say which was which.'

Instead of this, in the film the creatures outside merely have a momentary hallucination that the roomful of pigs have human faces. Whereupon they rebel.

The hopeful ending grafted on to the story is not the most unforgivable thing about the film. It may soften the pessimism which was so fundamental in Orwell, but it gives no promise that the new revolution will not have the same sad outcome as the old. In suggesting that history is cyclic, the film's ending does not deny its moral, so long as the moral is to be read as general. But once again it goes against the facts, giving a final demonstration that the film is not meant to be interpreted as a satire on the Soviet Union, that it might just as well be a 'savage satire on the Welfare State.'

It is, of course, arguable that the dramatic effect of an adaptation of

Orwell's book is likely to be heightened by suppressing local references in order to give it a more general relevance. This is all very well in theory; only it ignores everything that the book means to us. *Animal Farm* is not yet a *Gulliver's Travels*, nor can we know now whether it ever will be, whether it can ever transcend its immediate frame of reference to acquire a universal validity. So far as we are concerned, its validity is inextricably bound up with its particular historical references. For it tells a story in which we have been involved – the story of a process of disenchantment which almost every thinking person with any human sympathy born in the 20th century has shared. The future may see it otherwise, but for us *Animal Farm* is nothing if it is not the testament of Orwell's hatred of Stalinism. For us, its poignancy lies in its discovery of a dramatic pattern in that series of events known as 'The Betrayal of the Left.'[10] □

Sylvester's complaints against the adaptation reflect those of many critics who saw the film as a trivial, sub-Disney travesty of the original novel. Admittedly, the film was intended as a children's entertainment, but the simplifications that Sylvester points towards denude the text of much of its satirical power, and the comic novelty of talking, animate creatures was not sufficient to support the film's stripping of the novel to its bare message. Interestingly, the film received equally spirited criticism from all shades of the political spectrum. The conservative lobby in America condemned what it saw as the directors' Communist sympathies, whilst in *The Nation*, a magazine of the far Left, Robert Hatch dismissed not only the film but also the creative imagination behind it:

■ George Orwell had a poor opinion of revolutions, at least of the great revolution that occurred in his lifetime. When you eliminate a tyrant, he observed, you create a vacancy, and like as not a new tyrant will step nimbly into it, leaving you no better off – and very possibly much worse off – than before. On this generalisation he constructed *Animal Farm*, an allegory which stirred up a good deal of discussion in the war years. The arguments were not only between the pro-Russians and the anti-Russians but also between those who differed on whether or not Orwell was preaching the essential futility of any revolt against oppression. As a simplified but not inaccurate fable of what happened in Russia the book is no longer controversial, but it is still not clear what Orwell thought a people should do about oppression. I think he loved and pitied suffering humanity but had little hope for its future: people were sheep, geese, donkeys, oxen and plodding drayhorses, at the mercy of the scheming pigs.

Animal Farm has now come to the screen as an animated cartoon. It lends itself easily to this treatment but its animators, John Halas and

Joy Bachelor [*sic*] have taken no more than adequate advantage of the opportunity. . . . The tone is cute, pathetic or little-boy greedy, and the characterisations are superficial clichés of animal qualities. It is probably true, as advertised, that this is the first full-length cartoon on a serious theme; it is too bad that its British producers have executed it in a pedestrian style that cannot hold up for the required hour and a half.[11] □

For Hatch, as for many critics of the Left examined in this Guide, *Animal Farm* proposes only the continued subordination of the working classes and suggests that Orwell's sympathies with the oppressed were no more than cosmetic. Undoubtedly, the decision of Halas and Bacheler only to give speech to the pigs enabled and justified criticism along those lines. That such elitism was far from Orwell's intention is elided from the film and thus lost on the majority of the audience who had not previously read the novel. The animation could be argued to have done more harm than good to Orwell's reputation, as it tended to confuse viewers as to the colour of Orwell's politics. Given that *Animal Farm* had already given rise to many contradictory assertions of its meaning, the simplifications of the film only caused a deepening of the suspicion around Orwell's political affiliations.

The ending of the cartoon is perhaps the greatest deviation from the original text and is aesthetically the most difficult to justify. The conclusion to the novel pictures the animals clustering around the window of the farmhouse, whilst inside the pigs drink whisky and play cards with the other local farmers:

■ An uproar of voices was coming from the farmhouse. They rushed back and looked through the window again. Yes, a violent quarrel was in progress. There were shoutings, bangings on the table, sharp suspicious glances, furious denials. The source of the trouble appeared to be that Napoleon and Mr Pilkington had each played an ace of spades simultaneously.

Twelve voices were shouting in anger, and they were all alike. No question, now, what had happened to the faces of the pigs. The creatures outside looked from pig to man, and from man to pig, and from pig to man again; but already it was impossible to say which was which (p. 120). □

Of paramount importance is the fact that the pigs and humans have become indistinguishable – both are as greedy and power-hungry as each other and the fight reveals the full circle that has been traced from autocracy through democracy and back to autocracy. Of equal importance, however, is the extrinsic positions of the other animals. They are detached from the scene and, crucially, able to recognise that human and pig have become one. It is this intellectual distance that promises so much hope in Orwell's novel; because they recognise what has gone wrong in their system of collectivity there is still hope that they can rectify it. By making the human characters into pigs, Halas and Bacheler destroy the knowledge of ultimate betrayal that is perpetrated by the Manor Farm pigs. It also, as Sylvester suggests, implies that other local farms have been taken over by animals and focuses attention on the fact that the pigs are seen as naturally treacherous and not on the potential for corruption in all that Orwell sees at the root of power. This message is further obfuscated by the revolt against the pigs in the film which is instigated by Benjamin and which ousts the pigs from power. Again, this deviation from the original suggests the congenital malignity of the pigs and does not point towards the fallibility of all the animals. Above all, it suggests that revolutions can be successful; an issue which is surely debatable in Orwell's novel. One could claim that the second revolt of the animals brings about the true socialist democracy that Orwell craved, and thus the film extends his ideas beyond the book. The happy ending that is manufactured, however, ignores the bleak portent of the novel – that power demands both masters and slaves, and that revolution ultimately brings about a cyclical process of power abuse.

Despite its limitations and deviations, the animated *Animal Farm* cemented Orwell in the forefront of Cold War political discourse, at least in the mind of the general public, and maintained his reputation as an astute commentator on the nature and workings of power. It was soon followed by a screen version of *Nineteen Eighty-Four* from Columbia Pictures. Released in America in 1956 and designed to feed a popular interest in science fiction, the film contained serious editorial amendments to Orwell's text, which were justified as part of a process of free adaptation.[12] The film was British-made, but contained American actors in its lead roles, and the principal thematic focus shifted to the love of Julia and Winston. The producers, aware of the furore caused by the BBC adaptation of 1954, chose to produce two endings, one faithful to Orwell's text, the other showing the lovers refusing to be brainwashed and dying together in a hail of bullets as Winston defiantly proclaims 'Down with Big Brother'. It was this bowdlerised ending that was released in the United States and once again provoked questions about the integrity of the original art work and the colour of Orwell's politics. Financially, the film was not a success and its cultural significance lies in its indication of the taste of American audiences for sensationalism and for the championing of the individualistic over the collective.

The revival of interest in Orwell that characterised the run-up to 1984 saw a host of documentaries and screen biographies which reassessed his impact on post-war culture. Inevitably, the year itself also saw the production of a film of the book. Directed by Michael Radford and starring John Hurt (as Winston Smith), Suzanna Hamilton (as Julia), and Richard Burton (as O'Brien), the film strove to match the novel's pessimistic vision of the future. Naturalistic in setting, the film was shot during the months covered by Winston Smith's diary in the novel (April–June 1984), an interesting production decision which could be seen to reflect upon the contemporary political context. The decaying industrial fabric of the East End of London, which was used as a back-drop, intimates a politicised reading of the film as a commentary on the nature of Thatcherite Britain in the early 1980s. Images of industrial degeneration, such as the disused Battersea Power Station, punctuate the film and stand in symbolic relation to the perceived decay of Britain's international influence in both Orwell's novel and in 1984 itself. The film remained scrupulously faithful to the novel and largely abjured the sops to commercialism which had problematised the Columbia Pictures adaptation. Instead, the focus of the film was upon the compromised nature of human relationships under totalitarian systems and played heavily upon the psychological impact of Winston's betrayal first of his mother and sister and subsequently of Julia. O'Brien emerges as a combination of cruel tyrant and loving father, prepared equally to embrace and torture the recalcitrant Winston. Visually striking, the film melded the paraphernalia of Soviet society and propaganda with the sinister power of Nazi iconography; the Thought Police, dressed entirely in black uniforms, vividly recall the Third Reich's SS divisions. The film's *coup de grâce*, however, was the ubiquitous presence of the telescreens which provide an incessant commentary of war victories and production targets and endow the film with a very real sense of the repressive capabilities of the state.

In the context of this discussion of screen versions of Orwell, it is also worth mentioning the 1999 adaptation of *Animal Farm*, directed by John Stephenson and adapted from the novel by Alan Janes. Employing a mixture of computer simulations, puppets and specially trained animals, the film manages to convey the message of power corruption whilst decontextualising the story from any specific historical scenario. Apparently set at some point in the 1950s, the film makes little effort to connect that setting with any surrounding political context and, unlike the Bacheler and Halas version, the animals (all of whom are given speech) are not provided with recognisable voice characteristics that could correspond allegorically to any historical figure. Not surprisingly, perhaps, given the difficulties of filming animal performances, this adaptation of *Animal Farm* devotes a significant part of its plot to the human response to the rebellion and, in particular, to the plight of the ousted Jones. The most interesting, although predictable, element of the film, is the changed ending. Although the film retains the crucial final scene between man and pig, it deviates from the original in that the awareness of the corruption inspires in the more astute animals a desire to escape their tyranny. Having done this, they ultimately return in the wake of Napoleon's fall from power to find that new and more sympathetic human owners have installed themselves in the farm. The film, always sentimental in tone, concludes bizarrely with a rendition of Fats Domino's rock 'n' roll ballad *Blueberry Hill*. Again, the imperative of commerce and a desire to appeal to a young audience transforms Orwell's text into a parody of the original, and whilst there are interesting portrayals (such as Squealer's similarities to Josef Goebbels), the light touch which persists throughout renders any political comment negligible.

With the possible exception of Michael Radford's *1984*, the treatment of Orwell's last novels by the cinema and television has not therefore been greeted universally as successful, or even faithful to the political ideals of Orwell. In some ways, this has deepened and intensified the mystique surrounding both the novels' meanings and their author's intentions. The cult of personality which has both elevated and restricted Orwell, and indeed studies of Orwell, has also been at work on the screen. In any consideration of the filmic interpretations of his work, however, what comes across most forcibly is the degree to which the novels have outgrown their creator and have carved their own discrete niches within popular culture.

At the heart of Orwell's late fiction is a conviction that individual autonomy is under threat from a self-effacing bureaucracy which seeks to channel subjectivity into efficient productivity and effective self-management. This concern for the interaction of state and subject can be seen as an important motivating theme for post-1945 British and American culture. With the advent of the nuclear age and the ever-present menace of imminent annihilation, individual self-determination became a debatable concept – how autonomous could the individual subject be when faced by weapons of mass destruction, wielded by a distant and indifferent power? Orwell's *Nineteen Eighty-Four* vision of the state's indoctrination of its subjects into an acceptance of their subjection catches a *zeitgeist* of fear and impotence. In certain respects this anxiety is reflected in popular culture, as is demonstrated by some recent examples of films and television programmes that implicitly invoke Orwell's last fictions. To focus on the influence of Orwell's novels on filmic and televisual texts is not to suggest that equally apposite examples could not be drawn from other areas of popular culture, merely that the impact on screen culture is readily accessible as a test-case.

The 1960s television drama *The Prisoner* (1967) which starred Patrick McGoohan as the captive of a malevolent and faceless dictatorship featured the famous line 'I am not a number, I am a free man' which articulates an Orwellian reduction of the spirit to a numerical denominator, in much the same way as expressed in Zamyatin's *We*. Anthony Burgess's novel *A Clockwork Orange* (1962), later turned into a controversial film by Stanley Kubrick, clearly owes a debt to the apocalyptic nightmare of *Nineteen Eighty-Four*. The dystopia of Burgess's novel, with its manifestations of 'ultra-violence', can, in one light, be seen as the logical extension of the implied violence of Big Brother's state control. Alex's 'rehabilitation' also gestures towards the torture of Winston Smith by O'Brien.

One sees echoes of Orwell in much contemporary science fiction and equally in films such as *Bladerunner* (1982) which combines a technological futurism with a gritty naturalism in much the same way that Orwell bases Airstrip One on a wartime London but grafts onto that austere grimness a futuristic technology. Meanwhile, films of the mid-1980s such as *The Running Man* (1987) and *Robocop* (1987) focused on future dystopias where intensive media scrutiny has brought about the elimination of private space and recast the destruction of life as mass entertainment. Such dramas call to mind the films of fabricated war victories shown to the eager 1984 public and the obligatory Two Minutes Hate instituted by the regime. More recently, *The Truman Show* (1998) portrayed a character whose entire life was recorded and played live to television audiences who had the opportunity to influence the events that occurred to the unwitting 'star'. *The Truman Show* presents an Orwellian nightmare of surveillance, but takes the vision one step further by transmogrifying the process of monitoring into an invasive and manipulative form of popular entertainment. These echoes are of course only a sample of the intertextual relations to Orwell's work, but they do suggest that, particularly in mainstream cinema, the legacy of Orwell is still being addressed.

If one turns to look at the influence of *Animal Farm*, one sees in *Babe* (1995) and *Chicken Run* (2000) two reinterpretations of Orwell's story. The former, though based originally on a children's book, invariably calls *Animal Farm* to mind, especially with its principal character being a talking pig. One should perhaps not seek to stretch these analogies too far, but undoubtedly the text and the film draw on the popular appeal and knowledge of *Animal Farm* for their frames of reference. *Chicken Run*, an animated comedy, presents an even closer tie to Orwell's text. A combination of *Animal Farm* and *The Great Escape*, the film constitutes the malevolent and manipulative farmer in the role of Mr Jones and although the animals (in this case chickens) escape from the farm rather than rebel, there are clear undertones which evoke Orwell's text. Though such selections of intertexts barely scratch the surface of Orwell's influence, there is a serious point to be made about how all these films assume audience knowledge of the sources of their visual references. Again this reveals the extent to which Orwell has outgrown his own reputation and become a cross-cultural icon. More interestingly, it perhaps shows how *Animal Farm* and *Nineteen Eighty-Four* have actually out-grown Orwell and become discrete and independent popular cultural icons in themselves. This is evident in many areas of popular culture and two case studies will suffice to show its legitimacy: the BBC's comedy chatshow *Room 101* and Endemol Production's Channel Four programme *Big Brother*.

Orwell in Popular Culture – Two Case Studies

Room 101 is a long-running show in which celebrities are given the opportunity to consign to a notional Room 101 all the things that they most object to in life. Obviously, the programme is a light-hearted and casual rendition of an Orwellian concept, but both the set-design for the show and its presentation of what Room 101 represents reveal how Orwell's legacy is both understood and misunderstood. The design of the set has remained relatively static throughout the show's history and consists mainly of a hard, industrialised architecture that conveys a sense of the bare functionalism of Orwell's future, whilst at the same time invoking the diabolical brutality of the original Room 101. Alongside this industrial imagery is the equally prevalent imagery of bureaucracy, principally desks and filing cabinets where the personal horrors of the guests are supposedly classified. In early series, the title credits included an endless maze of filing cabinets receding into a bewildering distance. Those items that are 'condemned' to Room 101, on the arbitrary judge-ment of the show's host, disappear down a mock waste chute which draws together both imagistic modes: industry and bureaucracy. Clearly, an effort is being made to evoke the facelessness of Orwell's state; the guests' selections emerge from and return to filing cabinets in a gesture towards the freedom of individual choice which is simultaneously con-tained within the ordering structures of the bureaucratic system.

The Room 101 to which these personal hate-objects are consigned is at odds with that portrayed by Orwell. The format of the programme suggests that the room is distanced from the guests and from the audi-ence; it is a mythical and unattainable place where largely trivial objects are contained. It poses no threat and exists solely as a repository for all the world's undesirable things. As such, it is distinctly different from the concept envisaged by Orwell and is effectively desensitised both by its distance and by its largely comic contents. The threat of Room 101 for Winston Smith is its ever-increasing proximity; its power lies in the sug-gestion of horror that its contents convey and the tension around the room rests on the balance of whether or not Smith will be sent there. The terror that is implicit in the name Room 101 exists primarily in the intellectual and emotional contemplation of the worst private horror that could be imagined. The BBC's programme semantically castrates the name of its power by actualising that process of contemplation, and, more often than not, trivialising it by rendering it comic. What is evident, therefore, from the show is how familiar the watching audience is expected to be with Orwell's concept, particularly as Orwell's name is never mentioned; an assumption which places *Nineteen Eighty-Four* as a defining cultural symbol long after its moment has passed. And it is very much the novel, rather than Orwell, that is invoked by the programme; the idea of a chamber of horrors has a currency amongst a wide audience, a significant proportion of whom may never have read the novel.

Such a slippage of ownership between the author and his audience was also evident in the Channel Four programme *Big Brother*, which was screened in Britain throughout the summer of 2000. The format for the show, originally a Dutch conception, has been successfully transferred to a number of European countries and to North America, and has proved to be as popular with viewers as it has been unpopular with critics. The principle of the programme was that ten volunteers would be locked in an isolated house with no contact with the outside world for ten weeks. The house itself was constantly monitored by cameras and every area was accessible to the show's producers at any time. As an added ingredient, internet access to the show's cameras could also be obtained, meaning that potentially anybody outside the house could receive instant and unedited footage of the inhabitants. The volunteers were competing for a significant cash prize and each week one would be ejected based on a vote by the viewing public. The press coverage and controversy caused by the show were immense, as the following extracts from *The Observer* show. The first is by Barbara Ellen:

■ One can imagine that the contestants on *Big Brother* have been having more long dark nights of the soul than most recently. . . . *Big Brother* is the Channel 4 docu-soap, in which a group of youngish men and women live together in a house, cut off from society, with cameras recording their every move. The *1984* link is workable if you're inclined to be generous – watching the housemates flirt leadenly with each other, disrobe at every opportunity and drone on about sex is indeed a little like observing an Orwellian-themed 18–30 holiday in Swindon.

Apart from that, *Big Brother*'s basic premise is more Agatha Christie meets a high-school popularity contest than anything to do with George Orwell. One by one, the contestants are doomed to get 'offed' by their house mates and public opinion, until finally, some time in September, a sole survivor will collect the winner's purse of £70,000, as well as the usual plethora of invitations to open nightclubs and used-car salesrooms up and down the country.

Which sounds like quite a good deal until you actually see the programme and realise that 70 grand and a quick dab of micro-celebrity isn't nearly enough compensation for losing every scrap of dignity you might once have possessed.

That goes for viewers, too. . . . *Big Brother* is television heroin: addictive, full of garbage, and distinguished by the fact that those who consume it are as degraded by the experience as those who peddle it. We've all heard about the banality of evil – *Big Brother* brings you the banality of banality. Increasingly, over the last few weeks, the contestants' trials and tribulations have had an almost fairy-tale beat to them: who's going to sleep with who first? Who's going to burst into tears next?

As well as being voyeuristic and seedy, *Big Brother* manages to exude the most frigid of atmospheres . . . Even more worrying is that on our side of the dark glass, there seems to be a terrible pitilessness, which some seem to feel we have an automatic right to exercise.

What people in this country frequently seem to forget is that celebrity is as much a verb as it is a noun – and that, while people such as *Big Brother* contestants like to think they can 'do' celebrity', it more often than not ends up 'doing' them.[13] □

The second *Observer* extract is by Michael Collins:

■ In the early days of British television, Hughie Green bowed out of every show of *Opportunity Knocks* by turning to the camera and telling the viewers at home, most sincerely: 'Remember, it's your vote that counts.' It was the closest the viewer got to empowerment back in the Sixties and Seventies, beyond the interactivity of switching the set off. Shared experience is something else these days.

And the idea of putting the power in the hands of the viewer, while simultaneously removing the privacy of the viewed, is an idea that is beginning to dominate television and the surrounding territories. Later this month, a television programme makes the public privy to the kind of places that the camera has never before been granted access, while simultaneously claiming to put the viewer in control.

The event has been touted in some circles with the kind of zeal that accompanied the first footage of the Apollo Moon landings. But at the core of *Big Brother* is Hughie's first law – it really is your vote that counts. . . .

'Never before have people consented to being filmed under close scrutiny for so long,' says Liz Warner, C4's commissioning editor for the series. 'It's the first time in the UK that the audience can truly be involved and influence the destiny of the participants by voting for who stays and who goes.'

For nine weeks, 25 cameras and 30 microphones will watch over the every move of 10 volunteers, who have been selected from more than 40,000 applicants to live in a specially built house. Each will be subsidised by a daily fee of £30. Each week, the viewers vote on which member of the group is eliminated, until one emerges as the winner.

Big Brother takes our continuing preoccupation with voyeurism and exhibitionism into a new arena. The show is an attempt to transform exhibitionism from a voyeur's pastime into a viewer's sport. Exhibitionism is normally associated with things out of the ordinary. What's on show here is the sheer banality of ordinary lives.

Writing recently in the *New York Times* on the phenomenon, Marshall Sella made the point that exhibitionism is being marketed as a form of adventure: Exposure to media scrutiny is like being exposed to the elements. Only, the elements here are sight and sound, the heat of klieg lights instead of the sting of wind. We are asked to believe that this century's first explorers, our Scotts and Amundsens, are those who can withstand the pressures of the lens. *Big Brother* housemates travel down an Amazon of the self, unafraid to wash or weep (and not forgetting, please, to undress) in front of millions of strangers. And adversity, as everybody knows, breeds heroes.

Here the hurdles are the ups and downs of living within a confined space, with people you hardly know, and without certain creature comforts. The questions that beg to be asked are at what point would the camera be likely to be switched off? and how far would this go in the name of entertainment?

The participants emerging from the house of *Big Brother* abroad are treated like heroes, and immediately shrouded by a particular type of fame – the promise of recording contracts and modelling contracts, and the rounds of the chat-show circuit. This must be their prime motive for participating. ... What distinguishes *Big Brother* ... is that ... players within this show willingly hand over their privacy.

For the viewers of *Big Brother*, this programme is another chance to play God. But it's the networks that have most to gain, from the convergence of confessional culture and new media. In the light of the success of these shows abroad, networks here are now fighting for the next one out of the factory, in the way that was previously the case with docu-soaps. ... The two themes that dominate, that of a level of interactivity within the grasp of the audience, and an elimination of privacy on the part of the subject, are currently found away from the camera, and in art and performance.

Finally, the TV viewer has become like a punter at a peep show. As a showcase for what happy bedfellows the internet, television and the concept of the interactive viewer could become, at the most fundamental level, *Big Brother* is the perfect vehicle. Ultimately, there is too little time within a television programme to ponder the banality of ordinary lives in the manner of CCTV scanning the forecourt of a petrol station.

Something needs to happen, and in order to make it happen, something unreal has to be placed in the situation to create a narrative and the drama. In this instance, something has to be taken away. These characters are surrounded, and captured on film, by state-of-the-art technology, but they have to exist without the fundamental tools of communication – telephones, computers, television, faxes – that signpost their daily lives. This immediately makes the whole concept once removed from being the reality television that it claims to be.

However, the internet makes it possible to wait and witness everything that happens, unabridged, and in real time. Outside the regular visits to the house on [Channel] 4, there is the website to which everyone has access to all that's happening on the cameras all day and all night. ... ...

If *Big Brother* is, on one level, a webcam show for television, its internet site will take you to the parts that the TV show cannot reach, although television provided the platform for fans of the show to be privy to one of the participants going through their motions in the lavatory. ... ...

If *Big Brother* is a success here, within the realms of television and the internet, a further series would be expected to involve the viewer even more, in the manner of certain types of webcam pages. Not simply a case of choosing when someone is eliminated, but choosing when they defecate, fornicate, masturbate.

Of course, to stay in the game, they'll have to comply.[14] □

Both Barbara Ellen and Michael Collins point towards the fundamental paradox of 'reality tv', of which *Big Brother* has been the most successful example in Britain to date. The format is essentially voyeuristic and pornographic in the sense that it allows only a one-way relationship to develop between the viewer and viewed. It is a potentially sordid and self-gratificatory relationship in that viewers on the internet could, if so desired, focus on the most private of actions. Yet, as both Ellen and Collins acknowledge, the sense of disgust that is generated by such exposure is problematised by a deep-rooted fascination with the minutiae of others' lives and with the motives that drive the contestants willingly to surrender their privacy. Part of the complex public reaction to *Big Brother* was centred on the simultaneously banal and yet titillating prospect of total access to another person's life. The surreptitious pleasures that were to be gleaned derived mainly from a realisation of the lack of boundaries. The programme actively encouraged viewers into a moral stasis whereby the desire to pry into another's existence was seen not as an ethical taboo, but as a natural inquisitive response. The formulation of this ethical crisis as entertainment raised significant questions about the status of morality in relation to television. With the unstinting attention of the cameras, the participants in the game were denuded of the basic right of privacy, which in turn prompted for the viewer a difficult moral decision. Much of the fascination of the programme rested in the viewer's understanding of the lowest possible humanising factor and begged the question, what fundamental rights of existence can be withdrawn from an individual while still enabling them to remain human? Would the viewer therefore, knowing that they could/would not submit to that degree of scrutiny, continue to watch others being monitored and continue to suspend the moral decision-making process?

The programme's associations with Orwell derived mainly from the concept of the telescreen continually documenting the actions of the inhabitants of the house. All knew that they were under constant surveillance and that their actions could be broadcast. In some ways this situation did mirror the oppressiveness of *Nineteen Eighty-Four*, although clearly the gameshow format dictated a more or less benign attitude from the contestants towards the cameras and vice versa. In some cases this benignity merged with exhibitionism in a desire to promote future careers in the media or to make the most of the public's attention. There was little compulsion on the housemates to achieve anything constructive during their time in the house and the producers laid down few rules of conduct. What became increasingly apparent was the level of performance of self that was engaged in by some (if not all) of the contestants, who clearly saw the potential of a forum for spectatorship wherein their talents and qualities were displayed in an ostensibly 'natural' and spontaneous manner. Performativity itself became a necessary self-protection, but more cynically could be seen to have become a constitutive process whereby the public self effaces and displaces the private self. The notion of Big Brother thus became decontextualised and merely a suggestive monicker which pointed towards the omnipresence of an observing eye. For Winston Smith, Big Brother's presence is both a restriction on behaviour and a reminder of the way in which he, as a good citizen of Oceania, should behave. Orwell's vision of the telescreen comes much closer to the Foucauldian description of the panopticon – a prison designed in such a way that each prisoner can be constantly scrutinised. With the knowledge of one's surveillance always in mind, the observed begins to regulate their behaviour in accordance with the rules of the prison/society in which they live. The television version of this idea dispensed with this notion of discipline through observation and instead merely used the cameras as passive recorders of the contestants' behaviour. In this sense the programme could not be further removed from Orwell's original conception.

The Channel Four show also recalled Orwell in the persona (albeit disembodied) of Big Brother. The game's participants had recourse to a diary room where they could communicate with the production team through the notional figure of Big Brother. Their conversations were private in the sense that they were kept from the other members of the house, but public in that the viewing audience was privy to those thoughts. Interestingly, the housemates became increasingly dependent upon this very unstable privacy as a way of voicing concerns over the conduct of the game and of their fellow contestants. The Big Brother to whom they talked became a confidant and a benign outlet from the intensity of the isolation. In many ways, at least as far as the participants were concerned, Big Brother grew to be the caring fraternal influence that is suggested by the name and which Orwell ironises as a crude cover for indifference and cruelty. The Big Brother of the programme cared and provided for the housemates and protected them from the outside world. Again, we see how divorced this conception of an omnipresent force is from that of Orwell's novel, and see also how independently the iconography of *Nineteen Eighty-Four* exists without Orwell. The irony of the programme was that, whilst the title was originally intended to reflect the sinister omniscience of the enclosed and surveillanced microcosm of the show, it transpired that the Big Brother to which its title alluded was a very unironic and straightforward protector.

The debates and controversy which have surrounded the emergence of reality television bring this chapter full circle. The first screening of *Nineteen Eighty-Four* which caused such public dismay in 1954 initiated a heated discussion on the purpose and value of television. With the broadcasting of Big Brother in 2000, the arguments over the acceptable limits of televisual representation were reopened with Orwell once again at the heart of the issue. What the case studies of *Room 101* and *Big Brother* have striven to show is that within contemporary culture Orwellian imagery is still a dominant motif for describing the impinging of the nation state upon the autonomy of the subject/subjectivity. The playful and knowing relationship that existed between the cameras and media-conscious contestants on *Big Brother* intimates the degree to which the two-way interaction implicit in the telescreen has become a reality, even though that relationship has been shorn of much of its malignity. The distance which clearly exists between the 'horror' experienced in 1954 at the idea of Big Brother and the receptivity to the media evident in *Big Brother* reveals the wholesale renegotiation of the relationship between public and private and between self and other. The fear that the first screening of *Nineteen Eighty-Four* induced was stimulated partly by the intrusion of such images of violence into the sphere of the family; the violability of the private world became apparent. The process of watching *Big Brother* enables a two-way intrusion, based entirely upon that violability, which not only questions the barriers of real and represented, but also redefines the relationship between the public and private self.

Concepts such as Big Brother and Room 101 have passed so effectively into the cultural vocabularies of the Western world that they become repeatedly invoked and recycled as standard descriptors of totalitarianism or the threat of absolute state control. Unfortunately, in that process of invocation the connection between the original signifier (e.g. Room 101) and the signified (a place of private and individualised torment) becomes jeopardised by its casual application. What these two examples have shown is that the semiotic relations between concept and term have shifted so that although the associations with Orwell are generally understood, the exact connotations of the idea are realigned, reinterpreted or just simply misunderstood. It seems ironic and yet appropriate that, even when he is cut adrift from the concepts to which he gave life, Orwell is still the subject of contention, debate and political appropriation. As this Guide has shown, the critical histories of *Animal Farm* and *Nineteen Eighty-Four*, and the wrangling over his memory, reflect a deep ambivalence not only to Orwell's writings but to Orwell himself, an ambivalence which continues to this day and which still renders him one of the most contentious figures of twentieth-century British literature.

NOTES

INTRODUCTION

1 George Orwell, 'Why I Write', *Decline of the English Murder and Other Essays* (London: Penguin, 1965), p. 188.

2 James Joyce, *A Portrait of the Artist as a Young Man* (Harmondsworth: Penguin, 1976), p. 215.

3 For the purposes of this book, *Nineteen Eighty-Four* will be referred to as a novel, but with the acknowledgement that this definition includes the sub-generic presence of other forms such as the utopia, the political tract and the satire.

CHAPTER ONE

1 V. S. Pritchett, 'George Orwell', *New Statesman and Nation*, vol. 39, 28 January 1950, p. 96.

2 Quoted in John Rodden, *The Politics of Literary Reputation: The Making and Claiming of 'St. George' Orwell* (New York and Oxford: Oxford University Press, 1989), p. 43.

3 Figures quoted in Bernard Crick, *George Orwell. A Life* (Harmondsworth: Penguin, 1982), pp. 486–7.

4 Crick (1982), pp. 455–6.

5 Cyril Connolly, *Horizon*, September 1945, quoted in Jeffrey Meyers, *George Orwell: The Critical Heritage* (London and New York: Routledge, 1975), pp. 199–201.

6 Kingsley Martin, *New Statesman and Nation*, vol. 30, 8 September 1945, pp. 165–6.

7 Harry Scherman, 'A Statement', *Book-of-the-Month Club News*, August 1946, p. 1, quoted in Rodden (1989), p. 44.

8 Letter to Dwight Macdonald, 5 December 1946, quoted in Michael Shelden, *Orwell: The Authorised Biography* (London: Mandarin, 1992), p. 407.

9 Northrop Frye, *Canadian Forum*, December 1946, quoted in Meyers (1975), pp. 206–8.

10 Crick (1982), p. 309.

11 Crick (1982), p. 393.

12 Diana Trilling, *Nation*, 25 June 1949, quoted in Meyers (1975), pp. 259–61.

13 Daniel Bell, *New Leader*, 25 June 1949, quoted in Meyers (1975), pp. 262–6.

14 Frederic Warburg, *All Authors are Equal* (London: Hutchinson, 1973), pp. 103–4.

15 Warburg (1973), p. 104.

16 I. Anisimov, *Pravda*, 12 May 1950, quoted in Meyers (1975), pp. 282–3.

17 Quoted in Crick (1982), pp. 565–6.

18 Arthur Koestler, *Observer*, 29 January 1950, p. 4.

19 Rodden (1989), p. 46.

20 E. M. Forster, 'George Orwell', *Two Cheers for Democracy* (Harmondsworth: Penguin Books, 1965), p. 68.

21 John Atkins, *George Orwell: A Literary Study* (London: Calder & Boyars, 1971), p. 221.

22 Atkins (1971), pp. 252–4.

CHAPTER TWO

1 Letter to Peter Giles in Edward Surtz and J. H. Hexter, eds, *The Yale Edition of the Complete Works of St. Thomas More* (New Haven: Yale University Press, 1965) vol. 4: *Utopia*, p. 251.

2 Krishan Kumar, *Utopia and Anti-Utopia in Modern Times* (Oxford: Blackwell, 1987), pp. 21–32.

3 Vita Fortunati, '"It Makes No Difference": A Utopia of Simulation and Transparency', in Harold Bloom, ed., *George Orwell's 1984*, Modern Critical Interpretations Series (New York and Philadelphia: Chelsea House Publishers, 1987), p. 110.

4 F. R. Leavis, *The Great Tradition* (London: Chatto & Windus, 1948), p. 7.

5 Robert C. Elliott, *The Shape of Utopia: Studies in a Literary Genre* (Chicago and London: University of Chicago Press, 1970), pp. 108–11.

6 Sonia Orwell and Ian Angus, eds, *George Orwell: The Collected Essays, Journalism and Letters* (London: Secker & Warburg, 1968. Hereafter, *CEJL*), IV, p. 213.

7 Jeffrey Meyers, *A Reader's Guide to George Orwell* (London: Thames & Hudson, 1975), pp. 145–6.

8 See Bernard Crick, *George Orwell: A Life* (Harmondsworth: Penguin, 1982), p. 685.

9 Crick (1982), pp. 457–9.

10 Bernard Crick, 'Introduction' to *George Orwell, Nineteen Eighty-Four* (Oxford: Clarendon Press, 1984), p. 135.

11 David Lodge, 'Utopia and Criticism: The Radical Longing for Paradise', *Encounter*, vol. 32 (April 1969), p. 68.

12 Letter to F. J. Warburg, 31 May 1947, *CEJL*, IV, p. 378.

13 Kumar (1987), pp. 294–5.

14 Elliott (1970), pp. 85–7.

15 Quoted in Crick (1982), p. 468.

16 Christopher Hollis, *A Study of George Orwell: The Man and His Works* (London: Hollis and Carter, 1956), pp. 146–8.

17 *CEJL*, IV, p. 138.

18 Patrick Reilly, 'The Utopian Shipwreck', in Harold Bloom, ed., *George Orwell's Animal Farm*, Modern Critical Interpretations Series (New York and Philadelphia: Chelsea House, 1999), pp. 64–5, 88–9.

19 Lynette Hunter, *George Orwell: The Search for a Voice* (Milton Keynes: Open University Press, 1984), pp. 162–5.

20 Fortunati (1987), pp. 116–8.

CHAPTER THREE

1 Alaric Jacob, 'Sharing Orwell's "Joys" – But Not His Fears', in Christoper Norris, ed., *Inside the Myth – Orwell: Views From the Left* (London: Lawrence and Wishart, 1984), pp. 81–3.

2 Norman Podhoretz, 'If Orwell Were Alive Today', *Harper's*, vol. 266, January 1983, pp. 36–7.

3 Isaac Deutscher, '*1984* – The Mysticism of Cruelty', in Raymond Williams, ed., *George Orwell: A Collection of Critical Essays* (Englewood Cliffs, NJ: Prentice Hall Inc., 1974), pp. 119–32.

4 See John Rodden, *The Politics of Literary Reputation: The Making and Claiming of 'St. George' Orwell* (Oxford: Oxford University Press, 1989), p. 204.

5 John Mander, *The Writer and Commitment* (London: Secker and Warburg, 1961), p. 91.

6 Christopher Hollis, *A Study of George Orwell: The Man and his Works* (London: Hollis and Carter, 1956), pp. 152–3.

7 Raymond Williams, 'George Orwell', *Essays in Criticism*, January 1955, pp. 42, 55; and *Culture and Society* (London: Hogarth Press, 1958), pp. 285, 294.

8 Williams (1958), p. 288.

9 Raymond Williams, *George Orwell* (London: Fontana, 1971), p. 87.

10 Williams (1971), p. 96.

11 Williams (1971), pp. 1–3, 11–24, 90, 94–5.

12 Rodden (1989), pp. 189–200.

13 Stephen J. Greenblatt, *Three Modern Satirists: Waugh, Orwell and Huxley* (New Haven: Yale University Press, 1965).

14 [*Mander's Note:*] It may be objected that even if George Orwell wore no mask, Eric Blair did. The relations between George Orwell and Eric Blair are complex; but they belong, I feel, to the field of study of the psychoanalyst rather than of the literary critic. It is the literary personality, George Orwell, in whom we are interested.

15 Mander (1961), pp. 72–3.

16 Mander (1961), p. 73.

17 Laurence Brander, *George Orwell* (London: Longmans, Green and Co., 1954), pp. 14–16.

18 Frederick R. Karl, *A Reader's Guide to the Contemporary English Novel* (London: Thames and Hudson, 1963), pp. 165–6.

19 George Woodcock, *The Crystal Spirit: A Study of George Orwell* (London: Jonathan Cape, 1967), pp. 162–4.

20 Keith Alldritt, *The Making of George Orwell: An Essay in Literary History* (London: Edward Arnold, 1969), pp. 175–7.

21 Bernard Crick, *George Orwell: A Life* (Harmondsworth: Penguin, 1982), p. 526.

22 Williams (1971), pp. 39–40.

23 Sonia Orwell and Ian Angus, eds, *George Orwell: The Collected Essays, Journalism and Letters* (London: Secker & Warburg, 1968. Hereafter, *CEJL*), I, p. 20.

24 Richard Filloy, 'Orwell's Political Persuasion: A Rhetoric of Personality', in Graham Holderness, Bryan Loughrey and Nahem Yousaf, eds, *George Orwell* (Basingstoke: Macmillan, 1998), p. 59.

25 Letter to Brenda Salkeld, 27 July 1934, in *CEJL*, I, p. 160.

26 Brenda Salkeld, 'He Didn't Really Like Women', in A. Coppard and B. Crick, eds, *Orwell Remembered* (London: BBC, 1984), p. 68.

27 George Orwell, *The Road to Wigan Pier* (Harmondsworth: Penguin, 1969), p. 121.

28 Orwell (1969), p. 153.

29 Orwell (1969), p. 103.

30 George Orwell, 'Boys Weeklies', in *CEJL*, I, p. 505.

31 Deidre Beddoe, 'Hindrances and Help-Meets: Women in the Writings of George Orwell', in Christopher Norris, ed., *Inside the Myth – Orwell: Views From the Left* (London: Lawrence & Wishart, 1984), pp. 139–41.

32 Daphne Patai, *The Orwell Mystique: A Study in Male Ideology* (Amherst: University of Massachussetts Press, 1984), p. 17.

33 [*Patai's Note:*] Robert A. Lee, *Orwell's Fiction* (Notre Dame, Ind.: University of Notre Dame Press, 1969), notes that Boxer's stupidity 'suggests interesting qualifications about Orwell's reputed love of the common man, qualifications which become even stronger in light of the description of the proles in *1984*.' Lee further comments that 'Clover is more intelligent and perceptive than is Boxer, but

she has a corresponding lack of strength. Her "character" is primarily a function of her sex. Her instincts are maternal and pacifistic. She works hard, along with the other animals, but there is no picture of any special strength, as there is with Boxer. And even with a greater intelligence, her insights are partial' (p. 123). 'A paradigm appears,' Lee concludes: 'Boxer is marked by great strength and great stupidity; Clover has less physical power but has a corresponding increase in awareness; the equation is completed with Benjamin [the donkey] who sees and knows most – perhaps all – but is physically ineffectual and socially irresponsible' (p. 124). Lee's commentary on *Animal Farm* is far more interesting and insightful than most.

34 [*Patai's Note:*] Orwell's description of Clover as 'the motherly mare approaching middle life' recalls his preference for such maternal figures. In a column describing an ideal (imaginary) pub, 'The Moon Under Water,' he specifies that the barmaids 'are all middle-aged women' who call everyone 'dear' rather than 'ducky'; the latter, he says, is typical of pubs with 'a disagreeable raffish atmosphere' (*CEJL*, III, p. 45).

35 Patai (1984), pp. 205–16.

36 Richard Rees, *George Orwell: Fugitive from the Camp of Victory* (London: Secker & Warburg, 1961), pp. 106–8.

37 Beddoe (1984), pp. 147–8.

38 Irving Howe, 'Enigmas of Power', *New Republic*, 1982, p. 25.

39 Patai (1984), pp. 242–5.

40 Beatrix Campbell, 'Orwell – Paterfamilias or Big Brother', in Christopher Norris, ed., *Inside the Myth – Orwell: Views from the Left* (London: Lawrence and Wishart, 1984), pp. 131–3.

41 [*Rodden's Note:*] See, for example, Patsy Schweickart's enthusiastic review. Schweickart praises Patai for her 'thoroughness and cogency,' even as she notes 'the unrelieved negativity of her approach' and the fact that 'she makes almost no use of biographical information' and that her study often reads like just 'one more book about one more obnoxious male writer.' 'Orwell Revisited,' *Women's Review of Books*, 2 (November 1984), p. 3.

42 [*Rodden's Note:*] Elaine Hoffman Baruch, '"The Golden Country": Sex and Love in *1984*,' in *1984 Revisited: Totalitarianism in Our Century*, ed. Irving Howe (New York, 1983), p. 54.

43 Beddoe (1984), p. 153.

44 Patai (1984), p. 20.

45 Patai (1984), pp. 19, 263.

46 Patai (1984), p. 16.

47 Rodden (1989), pp. 217–8, 224–5.

48 Patai (1984), p. 244.

49 John Newsinger, *Orwell's Politics* (Basingstoke: Macmillan 1999), pp. 131–2.

CHAPTER FOUR

1 Raymond Williams, 'Introduction', in Raymond Williams, ed., *George Orwell: A Collection of Critical Essays* (Englewood Cliffs, NJ: Prentice Hall, 1974), p. 3.

2 Keith Alldritt, *The Making of George Orwell: An Essay in Literary History* (London: Edward Arnold, 1969), pp. 148–50.

3 George Orwell, *The Road to Wigan Pier* (Harmondsworth: Penguin, 1969), p. 121.

4 Laraine Fergenson, 'George Orwell's *Animal Farm*: A Twentieth Century Beast Fable', in Harold Bloom, ed., *George Orwell's Animal Farm*, Modern Critical Interpretations Series (Philadelphia: Chelsea House Publishers, 1999), pp. 113–18.

5 Patrick Reilly, 'The Fairy Tale Distances Us From the Terror', in Terry O'Neill, ed., *Readings on Animal Farm* (San Diego: Greenhaven Press, 1998), pp. 64–7.

6 Lynette Hunter, *George Orwell: The Search for a Voice* (Milton Keynes: Open University Press, 1984), pp. 178–80.

7 Robert A. Lee, *Orwell's Fiction* (Notre Dame, Ind. and London: University of Notre Dame Press, 1969), pp. 126–7.

8 Roger Fowler, *The Language of George Orwell* (Basingstoke: Macmillan, 1995), pp. 174, 177–8.

9 Alex Zwerdling, 'Orwell and the Left', in Terry O'Neill, ed., *Readings on Animal Farm* (San Diego: Greenhaven Press, 1998), pp. 92–7.

10 George Orwell, *The Penguin Complete Novels of George Orwell* (Harmondsworth: Penguin, 1983), p. 861.

11 Richard Rorty, 'The Last Intellectual in Europe', in Graham Holderness, Bryan Loughrey and Nahem Yousaf, eds, *George Orwell* (Basingstoke: Macmillan, 1998), pp. 139–40.

12 Elias Canetti, *Crowds and Power* (Harmondsworth: Penguin, 1981).

13 Alan Kennedy, 'The Inversion of Form: Deconstructing *1984*', in Graham Holderness, Bryan Loughrey and Nahem Yousaf, eds,

George Orwell (Basingstoke: Macmillan, 1998), pp. 92–5.

14 Sonia Orwell and Ian Angus, eds, *George Orwell: The Collected Essays, Journalism and Letters* (London: Secker & Warburg, 1968. Hereafter, *CEJL*), III, p. 222.

15 *CEJL*, III, p. 222.

16 Bernard Crick, *George Orwell: A Life* (Harmondsworth: Penguin, 1982), pp. 582–5.

17 Orwell's personal letter to a Mr Moss of 16 December 1943, cited by Bernard Crick (1982), p. 468.

18 Erika Gottlieb, 'Room 101 Revisited: The Reconciliation of Political and Psychological Dimensions in Orwell's *Nineteen Eighty-Four*', in Peter Buitenhuis and Ira B. Nadel, eds, *George Orwell: A Reassessment* (Basingstoke: Macmillan, 1988), pp. 53–6.

19 [*Gottlieb's Note:*] Murray Sperber, for example, focuses on Winston's paranoia ('Gazing into the Glass Paperweight: The Structure and Philosophy of Orwell's *Nineteen Eighty-Four*', *Modern Fiction Studies*, 26, [1982], p. 22), while Gerald Fiderer concentrates on Winston's masochism and his 'homosexual resolution of the Oedipus triangle' ('Masochism as Literary Strategy: Orwell's Psychological Novels', *Literature and Psychology*, 20, [1970], p. 20). Finally, Marcus Smith considers Winston's phobia of the rats the conclusion of a fixation on the mother. Since Winston also feels that he had offended against his mother, he seeks his punishment through the rats as a condition to be allowed to return to the womb ('The Wall of Blackness', *Modern Fiction Studies*, 14, [1968–9]), pp. 423–433.

20 Gottlieb (1988), pp. 58–9, 71–3.

21 Sigmund Freud, *Civilisation and its Discontents*, trans., Joan Riviere (Garden City: Doubleday, 1960), pp. 77, 79.

22 *CEJL*, IV, p. 65.

23 Mason Harris, 'From History to Psychological Grotesque: The Politics of Sado-Masochism in *Nineteen Eighty-Four*, in Peter Buitenhuis and Ira B. Nadel, eds, *George Orwell: A Reassessment* (Basingstoke: Macmillan, 1988), pp. 44–6.

24 [*Rorty's Note:*] Or even, I would add, to use as a reference point for clear and distinct ideas about the equality of two twos with four. But this is a philosophical quarrel about the 'status' of mathematical truth which need not be pursued here.

25 Rorty (1998), pp. 147–50.

26 Lee (1969), pp. 152–4.

27 *CEJL*, IV, p. 136.

28 *CEJL*, IV, p. 137.

29 *CEJL*, II, p. 108.

30 Alok Rai, *Orwell and the Politics of Despair: A Critical Study of the Writings of George Orwell* (Cambridge: Cambridge University Press, 1988), pp. 122–3, 128–9, 130–3.

CHAPTER FIVE

1 Alan Sandison, *George Orwell: After 1984* (Basingstoke: Macmillan, 1986), p. 191.

2 [*Rodden's Note:*] Created by Tim Keefe and Howard Levine, the calendar aimed to 'demonstrate the validity and relevance of Orwell's commentary regarding the U.S. in this century'. 'Obviously' note the authors in their introduction, 'ours is not exactly the same as the society Orwell warned us of. We believe the differences are in degree rather than in kind'.

3 '1984 Is Here', *Welding Journal*, February 1984, p. 2.

4 Ralph Monti, 'Casually Speaking: Here Comes 1984', *Casual Living Monthly*, January 1984; 'The State of the Handgun Market Today', *The Shooting Industry*, October 1983.

5 Mildred Tober, 'Where Will the Orwellian Fascination End?', *Fort-Wayne Journal Gazette* (Ind.), 2 January 1984.

6 *Time*, 2 February 1981.

7 John Rodden, *The Politics of Literary Reputation: The Making and Claiming of 'St. George' Orwell* (Oxford: Oxford University Press, 1989), pp. 239–42.

8 Sonia Orwell and Ian Angus, eds, *George Orwell: The Collected Essays, Journalism and Letters* (London: Secker & Warburg, 1968. Hereafter, *CEJL*), IV, p. 502.

9 *CEJL*, IV, p. 502.

10 *CEJL*, IV, p. 8.

11 *CEJL*, IV, p. 371.

12 *CEJL*, IV, p. 371.

13 *CEJL*, IV, p. 8.

14 Raymond Williams, *George Orwell* (London: Fontana, 1984), pp. 100–3, 105–11.

15 George Woodcock, *Orwell's Message: 1984 and the Present* (Madeira, BC: Harbour Publishing, 1984), pp. 151–4.

16 Woodcock (1984), pp. 158–61.

17 [*Miller's Note:*] Elaine Hoffman Baruch advances this position in '"The Golden Country": Sex and Love in *1984*', in Irving Howe, ed., *1984 Revisited* (New York: Harper and Row, 1983), pp. 47–56.

18 Miller's discussion here relates quite

closely to the discussion of television's appropriation of Orwell contained in Chapter Six. His arguments about the neutralising effect of television can be read in the context of Channel Four's *Big Brother* in particular.

19 Mark Crispin Miller, 'Big Brother is You, Watching', in Robert Mulvihill, ed., *Reflections on America, 1984 An Orwell Symposium* (Athens and London: University of Georgia Press, 1986), pp. 189–92, 194–5, 196–7.

20 Anthony Burgess, *1985* (London: Arrow Books, 1978), pp. 98–100.

21 Tom Winnifrith and William V. Whitehead, *1984 And All's Well?* (London: Macmillan, 1984), pp. 7–11.

22 Winnifrith and Whitehead (1984), pp. 32–3.

23 Donald McCormick, *Approaching 1984* (Newton Abbot and London: David & Charles, 1980), pp. 24–6.

24 McCormick (1980), pp. 44–6, 48–9, 51–2.

CHAPTER SIX

1 John Rodden, *The Politics of Literary Reputation: The Making and Claiming of 'St. George' Orwell* (Oxford: Oxford University Press, 1989), p. 273.

2 Rodden (1989), p. 275.

3 Rodden (1989), p. 274.

4 '*1984*: Wife Dies As She Watches', *Daily Express*, 14/12/54, quoted in Rodden (1989), p. 275.

5 '*1984* Shocks Viewers', *The News Chronicle*, 13/12/54, quoted in John Sutherland, 'The Drama Caused by the Camera in Room 101', *The Times Higher Education Supplement*, 30/12/83, p. 8.

6 Sutherland (1983), p. 8.

7 Philip Hope Wallace, 'Drama: Thirty Years On', *The Listener*, 52, 23/12/54, pp. 116–17.

8 William Salter, 'Look and Listen', *New Statesman and Nation*, 48, 25/12/54, p. 854.

9 Sutherland (1983), p. 8.

10 David Sylvester, 'Orwell on the Screen', *Encounter*, 4/3/55, pp. 36–7.

11 Robert Hatch, 'Films', *The Nation*, 22/1/55, p. 85.

12 See Rodden (1989), p. 284.

13 Barbara Ellen, 'Why we are Watching *Big Brother*', *The Observer*, 13/8/00.

14 Michael Collins, 'The Greatest Peep Show on Earth', *The Observer*, 9/7/00.

SELECT BIBLIOGRAPHY

Editions of Orwell Works

Wherever possible, references in the body of this Guide have been made to the latest editions of *Animal Farm* and *Nineteen Eighty Four* (produced in 1989). Other editions consulted are included below.

Animal Farm (Harmondsworth: Penguin, 1989).
Animal Farm (Harmondsworth: Penguin, 1951).
Nineteen Eighty-Four (Harmondsworth: Penguin, 1989).
Nineteen Eighty-Four (Harmondsworth: Penguin, 1954).
The Road to Wigan Pier (Harmondsworth: Penguin, 1969).
Decline of the English Murder and Other Essays (Harmondsworth: Penguin, 1965).
George Orwell: The Collected Essays, Journalism and Letters, 4 volumes, Sonia Orwell and Ian Angus, eds (London: Secker & Warburg, 1968).

Biographies of Orwell

Crick, Bernard, *George Orwell: A Life* (Harmondsworth: Penguin, 1980).
Shelden, Michael, *Orwell: The Authorised Biography* (London: Minerva, 1992).

Obituaries

Koestler, Arthur, *Observer*, 29 January 1950, p.4.
Pritchett, V.S., 'George Orwell', *New Statesman and Nation*, vol. 39, 28 January 1950, p.96.

Early Reviews

Animal Farm

Connolly, Cyril, *Horizon*, September 1945, quoted in Meyers (1975[B]), pp.199–201.
Frye, Northrop, *Canadian Forum*, December 1946, quoted in Meyers (1975[B]), pp.206–8.
Martin, Kingsley, *New Statesman and Nation*, vol. 30, 8 September 1945, pp.165–6.

Nineteen Eighty-Four

Anisimov, I., *Pravda*, 12 May 1950, quoted in Meyers (1975[B]), pp.282–3.
Bell, Daniel, *New Leader*, 25 June 1949, quoted in Meyers (1975[B]), pp.262–6.
Rahv, Philip, 'The Unfuture of Utopia', *Partisan Review*, 16:7 (1949), pp.743–9.
Trilling, Diana, *Nation*, 25 June 1949, quoted in Meyers (1975[B]), pp.259–61.

General Orwell Criticism

Alldritt, Keith, *The Making of George Orwell: An Essay in Literary History* (London: Edward Arnold, 1969).

Atkins, John, *George Orwell* (London: John Calder, 1954).

Beddoe, Deidre, 'Hindrances and Help-meets: Women in the Writings of George Orwell', in Christopher Norris, ed., *Inside the Myth – Orwell: Views from the Left* (London: Lawrence and Wishart, 1984), pp. 139–54.

Bloom, Harold, ed., *George Orwell, Modern Critical Views* (New York, New Haven, Philadelphia: Chelsea House, 1987[A]).

Brander, Laurence, *George Orwell* (London: Longmans Green & Co., 1954).

Buitenhuis, Peter and Nadel, Ira B., eds, *George Orwell: A Reassessment* (London: Macmillan, 1988).

Calder, Jenni, *Chronicles of Conscience* (London: Secker & Warburg, 1968).

Campbell, Beatrix, 'Orwell – Paterfamilias or Big Brother', in Christopher Norris, ed., *Inside the Myth – Orwell: Views from the Left* (London: Lawrence and Wishart, 1984), pp. 126–38.

Chilton, Paul, 'Orwell's Conception of Language', in Benoit Suykerbuyk, ed., *Essays from Oceania and Eurasia: George Orwell and 1984* (Antwerp: Universitaire Instelling Antwerpen, 1984), pp. 99–110.

Collins, Michael, 'The Greatest Peep Show on Earth', *The Observer*, 9 July 2000.

Coppard, A. and Crick, B., eds, *Orwell Remembered* (London: BBC, 1984), p. 68.

Davison, Peter, *George Orwell: A Literary Life* (Basingstoke: Macmillan, 1996).

Ellen, Barbara, 'Why we are Watching Big Brother', *The Observer*, 13 August 2000.

Filloy, Richard, 'Orwell's Political Persuasion: A Rhetoric of Personality', in Graham Holderness, Bryan Loughrey and Nahem Yousaf, eds, *George Orwell, New Casebooks* (Basingstoke: Macmillan, 1998), pp. 47–63.

Forster, E. M., *Two Cheers for Democracy* (Harmondsworth: Penguin, 1965).

Fowler, Roger, *The Language of George Orwell* (Basingstoke: Macmillan, 1995).

Greenblatt, Stephen J., *Three Modern Satirists: Waugh, Orwell and Huxley* (New Haven: Yale University Press, 1965).

Hall, Stuart, 'Conjuring Leviathan: Orwell on the State', in Christopher Norris, ed., *Inside the Myth – Orwell: Views from the Left* (London: Lawrence and Wishart, 1984), pp. 217–41.

Hatch, Robert, 'Films', *The Nation*, 22/1/55, p. 85.

Holderness, Graham, Loughrey, Bryan and Yousaf, Nahem, eds, *George Orwell, New Casebooks* (Basingstoke: Macmillan, 1998).

Hollis, Christopher, *A Study of George Orwell: The Man and his Works* (London: Hollis and Carter, 1956).

Hope Wallace, Philip, 'Drama: Thirty Years On', *The Listener*, 52, 23/12/54, pp. 116–17.

Hunter, Lynette, *George Orwell: The Search for a Voice* (Milton Keynes: Open University Press, 1984).

Jacob, Alaric, 'Sharing Orwell's "Joys" – But Not His Fears', in Christopher Norris, ed., *Inside the Myth – Orwell: Views from the Left* (London: Lawrence and Wishart, 1984), pp. 62–84.

Lee, Robert A., *Orwell's Fiction* (Notre Dame and London: University of Notre Dame Press, 1969).

Mander, John, *The Writer and Commitment* (London: Secker & Warburg, 1961).

Mellor, Anne, '"You're Only a Rebel from the Waist Downwards": Orwell's View of Women', in Peter Stansky, ed., *On Nineteen Eighty-Four* (New York: Freeman and Company, 1983), pp. 115–25.

Meyers, Jeffrey, *A Reader's Guide to George Orwell* (London: Thames and Hudson, 1975[A]).

Meyers, Jeffrey, ed., *George Orwell: The Critical Heritage* (London: Routledge, 1975[B]).

Newsinger, John, *Orwell's Politics* (Basingstoke: Macmillan 1999).

Norris, Christopher, ed., *Inside the Myth – Orwell: Views from the Left* (London: Lawrence and Wishart, 1984).

Oxley, B. T., *George Orwell* (London: Evans Brothers, 1967).

Patai, Daphne, *The Orwell Mystique: A Study in Male Ideology* (Amherst: University of Massachussetts Press, 1984).

Podhoretz, Norman, 'If Orwell Were Alive Today', *Harper's*, 266 (January 1983), pp. 30–7.

Rai, Alok, *Orwell and the Politics of Despair: A Critical Study of the Writings of George Orwell*, (Cambridge: Cambridge University Press, 1988).

Rees, Richard, *George Orwell: Fugitive from the Camp of Victory* (London: Secker & Warburg, 1961).

Rodden, John, *The Politics of Literary Reputation: The Making and Claiming of 'St. George' Orwell* (Oxford: Oxford University Press, 1989).

Rorty, Richard, 'The Last Intellectual in Europe', in Graham Holderness, Bryan Loughrey and Nahem Yousaf, eds, *George Orwell, New Casebooks* (Basingstoke: Macmillan, 1998), pp. 139–60.

Rothbard, Murray N., 'George Orwell and the Cold War: A Reconsideration', in Robert Mulvihill, ed., *Reflections on America, 1984 An Orwell Symposium* (Athens and London: University of Georgia Press, 1986), pp. 5–14.

Salter, William, 'Look and Listen', *New Statesman and Nation*, 48, 25 December 1954, p. 854.

Small, Christopher, *The Road to Miniluv: George Orwell, the State and God* (London: Victor Gollancz, 1975).

Sutherland, John, 'The Drama Caused by the Camera in Room 101', *The Times Higher Education Supplement*, 30 December 1983, p. 8.

Sylvester, David, 'Orwell on the Screen', *Encounter*, 4 March 1955, pp. 35–7.

Trilling, Lionel, 'George Orwell and the Politics of Truth', in Raymond Williams, ed., *George Orwell: A Collection of Critical Essays*, Twentieth Century Views Series (Englewood Cliffs, NJ: Prentice-Hall, 1974), pp. 62–79.

Warburg, Frederic, *All Authors Are Equal* (London: Hutchinson, 1973).

Wemyss, Courtney and Ugrinsky, Alexej, eds, *George Orwell* (New York: Greenwood Press, 1987).

Williams, Raymond, *Culture and Society* (London: Hogarth Press, 1958).

Williams, Raymond, *George Orwell* (London: Fontana, 1984).

Williams, Raymond, 'Introduction', in Raymond Williams, ed., *George Orwell: A Collection of Critical Essays*, Twentieth Century Views Series (Englewood Cliffs, NJ: Prentice-Hall, 1974), pp. 1–9.

Williams, Raymond, ed., *George Orwell: A Collection of Critical Essays*, Twentieth Century Views Series (Englewood Cliffs, NJ: Prentice-Hall, 1974).

Wollheim, Richard, 'Orwell Reconsidered', *Partisan Review*, 27:1 (1960), pp. 82–97.

Woodcock, George, *The Crystal Spirit: A Study of George Orwell* (London: Jonathan Cape, 1967).

Wykes, David, *A Preface to Orwell* (London and New York: Longman, 1987).

Zwerdling, Alex, 'Orwell and the Left', in Terry O'Neill, ed., *Readings on Animal Farm* (San Diego: Greenhaven Press, 1998), pp. 91–102.

Criticism Related Specifically to *Animal Farm*

Bloom, Harold, ed., *Animal Farm, Modern Critical Interpretations* (Philadephia: Chelsea House, 1999).

Fergenson, Laraine, 'George Orwell's *Animal Farm*: A Twentieth-Century Beast Fable', in Harold Bloom, ed., *Animal Farm, Modern Critical Interpretations* (Philadephia: Chelsea House, 1999), pp. 109–18.

Kerr, Douglas, 'Orwell, Animals and the East', *Essays in Criticism*, 49:3 (1999), pp. 234–55.

Letemendia, V. C., 'Revolution on *Animal Farm*: Orwell's Neglected Commentary', *Journal of Modern Literature*, 18:1 (1992), pp. 127–37.

O'Neill, Terry, ed., *Readings on Animal Farm* (San Diego: Greenhaven Press, 1998).

Peters, Michael, 'Animal Farm Fifty Years On', in Harold Bloom, ed., *Animal Farm, Modern Critical Interpretations* (Philadephia: Chelsea House, 1999), pp. 131–3.

Reilly, Patrick, 'The Fairy Tale Distances Us From the Terror', in Terry O'Neill, ed., *Readings on Animal Farm* (San Diego: Greenhaven Press, 1998), pp. 61–9.

Reilly, Patrick, 'The Utopian Shipwreck', in Harold Bloom, ed., *Animal Farm, Modern Critical Interpretations* (Philadephia: Chelsea House, 1999), pp. 61–89.

Rodden, John, ed., *Understanding Animal Farm* (Westport, CT: Greenwood Press, 1999).

Sedley, Stephen, 'An Immodest Proposal: *Animal Farm*', in Christopher Norris, ed., *Inside the Myth – Orwell: Views from the Left* (London: Lawrence and Wishart, 1984), pp. 155–62.

Smyer, Richard I., '*Animal Farm*: The Burden of Consciousness', in Harold Bloom, ed., *Animal Farm, Modern Critical Interpretations* (Philadephia: Chelsea House, 1999), pp. 25–8.

Solomon, Robert, 'Ant Farm: An Orwellian Allegory', in Harold Bloom, ed., *Animal Farm, Modern Critical Interpretations* (Philadephia: Chelsea House, 1999), pp. 91–107.

Criticism Related Specifically to *Nineteen Eighty-Four*

Bloom, Harold, ed., *1984, Modern Critical Interpretations* (New York and Philadelphia: Chelsea House, 1987[B]).

Bolton, W. F., *The Language of 1984* (Oxford: Basil Blackwell, 1984).

Burgess, Anthony, 'Utopia and Science-Fiction', in Benoit Suykerbuyk, ed., *Essays from Oceania and Eurasia: George Orwell and 1984* (Antwerp: Universitaire Instelling Antwerpen, 1984), pp. 3–18.

Burgess, Anthony, *1985* (London: Arrow Books, 1980).

Connors, James, '"Do it to Julia": Thoughts on Orwell's *1984*', *Modern Fiction Studies*, 16 (1970), pp. 463–73.

Crick, Bernard, 'Reading *Nineteen Eighty-Four* as Satire', in Robert Mulvihill, ed., *Reflections on America, 1984 An Orwell Symposium* (Athens and London: University of Georgia Press, 1986), pp. 15–45.

Croft, Andy, 'Worlds Without End Foisted Upon the Future – Some Antecedents of *Nineteen Eighty Four*, in Christopher Norris, ed., *Inside the Myth – Orwell: Views from the Left* (London: Lawrence and Wishart, 1984), pp. 183–215.

Deutscher, Isaac, '*1984* – The Mysticism of Cruelty', in Raymond Williams, ed., *George Orwell: A Collection of Critical Essays*, Twentieth Century Views Series (Englewood Cliffs, NJ: Prentice-Hall, 1974), pp. 119–32.

Fortunati, Vita, '"It Makes No Difference": A Utopia of Simulation and Transparency', in Harold Bloom, ed., *1984, Modern Critical Interpretations* (New York and Philadelphia: Chelsea House, 1987[B]), pp. 109–20.

Gauffenic, Armelle, '*1984*: From Fiction to Reality', in Benoit Suykerbuyk, ed., *Essays from Oceania and Eurasia: George Orwell and 1984* (Antwerp: Universitaire Instelling Antwerpen, 1984), pp. 121–57.

Gottlieb, Erika, 'Room 101 Revisited: The Reconciliation of Political and Psychological Dimensions in Orwell's *Nineteen Eighty-Four*', in Peter Buitenhuis and Ira B. Nadel, eds, *George Orwell: A Reassessment* (London: Macmillan, 1988), pp. 51–76.

Hadomi, Leah, '*Nineteen Eighty-Four* as Dystopia', in Courtney Wemyss and Alexej Ugrinsky, eds, *George Orwell* (New York: Greenwood Press, 1987), pp. 119–33.

Harris, Mason, 'From History to Psychological Grotesque: The Politics of Sado-Masochism in *Nineteen Eighty-Four*, in Peter Buitenhuis and Ira B. Nadel, eds, *George Orwell: A Reassessment* (London: Macmillan, 1988), pp. 32–50.

Hewitt, Janice L., 'More to Orwell: An Easy Leap from *Utopia* to *Nineteen Eighty-Four*', in Courtney Wemyss and Alexej Ugrinsky, eds, *George Orwell* (New York: Greenwood Press, 1987), pp. 127–33.

Kennedy, Alan, 'The Inversion of Form: Deconstructing *1984*', in Graham Holderness, Bryan Loughrey and Nahem Yousaf, eds, *George Orwell, New Casebooks* (Basingstoke: Macmillan, 1998), pp. 76–96.

McCormick, Donald, *Approaching 1984* (Newton Abbot and London: David & Charles, 1980).

Macklin, Ruth, 'Modifying Behavior, Thought and Feeling: Can Big Brother Control From Within?', in Robert Mulvihill, ed., *Reflections on America, 1984 An Orwell Symposium* (Athens and London: University of Georgia Press, 1986), pp. 159–78.

Miller, Mark Crispin, 'Big Brother is You, Watching', in Robert Mulvihill, ed., *Reflections on America, 1984 An Orwell Symposium* (Athens and London: University of Georgia Press, 1986), pp. 179–201.

Mulvihill, Robert, ed., *Reflections on America, 1984 An Orwell Symposium* (Athens and London: University of Georgia Press, 1986).

Rademacher, Michael, 'Orwell and Hitler: Mein Kampf as a Source for *Nineteen Eighty-Four*', *Zeitschrift für Anglistik und Amerikanistik*, (1999), pp. 38–53.

Roazen, Paul, 'Orwell, Freud, and *1984*', *Virginia Quarterly Review*, 54 (1978), pp. 675–95.

Rothbard, Murray, 'George Orwell and the Cold War: A Reconsideration', in Robert Mulvihill, ed., *Reflections on America, 1984 An Orwell Symposium* (Athens and London: University of Georgia Press, 1986), pp. 5–14.

Sandison, Alan, *George Orwell: After 1984* (Basingstoke: Macmillan, 1986).

Sargent, Lyman T., 'Social Control in Contemporary Dystopia', in Benoit Suykerbuyk, ed., *Essays from Oceania and Eurasia: George Orwell and 1984* (Antwerp: Universitaire Instelling Antwerpen, 1984), pp. 35–42.

Skovmand, Michael, ed., *George Orwell and 1984: Six Essays, The Dolphin*, 10 (1984).

Skovmand, Michael, 'The Battleground of *1984*: Readings and Appropriations', in Michael Skovmand, ed., *George Orwell and 1984: Six Essays, The Dolphin*, 10 (1984), pp. 47–58.

Smith, Marcus, 'The Wall of Blackness: A Psychological Approach to *1984*', *Modern Fiction Studies*, 14 (1968), pp. 423–33.

Stansky, Peter, ed., *On Nineteen Eighty-Four* (New York: Freeman and Company, 1983).

Steinhoff, William, *The Road to 1984* (London: Weidenfeld & Nicholson, 1975).

Suykerbuyk, Benoit, ed., *Essays from Oceania and Eurasia: George Orwell and 1984* (Antwerp: Universitaire Instelling Antwerpen, 1984).

Winnifrith, Tom and Whitehead, William, eds, *1984 And All's Well?* (London: Macmillan, 1984).

Woodcock, George, *Orwell's Message: 1984 and the Present* (Madeira Park, British Columbia: Harbour Publishing, 1984).

Film and Television Adaptations

Animal Farm (1955), John Halas and Joy Bacheler (dir.), De Rochement Films (prod.).

Animal Farm (1999), John Stephenson (dir.), Hallmark Entertainment (prod.).

Nineteen Eighty-Four (1954), Nigel Kneale (dir.), BBC TV.

Nineteen Eighty-Four (1956), Michael Anderson (dir.), Columbia Pictures (prod.).

Nineteen Eighty-Four (1984), Michael Radford (dir.), Virgin Films/Umbrella-Rosenblum Films (prod.).

Additional Texts Consulted

Canetti, Elias, *Crowds and Power* (Harmondsworth: Penguin, 1981).

Elliott, Robert C., *The Shape of Utopia: Studies in a Literary Genre* (Chicago, London: University of Chicago Press, 1970).

Freud, Sigmund, *Civilisation and its Discontents*, trans., Joan Rivière (Garden City: Doubleday, 1960).

Joyce, James, *A Portrait of the Artist as a Young Man* (Harmondsworth: Penguin, 1976).

Karl, Frederick R., *A Reader's Guide to the Contemporary English Novel* (London: Thames & Hudson, 1963).

Kumar, Krishan, *Utopia and Anti-Utopia in Modern Times* (Oxford: Basil Blackwell, 1987).

Leavis, F.R., *The Great Tradition* (London: Chatto & Windus, 1948).

ACKNOWLEDGEMENTS

The editor and publisher wish to thank the following for their permission to reprint copyright material: Arnold (for material from *The Making of George Orwell: An Essay in Literary History*); Calder Publications (for material from *George Orwell: A Literary Study*); Lawrence and Wishart (for material from *Inside the Myth – Orwell: Views From the Left*); Addison Wesley Longman (for material from *George Orwell*); Arrow Books (for material from *1985*); *The Observer* (for material from 'The Greatest Peep Show on Earth'); Oxford University Press (for material from *George Orwell: The Critical Heritage*; and *The Politics of Literary Reputation: The Making and Claiming of 'St. George' Orwell*); University of Chicago Press (for material from *The Shape of Utopia: Studies in a Literary Genre*); Chelsea House Publishers (for material from *Modern Critical Interpretations: George Orwell's Animal Farm*; and *George Orwell's 1984*); Macmillan (for material from *George Orwell*; *The Language of George Orwell*; *George Orwell: A Reassessment*; *Orwell's Politics*; and *1984 And All's Well?*); Open University Press (for material from *George Orwell: The Search for a Voice*); Blackwell (for material from *Utopia and Anti-Utopia in Modern Times*); University of Notre Dame Press (for material from *Orwell's Fiction*); David and Charles (for material from *Approaching 1984*); University of Georgia Press (for material from *Reflections on America, 1984: An Orwell Symposium*); University of Massachusetts Press (for material from *The Orwell Mystique: A Study in Male Ideology*); Harper's (for material from 'If Orwell Were Alive Today'); Cambridge University Press (for material from *Orwell and the Politics of Despair: A Critical Study of the Writings of George Orwell*); Secker and Warburg (for material from *George Orwell: Fugitive from the Camp of Victory*); Greenhaven Press (for material from *Readings on Animal Farm*); Fontana (for material from *George Orwell*); Harbour Publishing (for material from *Orwell's Message: 1984 and the Present*); Jonathan Cape (for material from *The Crystal Spirit: A Study of George Orwell*).

There are instances where we have been unable to trace or contact copyright holders before our printing deadline. If notified, the publisher will be pleased to acknowledge the use of copyright material.

The editor would like to thank Helen Rogers for all her help and support during the production of this text, and Diana Spencer for many years of inspiration.

INDEX